RECENT THOUGHT IN FOCUS

RECENT THOUGHT IN FOCUS

by

DONALD NICHOLL

SHEED AND WARD
LONDON AND NEW YORK

FIRST PUBLISHED 1952
BY SHEED AND WARD, LTD.
110-111 FLEET STREET
LONDON, E.C.4.
AND
SHEED AND WARD, INC.
840 BROADWAY
NEW YORK 3

PRINTED IN GREAT BRITAIN
BY PURNELL AND SONS LTD.
PAULTON (SOMERSET) AND LONDON

CONTENTS

THE PURPOSE OF THIS BOOK

It is always advisable, when beginning a discussion, to try to start off from some fact upon which everyone is agreed. Most people nowadays would agree that the world in which we live bears a striking resemblance to the Tower of Babel, everyone talking with breathless speed and as loudly as possible in a language which no one else can understand; if you possess a broadcasting station or run a fashionable magazine you enjoy the advantage of being heard but have scarcely more chance of being understood than anyone else. On one wave-length the praise of "democracy" means eliminating your opponents, on another wave-length "democracy" means lying so successfully that your opponents eventually accept your lies. On one wave-length "freedom" means doing what you are told by a commissar, on another wave-length it means doing what you are told by a civil servant. Until some of those who are broadcasting on one of these wave-lengths take some time off to listen to those broadcasting on the other one, disputes about true democracy or true freedom cannot but be fruitless.

Such is the position in politics, as is well known. Less well known is the fact that the world of learning cannot claim to be in any happier condition—perhaps, as a matter of fact, it is the world of learning which is responsible for the general chaos, since the politicians by their actions are often trying to put into force ideas which they have learnt from the thinkers. If so, the world of learning might be expected to display the same chaos as we meet in practical affairs. It does so with a vengeance. Anyone wishing to test this statement should take the opportunity to spend some weeks reading the vast number of learned periodicals which are to be found in large public libraries. There they will find scores of periodicals on biology, astrophysics, ascetical theology, geophysics, microbiology, history, philosophy, logic, philology, and all the other studies

which engage the most brilliant minds of our day. After a few
weeks of trying to get the drift of modern learning the general
reader will probably emerge from this maze of periodicals
wondering how any one person could manage to read all these
different books.

The answer, of course, is that no-one does. It would be a
physical impossibility, apart from the intolerable strain on one's
mind. Even by reading solidly for ten hours a day every week
of the year a European historian could read nothing more than
a fraction of the studies on European history which are being
turned out each day of the week. Which means to say that
anyone who tried to master all the different branches of modern
learning would simply go mad in the process!

What hope, then, can we hold out of satisfying another wish
that would inevitably come upon the general reader as he
turned away mournfully from his vast array of periodicals?
The wish, namely, that some synthesis could be made of all
this industrious research, so that ordinary men might pick up
some clue about the purpose it all serves and how it enables us
to gain a fuller view of life? "We must make a synthesis",
cries modern man in face of all this complicated research. But
he does not always realize quite how much he is asking. Does he
mean, for instance, that someone should gather all the results
of the geneticist's experiments, the ethnologist's discoveries
and the psycho-analyst's case-work into a vast encyclopædia
where the latest references could be picked up immediately?
If so, he is asking for the moon; because no sooner would the
encyclopædia be in the press than it would have to be withdrawn to include fresh material that had been gathered since the
encyclopædia was in manuscript.[1] It would scarcely be in the
press again before it would once more have to be withdrawn.

But perhaps he means something different when he says, "We
must make a synthesis." Not an encyclopædia, but a *Summa* is
what he wants, a series of volumes in which the labours of
scholars are represented according to their value, only the more
important theories receiving a place there. Those who ask for
such a synthesis are usually longing for a *Summa* such as St.
Thomas Aquinas produced for the Middle Ages, in which each

of the sciences received its place according to its value; crowning this wealth of learning came theology, followed by metaphysics, ethics and the sciences of nature, each fitting into the synthesis in strict subordination according to the certainty of their principles, the certainty of the principles in the higher sciences guaranteeing the principles of those subordinate to them. Only a genius such as St. Thomas could have worked out such a scheme even in the thirteenth century when he was able to assume a general agreement amongst his fellows as to the relative importance of the various disciplines. But even a St. Thomas could scarcely hope for a similar success in the present century, because the very first principles which he could assume are now called into question. The logic which he used, that of Aristotle, is scorned in some quarters, and others would actually question the basic assumption of his ethical teaching: that all men desire happiness. As for his arrangement of the sciences according to their value, with theology as the noblest because it is concerned with God, that also would be rejected on the ground that there is doubt as to whether God exists. Any summary of modern learning which ordered the sciences according to their object (the formal object of the science of theology being God, of metaphysics "being as such", and of biology, "living being") would be met with the sceptical query, "And what is God? What do you mean by 'being as such'?"; "How", the critic would ask, "can you speak as though you know the formal object of your science when it is the task of your science to discover that object? It is because we do not know it that we have to look for it."

It seems, then, that we have no solution to offer for those who are searching for a synthesis of modern learning on the lines of the *Summa*. Does that mean that we can only throw up our hands in despair and allow the experts to pursue their mad careers, talking to themselves in their obscure languages and becoming ever less intelligible to ordinary people? It does not; at least we can check this mad career by asking the experts questions in everyday language in order to find out where they imagine they are going, what they think they are doing. And even if they reply that they cannot tell us, because the goal is unknown, we can at any rate find out *how* they propose to arrive at this unknown goal—for no matter how soon they lose themselves in their expertness they do at least begin at the same place as ourselves, being human and talking human language. In other words, we can find out the *methods* they employ and see what results may be expected from such methods. Much of this book will be concerned, therefore, with the study of *method*, with seeing what results we can expect from employing different methods of investigation, and with observing the commonest failings of scholars who are unaware of the limitations in their own particular method. We shall simply be examining at the level of scholarship a failing common to us all. Unless it were common, advertisers, for instance, would never bother to tell us that their kind of tooth-paste is recommended by Mr. X, a well-known cricketer. They are hoping that we shall accept him as a judge of tooth-paste because his method of hitting a cricket ball proves very successful. In fact the methods of cleaning teeth and hitting cricket balls have very little in common and throw scarcely any light on each other, and it is foolish to treat them as if they did. But, as we shall see, many scholars make mistakes about method just as ridiculous as those into which advertisers seek to lure us.

To say that the experts can be saved from madness in this way, by asking them simple questions, is not to claim too much. Madness, after all, means losing contact with reality, going out of communication; it is no accident that the French speak of madness as "aliénation", since a madman is one who is alienated from society, out of communication. By constantly questioning the leaders of learning one may hope to check this disintegration, to make them pause before they flatly contradict each other and common sense. The disintegration may be arrested in this way; but something more positive is surely demanded—some effort at a synthesis—if the disintegrating process is to be turned into one of real integration, if wholeness is to be achieved. And yet reasons have already been given for doubting whether such a synthesis in terms of hierarchically ordered principles can be achieved nowadays. What other possibility remains?

There remains the possibility of a person's evaluating the various sciences in the light of his own thought and experience, in the hope that his readers will agree with that evaluation. If the evaluation carries conviction they may see it as a reflection of the light that is in him and in them, and they may come to share that light, to see things with the same vision as he does. If he himself has been faithful to the light that is in him, such vision, coming from the one simple light, will be simple and unitive, not broken into shadows and darkness but revealing things in their wholeness, a wholesome vision. Should he have been unfaithful to his inner light and have distorted its rays, still his readers, by being faithful to their own, may gather the scattered lights into one and enjoy a vision clearer than his. It is possible, as St. Augustine maintains, for a teacher to teach better than he knows—the truth so often communicates itself in glorious independence of its instruments.

In such a manner much more is learnt than by point-to-point reasoning in an age where both the point of departure and the goal are disputed. Dispute as one may over the point-to-point reasoning, in the end the opinion which prevails is that which enables us to appreciate the rich variety of the universe, which does not flinch before the evil nor ignore the tragedy but which sees things as they are and sees that they are good. Because he so faithfully described the world as it was revealed to him by his inner light, because his mind's eye penetrated into the furthest corners of human life, the poet Dante has been a source of inspiration to generation upon generation of his fellows. It was not that he demonstrated the universe to be good and beautiful by point-to-point reasoning; he simply described what he saw, enabling others for the first time to see this universe, and to see that it is good, thus drawing them to the source of his life, bringing them to the centre of his vision by sharing the goodness and beauty with them.

After a much more humdrum fashion this book offers to share with the reader a view of the world which will enable him to see it in the light of modern learning, and to see that it is good. It is an attempt to see through modern thought—not to "see through" in the sense of debunking it, but literally to see through it to the world, using this light as a medium in order to appreciate more fully the infinite variety of our universe, to see it naked. Nor is it timidity which prompts us to avoid opening the discussion by proving our first principles, by justifying the light. (Contrary to general opinion one cannot begin by justifying first principles; one must begin by using them. First principles being the highest—and the deepest—we, who are creatures, have to work our way up to them, into their light—and dig our way down to them, into their riches.) Once we have allowed this light to play upon the earth we may find ourselves in a position to know its source, its first principle, but if we begin by trying to look at the source we shall only be blinded and shall stumble unseeing past the loveliness of each single thing. Only at the end do we discover the first principles and know that the beginning and end are one; at the end only we discover where we are, where we have been from the beginning.

All of which sounds shocking, no doubt, to those parts of our minds which are convinced that they know what is meant by "first principles". The shocked objections to our proposed procedure might be summed up by saying that it does not propose strict proofs; that it is not rational; that it is subjective, and not objective; that it is not scientific. Four objections upon which we may profitably dwell for a time since they are current *clichés* which conceal readily accepted half-truths.

The question of how to prove something could not be fully dealt with even within the space of a volume, but a few observations on it might help the process of discussion to flow more smoothly. An instance of confusion about proof occurred recently in the publication of a book entitled, *Is Evolution Proved?*, a volume of several hundred pages. At the end of it the two men concerned in the debate came to opposite conclusions; both were faced with the same facts, yet ultimately one of them thought that "evolution" is proved and the other that it is not. Since they were both faced with the same facts it seems obvious enough that they had different views of what constitutes a proof. In the same way certain apologetes for centuries have kept on repeating the proofs for the existence of God to their own satisfaction, if to no-one else's. They do not seem to have been sufficiently worried by the fact that many of the people to whom they have stated their proofs do not accept the existence of God. With all respect it is tempting to recall Glendower's boast, "I can call spirits from the vasty deep" and Hotspur's crushing reply, "Why, so can I, or so can any man, but will they come when you do call for them?" This incident discloses to us the mistake about "proof" which these apologetes and the debaters on evolution have been making: it takes two to make a proof, and the call to the spirits is not effective unless they actually do come from the vasty deep.

Once we recognize that a proof involves at least two persons in relationship we may be less inclined, perhaps, to announce glibly that we have a universal proof for something or other. How rarely do we get the three factors which are necessary before we can prove any truth even to a single person—i.e., ourselves, completely ready to bear witness to the truth, the other person wholly open to the truth, and, thirdly, a means of communication which does not distort the truth. Normally one has to assume, of course, that the giver and receiver are perfectly honest, no matter how frequently one is deceived, and it then becomes necessary to concentrate upon perfecting the means of communication; but this perfecting itself presents untold difficulties. To begin with, not every human being can hear (some are deaf); not every human being can read, and even when people can, their languages differ so vastly that translation into some languages cannot be done. Nor is this matter of translation sheer quibble, for what prevents translation is that the thought-processes underlying the languages cannot be equated; one cannot, for instance, translate Greek terms into Malayalam, because the South Indian does not think in Greek concepts. "But", the defender of Greek thought might object, "if only the South Indian could see a concept as I see it then he would be forced to accept the proofs which I present to him by inferences from those concepts; he would see that my proofs are universally binding." Precisely, if only the South Indian saw things as the Greek sees them. But then there would be no need to present him with any proofs! The whole task of persuading someone of a truth is to get him to see things in a certain way, which explains the procedure adopted in this book.

On the face of it the previous remarks seem to make the chances of proving anything very slender and narrow down the effectiveness of our universal proofs and remedies. At the same time, however, this extends the notion of proof in other directions. For if a proof means any process of communication between one person and another which leaves the second person convinced of some truth which he did not previously hold, then there are many ways of proving truths other than by logical demonstration. For instance, a person may live such a good life that the people around him see his beliefs em-bodied, incarnate in him; the truth shines out of him, and they are convinced that his opinions are true. In this way the Christian martyrs, by their deaths, proved the truth of Christianity to many of the bystanders. Their martyrdom was a proof, not a logical demonstration—even though logical thinking was necessary subsequently to show precisely *what* truths such deaths did reveal.

A further advantage in this use of the word "proof" is that it has been consecrated by the traditions of many peoples. "Proving" someone has meant finding out whether his beliefs were genuine or whether they were only a form of lip-service; in the Old Testament God proved Job by subjecting him to the loss of his worldly prosperity, and in this way medieval knights proved their love for their ladies by their valorous deeds. A truth stated in a proposition rarely carries the same conviction as a truth embodied in a person.

"That it is not rational", ran the second objection to the way in which we have proposed to deal with modern learning. There are many meanings in that word "rational". Often it is used in a commendatory fashion as if the whole process of our reasoning could be termed "rational" in the sense of point-to-point, discursive reasoning. Simple consideration of an elementary process should quickly convince us to the contrary. All are agreed that $2 + 2 = 4$; all should be agreed that this elementary sum involves another factor besides that of discursive

reason, for before we can add 2 and 2 and see that they equal
4 we have first of all to grasp the meaning of "2", of "+", of
"=" and of "4"; these are the points at which our minds rest
in this movement of addition and equation. Without these
points there would be nothing to move from nor anything to
move towards; in grasping the meaning of "2" and "+", etc.,
we are exercising our intuition—not a rare faculty which per-
mits us to sound other persons' souls, but an everyday one by
which we carry out our normal reasoning. Complementary to
discursive reasoning, then, and equally reasonable, is intuition.
But for the moment it is not the distinction between intuition
and discursive reason that we wish to stress so much as the
proper use of the word "reasonable". In one sense it is rightly
used to describe discursive reasoning, but it includes a far
richer sense, and one which the average man acknowledges
when he says of the explanation of some event that it is reasonable. He is saying that once we accept the explanation (even
though we cannot demonstrate it by logic), then the explanation
throws light on the event and shows the ordering of it. This
richer sense receives its classic application amongst Christians
in the doctrine of the Trinity. The doctrine of the Trinity is not
reasonable in the sense that one can demonstrate logically from
first principles that the Father begets the Son, and the Holy
Spirit proceeds from both; but it is reasonable in the sense that
its acceptance makes it possible to see the order in the universe;
the doctrine, as it were, provides the points upon which discursive reasoning can proceed, and without which it would be
helplessly suspended in mid-air. Therefore when the shocked
mind objects to our plan of work that it is not rational, we must
distinguish; that it is not rational, in the sense of not beginning
by justifying our discursive reasoning, I concede; that it is not
rational, in the sense of unreasonable, I deny.

We could further concede the third objection, that our procedure is subjective, if it were not taken to mean that it thereby
excludes objectivity. To write off some statement on the
grounds that it is "subjective" cannot be justified unless it is
meant that the person making the statement has allowed his
particular feelings and prejudices to lead him into falsehood—

in which case his statement should be described, not as subjective but as untrue! For every statement made by any human being is subjective in the sense that it attempts to express the truth as seen from the standpoint of a limited creature—it is subjective; anyone claiming to make a statement that is not subjective is, in effect, claiming to be able to jump out of his creaturely skin. Does this mean to say that one can never arrive at objective truth, that we are for ever shut up within our own subjectivity? Not in the least. This would only follow if the terms "subjective" and "objective" were mutually exclusive, and if the fact of seeing the truth from a limited viewpoint meant to say that one were not seeing the truth at all. Both of which assumptions are clearly absurd. Subject and object are complementary terms describing two things in their relationship to each other; they are complementary. To stand towards the king in the relation of subjectivity, to be the king's subject, for instance, does not make the king any less "objective".

In the same way, because a creature can only see the truth from a limited standpoint it does not follow that he is not seeing any of the truth. It would be absurd to say that I am not seeing Edinburgh Castle at all because I can only look at it from one side at one time. What I am seeing is Edinburgh Castle as a whole but not every detail of it. Similarly I am unable to know the whole truth about the universe; to imagine that I therefore know nothing about the universe is to commit one of the greatest and most common errors about the relation between a whole and a part (an error which will be dealt with on a later page).

An interesting illustration of how even those most accustomed to claim for themselves objectivity have had to accept their own subjectivity has occurred in recent years through the development of quantum physics. Physicists of the last century would have been highly offended if one had suggested that their discipline was not purely objective, and that subjective elements entered into it. Now, however, those very instruments of theirs, which they regarded as the guarantee of objectivity, have taught them to acknowledge themselves as limited creatures, unable to know the whole truth about the physical universe. For they have discovered, in dealing with those parts of the world beyond the reach of the microscope, that even their most delicate measuring instruments actually affect what they are trying to measure; so that each of their measurements must be inaccurate to some extent. Never can they hope to achieve a purely objective measurement.

Enough has been said to show that "objective" and "subjective" are not exclusive, but complementary terms. In the course of our argument a clue has also been given as to the proper method of exchanging opinions, which is what we are here about. The proper method, that is to say, is not for us to pretend that we are not subjects and to deny our subjectivity by making a quick jump into so-called objectivity. No. We must begin by recognizing the apparent paradox that what men have in common is their subjectivity, their relationship as subjects towards the world, towards other persons, towards God; by affirming this relationship, this subjectivity, it is then possible to find common ground in that by which they are related—the world, other persons and God. If one were to deny this relationship in the name of objectivity one would be cutting oneself off from all relationships and all possibility of finding common ground. There would be no discussion, in fact.

The procedure which we have outlined for this book has to meet a further objection, though one from which much of the force has already been taken; that it is "not scientific". In view of the disagreement amongst contemporary thinkers about the definition of science one may be excused for confining oneself to two comments, one on a fallacy and one on a neglected truth. The fallacy lies in believing that there is a *thing* called "science" (usually physical science) to which reference may be made whenever one is in doubt upon some subject. It is really extraordinary to notice how common this mistake about science has become of recent years, how readily people objectify knowledge and imagine that knowledge can be stored up in vast reference-works in much the same way as one stores up meat in a great refrigerator. Therefore a salutary practice on occasion is to remember that knowledge cannot be stored anywhere but in the human mind, that the statements made in scientific books are not made by "science" but by other human beings who are just as much searching for the truth as the reader. One way of clearing the atmosphere of mystery which has gathered around this "science" (which only exists in minds and cannot be carried around like a table) is by remembering from time to time that the "statements" in books do not say anything! Strictly speaking those heaps of dry ink on paper should only be described as "statements" when someone is interpreting them by reading the book; those heaps of dry ink on paper only "say" whatever the reader is prepared to let them "say"; unless there is a reader they return once more to the status of heaps of dry ink on paper.

So much for the fallacy, which presents us with an insight into the neglected truth. The truth is expressed in the ancient description of science not as a body of doctrine easily referred to but as a *habitus mentis*, a disposition of the mind, a way of seeing things. This description locates science in its proper place, i.e. the human mind, and at the same time shows how the various sciences may be brought into a true relationship. For the mere fact of binding the opinions of biologists, anthropologists and philosophers within the same book-backs does not constitute a synthesis—it is merely an assemblage of heaps of dry ink. In order that the various sciences may be related they have to be brought into relationship where alone they can exist, that is to say, in the human mind. Clearly the view of science as a *habitus mentis*, a disposition of the mind, makes this synthesis possible, whereas the attitude which treats each science as a body of doctrine makes it quite impossible—all that can result is a heap of bodies. The attempted synthesis, then, of which we spoke at the beginning is not so utterly impracticable as it had seemed, because it is conceivable that one person should be able to acquire, in a limited fashion, the various mental dispositions which are characteristic of different kinds of scientists. He should be able, in other words, to develop the psychologist's way of seeing things (his science), the physicist's way of seeing things, and so on, whilst at the same time retaining his own identity as a human being with interests beyond the various sciences. Making use of all these different dispositions each one of us should be able to achieve a unifying view of the world, a harmonious balancing of his very diverse mental habits bringing with it wholesomeness, so that he can see the world in its naked beauty and terror, and see that it is good. Such a synthesis of modern learning will not be some *thing* that can be passed on complete from one person to another in the same way that one can pass on a loaf of bread, or even a formula; for whoever is going to receive it must himself acquire the necessary mental dispositions and bring them into harmony. Like any other habits which are worth having these scientific habits demand discipline and courage for their formation, which explains why the branches of learning are so rightly termed disciplines.

Even now that we have considered these objections to our method of working, doubts might still arise because it fails to offer something which most books do offer; that is, the guarantee that you will be convinced if only you read until the end— the kind of guarantee which one might make to a chocolate as it goes into one end of the conveyor belt—that if only it remains still it will certainly and mechanically be packed. In a technical age similar mechanical effects are expected of discussions; what comes out at the end is the sole criterion for their value. Wiser ages thought otherwise; they saw that all truly human discussion takes place between persons, each responding freely to the other and respecting the other's freedom. Thus men were able to address each other as brothers instead of one of them regarding another as an object to be submitted to a mechanical process. And the knowledge acquired was achieved through the exercise of their freedom; habits were formed through the discipline it provided; and even though new formulæ seldom emerged, there often emerged a new man, who had learnt those mental dispositions which are both science and wisdom. Not that discussion was soft—any more than the subsequent pages will be—for it was in earnest that they wrestled with each other, and wrestling cannot be had except between free men; but their struggle was a veritable *lutte fraternelle*, a struggle between brothers, not a cry of "Stand, and deliver the goods" as our technical age would have it. There is no intention here of trying to compel assent in this mechanical fashion, not even by brandishing of syllogisms; only in freedom can one see the world as it is, and see that it is good.

With a further lingering suspicion more drastic measures need to be employed; the suspicion that anyone trying to make a synthesis will be trespassing on "the field of the expert". That is precisely our aim, to go prospecting in the fields appropriated by experts. Why it should be deemed trespassing one cannot imagine, unless because the expert has persuaded everyone else to accept his own opinion of himself. That, indeed, seems to be the case, an absurd position to say the least of it, and one which ultimately harms the expert more than anyone else. There are few more pitiable sights than to see a man mark out for himself a little kingdom of learning (it may be on the behaviour of beetles or the handwriting of medieval kings), and then to see him trying to defend his precious kingdom against all comers, using the weapons of scorn and misrepresentation until his very soul becomes shrivelled to the size of his kingdom, his beetles or his manuscripts. Small though his kingdom may be, he still comforts himself with the reflection that he is master in it; imagining that there he wields absolute power—better to rule in Hell than serve in Heaven.

Granted, however, that the expert often does become this caricature of a human being, is it justifiable to venture onto his field? Would that not betoken the same lack of humility which is deplored in the expert? That is true, and the caution would be merited if it were intended, for instance, to deny the expert's competence in his own line and to start telling him that the results of his experiments were quite preposterous and that no one should accept them. But it does not offend against humility to refuse to leave the demarcation of his field to the expert himself, because in the end he will tend to draw the demarcation line round the rest of the world, so that all fall beneath his power. Take, for instance, some of the early nineteenth-century economists in England. These specialists in economics maintained that the profits which their manufacturing friends were making out of their factories and mills were all made in the last two hours of work. Up to the beginning of the last two hours the mill was, so to speak, keeping up with itself, production balancing expenditure; only during the last two hours was any profit made, and, therefore, the country's industry would be ruined if Factory Acts were passed to limit the men's hours. Therefore the men would just have to go on working for twelve hours a day. So spoke the experts. Fortunately there were in England men of common sense who turned round to the economists and gave the only possible answer; they told them not to be so silly.

Frequently that is the only answer for the expert. He must be told to stop being silly; on those occasions, that is, when he starts running other people's lives, when he reaches the very height of elation at his own powers. A less inflated stage has to be dealt with less severely. When experts disagree, for example, about what seems to be their special discipline, the rest of us may take it as a likely sign that they have abandoned their discipline and are promiscuously extending their *expertise*. Such disagreement exists, to quote one case, amongst the biologists on the question of man's evolution. Most biologists assume some theory of evolution but some believe that man is descended from the great apes; others that man and the apes are both descended from a common ancestor which was unlike any existing creature; others hold that man never passed through an anthropoid state at all. An outsider encountering this extreme diversity of opinion amongst experts may legitimately conclude that they are disagreeing upon the subject simply because the method of their special discipline does not permit them to decide the question at issue. In which case the outsider, having mastered the results which the method in question *does* guarantee, has every right to form his own opinion on the subject, basing his views on that reasoning of which he is no less capable than the expert.

A more delicate situation arises when one is faced with agreement amongst the specialists, because one presumably has no choice but to accept their findings. Yet even at this level, where the expert should be the complete master of the situation, pitfalls cannot always be avoided, and the findings accepted.

A classic illustration of which occurred when a famous scientist was invited to look through the telescope at the canals running across the face of Mars; having looked long through the telescope he announced to everyone's consternation that he could not see any canals there! Nor, when they who had previously "seen" the canals again looked at Mars, were they able to detect them! This is an extreme case, and very rare—we hope, for there is no way of testing whether it is! Not so rarely, experts simply deny or ignore the evidence of their own, or other people's senses because the evidence seems to conflict with what they regard as the cherished principles of their special discipline. Of this failing, illustrations could be given almost *ad infinitum*.[2] When certain objects were reported to have struck the earth in 1791 many scientists refused to believe that these bodies had come from outer space on the grounds that it was not possible for them to do so. In other words, if their theories did not permit bodies from the outer spaces to strike the earth then they would deny the facts which implied that they do strike the earth! A more subtle way of preserving an appearance of agreement amongst experts lies in ignoring awkward facts. It would be awkward, for example, if the experiment upon which modern physicists originally based the special relativity theory were proved to give different results from those they have stated. Yet an American physicist, D. C. Miller, claims that he has constantly carried out the experiment in question, the Michelsen-Morley experiment, and that his results are the opposite of what physicists had previously assumed[3]. How is the non-expert to decide which results are correct? Here the experts are in disagreement even as to the results of an experiment. And it is no help to say that one should follow the majority, because experience has taught us how often the majority have been wrong.

The attitude of the specialist who refuses in this way to face facts which might disturb his hardened prejudices is well summed up in William James' reference to the suspicion cast over the truly scientific investigation of telepathy. "Why do so few 'scientists' ever look at the evidence for telepathy, so-called? Because they think, as a leading biologist, now dead, once said to me, that even if such a thing were true, scientists ought to band together to keep it suppressed and concealed. It would undo the uniformity of nature and all sorts of other things without which scientists cannot carry on their pursuits."[4]

Probably few mistakes about the actual facts which the specialist puts before us result from so blatant a refusal to examine them as William James' biologist was guilty of. Usually they arise out of an unconscious prejudice in favour of some theory. A classic illustration of a preconceived theory deluding investigators into believing that they had found certain "facts" is the case of the "Kallikak" family.[5] The case begins with an investigator wishing to discover if the ancestry of a certain feeble-minded girl (to whom the investigator gave the fictitious family-name "Kallikak") bore out the thesis that feeble-mindedness is hereditary. His researches revealed that her ancestors were a crowd of alcoholics, illegitimates, keepers of disorderly houses, and so forth; from which he concluded that "feeble-mindedness is hereditary in a large percentage of cases". The argument certainly appeared to be a weighty one. But some years later other investigators went over the ancestry of the Kallikak family again, only to discover that the evidence for their being a crowd of alcoholics, illegitimates and keepers of disorderly houses was terribly flimsy, and could not be accepted as grounds for the thesis of hereditary feeble-mindedness. In other words, the first investigator had "found facts" to support his preconceived theory—not out of a desire to deceive anyone but simply because the expert, like every other human being, has an inclination to find things that are convenient.

Instead of continuing this list of instances of the care with which one has to treat these expert "findings" let us now try to point the moral of it. That should hardly be necessary, it is so obvious: no sane person will allow his view of the world to be determined for him by experts of any kind, because an expert sometimes contradicts himself, and sometimes contradicts the other experts. Specialists have the same means of deciding their view of the world as everyone else, i.e. their own persons (their senses, their reason and will). It is true that they receive opportunities of refining their persons (a microscope or a telescope can be regarded as a refinement of their senses; reading and thinking as a refinement of their reason and will); but every human being has these opportunities; a refined perception of the world is the prerogative of no man, and may just as easily be met with in a shepherd from the Border Country as in a philosopher from Göttingen.

There is a story of a professor which drives home to us the foolishness of regulating one's life according to the researches of experts. This professor said that there was only one piece of evidence about the Bible which he needed in order to believe in Christianity. All the years of his life he spent looking for this one piece of evidence, but he never found it; and eventually he died. The day after his death the evidence was found by a Biblical scholar. If only the professor had known this evidence earlier he might have been a radiant follower of Christ instead of a life-long searcher for one piece of evidence. If only he had realized that no sane person allows his view of the world to be determined for him by experts of any kind!

So much needed to be said, to begin with, in justification of our procedure in these pages, to show that it is reasonable, scientific and not purely subjective, and to justify the survey by an outsider of the specialized branches of modern learning. A few words more are necessary as a help to reading what follows, in order to see what mental habits are responsible for its evaluations and judgements.

And first of all an old distinction about different sorts of knowledge must be invoked. Aristotle used to distinguish two sorts of knowledge, that in which certainty is easily gained, and that in which certainty is worth gaining. The two sorts do not necessarily exclude each other, obviously; they overlap, but they may be distinguished. Included in the sort of knowledge wherein certainty is easily gained are all those answers to questions about number and measurement. For example, one might set out to discover how many hot-water taps there are in this house, how many books there are, what amount of cubic space there is for each occupant, how many calories each person received in his last meal, and so on. In all of these questions it is possible to arrive at a certainty which few would bother to doubt.

Nearly all the problems which are dealt with by natural science come under this sort of knowledge; they can all be answered by counting. This is worthwhile bearing in mind, because it explains the ease with which the natural scientist dealing with inorganic matter can give a mathematical expression to his theories; he can produce formulæ. When an astronomer works out a law about the periodic movements of the constellations he is telling us that at a certain time and in a certain place he (or someone whose results he accepts) noticed a change produced on his refined means of sensation (his instruments); then he attributed this change to a certain light, counted its effect as compared with past effects which he had attributed to the same light, and then counted the number of units of space through which he calculates the light to have passed. Having calculated the distance between the source of the light and its impact on his instruments he then repeated the counting-process at other times and noted the differences. These differences he then expressed either in a living language or else in a mathematical formula. If he uses a living language he has to rely upon analogies between events of daily experience and events in outer space in order to put across his discoveries. Since the exactness of his formulation will depend upon the exactness of his analogy this way of putting over his discoveries must almost inevitably prove misleading, because there is no method whatsoever of guaranteeing analogies between the events in outer space and the human events for which the living language was formed. Because of the almost inevitable confusion in using a living language for these specialized purposes most scientists have rightly been reluctant to popularize their results (exceptions being Eddington, Jeans and Hoyle).

The other course open to the astronomer is for him to express his findings in a mathematical way, that is, by using a counting-formula, which puts into a mathematical form the relationship between his various processes of counting. Therefore the complicated-looking equations which come at the end of his work represent a transposition from one system of counting to another, more complex, system of counting. A mathematical formula is a record of counting operations performed either by a present-day mathematician or by generations of them, which prompts the interesting reflection that Einstein's $\dfrac{MC^2}{\sqrt{1-\dfrac{U^2}{C^2}}}$, the relativity formula, represents the counting-autobiography of generations of mathematicians !

It is not surprising, then, that those scientists who deal with inorganic matter find it easy to express their results in a mathematical form, because what they have been doing *all the time* is counting !

In relation to the Aristotelian division of knowledge, then, mathematics is the science which offers the most easily obtained certainty, and the only difficulties facing those who use mathematics arise when the physical conditions for counting are unfavourable, e.g. in dealing with units beyond immediate observation by either microscope or telescope.

The certainty which most human beings consider worthwhile, however, is not so easily obtainable: the answers to such questions as, Have I inherited cancer? Is there an eternal life? Am I my brother's keeper? Is there a God? Why do I regard that person as beautiful? Few would maintain that such questions can easily be answered, and yet they are the ones which most preoccupy the human mind. The distinction between the knowledge for which they reach out and the knowledge discussed previously can be simply proved. Suppose you asked a person to count the number of windows in this house. After he had counted them, and said there were 105, suppose you then brought before him a thousand other people each of whom claimed to have counted 106. You next tell him that you will execute him unless he agrees that there are 106. Do you think he would regard it as reasonable to sacrifice his life for the sake of saying that there are 105 windows in the house? Might he not have made a mistake in counting? and even if he had not, would it be worthwhile to leave his family and friends for the sake of maintaining his ability to count better than a thousand other people? Of course, the situation is unimaginable, because it would be absurd to attach so much importance to mathematical certainty. And yet thousands of people *have* staked their lives for the other kind of knowledge, the knowledge which is so difficult to obtain, and whose certainty is so very difficult to demonstrate logically (perhaps, for most people, impossible). Thousands of people have died for the sake of their belief in God, confident in the knowledge that there is an eternal life— even though learned philosophers still dispute about such tenets and produce many arguments against them. What other proof does anyone need that this distinction between different kinds of knowledge is deeply rooted in our very natures? Besides easily obtainable knowledge there is another kind of knowledge, no less certain in its own mode, but hard to come by and precious enough to die for.

On the whole these pages are devoted to this latter kind of knowledge, though not out of disparagement for the other kind. For they overlap, and a knowledge of statistics may often help one to answer very worthwhile questions concerning, say, housing, or sanitation, or a just wage. Such knowledge must not be despised, but it must always be subordinated to aims suggested to us by our knowing what is worthwhile. Believing that these pages have an aim I naturally concentrate on what is worthwhile.

One of these aims, in a way the source of all the others, springs from the desire to turn all learning into worthwhile learning, to see the positive value embodied in even the most wrong-headed opinions. Sanctions for this approach may be found in St. Thomas Aquinas' teaching that one should not ask who said a certain thing but whether it is true; truth is not partisan, for all truth comes from the Truth. No matter how much he may have given himself to untruth and darkness, hardly any man has so completely extinguished the light in him that one cannot draw upon that light and share in it. St. Thomas himself drew largely upon the pagan Aristotle, as his followers should be ready to draw upon Marx and Darwin, Freud and Bertrand Russell. If these people have some truth in them why not claim it for the Truth? Surely it would be a sin against one's own conscience to deny that it is true simply because it is *they* who proclaim it?   ·

This continual effort to indicate the positive values of theories and events may have very practical consequences. Consider, for instance, the fact of the atomic bomb, a consideration from which it is undoubtedly difficult to draw much positive value ! A negative person would say that nothing good whatsoever · could come out of its appearance in world-history, and would assure us that we are living in the last days, that civilization is doomed and so on; everyone has heard the lamentations. A positive person, however, whilst fully recognizing the terrible possibilities of the bomb, would be inclined to say, "Now that human beings have discovered the atomic bomb the human race, as a race, could commit suicide. This has never been possible; hitherto advocates of suicide, such as Schopenhauer, have refused to carry out what they advocate, on the grounds that even if enlightened individuals such as themselves were to do so, their gesture would be in vain, because the rest of humanity would just go on breeding at the usual rate. A changed situation has come about ; humanity can destroy itself if it chooses." There is the key-phrase, "if it *chooses*"; previously the human race has gone on living, having no choice about it, but now it can really *choose* to do so, making a positive affirmation in favour of life, seeing that it is good. The temptation to suicide to which young people are often subjected now has its parallel in the temptation before the race as a whole; and just as the young person who overcomes the temptation emerges a mature and responsible soul, similarly the human race, by overcoming the danger of the atomic bomb, will rise to maturity and achieve a profounder liberty.

A mode of reasoning likely, no doubt, to incur the scorn of many disillusioned people of our age. Yet what would such disillusioned people have said if they had been living after the fall of Adam and before the coming of Christ? Would their minds not have been so obsessed with the evil done that they would have murmured, "No good can come out of this?" All of us know the Christian Church's answer to such despairing pessimism, as we hear in the Easter cry, *Felix culpa*—Adam's fault, the Church says, was a "happy fault"; God brought good out of evil, since everything works together unto good for those who love God. In the Christian tradition one has the strongest sanction for a positive attitude to each event in this life, and in it is no countenance for the negative one. The fall of man itself has its positive side in the lifting up of man by Christ.

Notice, however, that man does not lift himself—it is God who does so; it is not nature but grace which perfects nature; similarly it is not man in reliance upon his own powers who will draw out the positive value in Marx and Freud; nor can man give himself a vision of the mature liberty opened up to him by the advent of the atomic bomb—only God can do so. Consequently, when a person strives to unveil the light shining obscurely in pagan thinkers he should not rely upon his own strength to do so; he should trust in the all-powerful light of God. The people who walked in darkness have seen a great light; they did not manufacture it.

In such an enterprise, all the same, man has to develop his discernment as best he can by using his natural faculties. Such discernment depends particularly upon grasping the right methods of work and investigation, learning how to distinguish between what results may, and may not, be expected of each separate method. In popular language, we have to learn how to see the wood as well as the trees, to see the trees and see that they are wood. One hopes that this survey of modern thought will prove an effective way of learning the lesson. Certainly after a person has laid bare the fallacies in one discipline such as history he finds it easier to detect the fallacies in other disciplines such as philosophy or sociology, partly because the historian and philosopher are both human beings liable to make the same mistakes, and partly because he himself has begun to acquire a scientific attitude, developing appropriate mental habits. A sharp knife cuts meat as well as bread.

Let us illustrate what we mean.

A university lecturer in history was once giving a course upon the historical foundations of European unity. During the course he had occasion, not surprisingly, to refer to the Catholic Church. He explained to his innocent students that the Bishop of Rome's primacy over Christianity was, as he said, "purely natural. There was nothing supernatural about it". In support of this statement he explained that Rome had, of course, been the centre of the ancient world and retained this position in Christian days; all roads led to Rome, the communications, the commerce, the learning and the administration of the Mediterranean were all centred upon Rome, and therefore Rome naturally became the head of the Christian Church; "there was nothing supernatural about it". Now all the evidence which he brought forward can readily be granted; furthermore one can grant that it was natural for Rome to become the centre of Christianity. What one cannot allow is that it was therefore "purely natural"—the fallacy lies in the "purely". By saying "purely natural, therefore not supernatural" the lecturer was making what is perhaps the commonest mistake in method; he was saying, "because factor A [i.e. the 'natural'] was present, therefore only factor A [i.e. now, the 'purely natural'] was present, therefore factor B [i.e. the 'supernatural'] was absent."

The lecturer may readily be forgiven for his elementary mistake on this issue since it was a false notion of the natural and supernatural which led him into it. He was saying, in effect, "natural, therefore not supernatural" (and many misguided Christians think similarly); or, expressing his thought in the order which it first took, "if it had been supernatural it would not have been at all natural; not natural, therefore 'spooky', queer. I have never come across evidence for 'spooks' killing antagonists of the Roman primacy; the 'spooks' were not on the Roman side, therefore it was by purely natural means that Rome secured the primacy." If this seems to be a travesty of his thought that is because originally his thought travestied Christian teaching. According to Christian teaching the grace of God does not destroy our nature but supposes and perfects it; therefore when we receive his grace we do not suddenly find that our nature has been destroyed and another nature substituted for it, as would happen, for instance, if we developed powers natural to an angel—which has a different nature. On the contrary, grace enables us to overcome those defects which prevent us from realizing our true human nature; this would be impossible without grace. It means that grace enables us to become perfect in our nature, to become *perfectly* natural; when a human being is perfectly natural he is so in virtue of super-natural grace. And so the Christian who believes in the Roman primacy would see how perfectly natural it all was, how supernatural! Given that the Church had to be administered from somewhere he would hardly have expected St. Peter and his successors to go to Timbuctoo to do it—this would not have been a perfection of the natural but a contra-diction of it, which is not the way that grace operates.

It may be useful to restate the form taken by this fallacy, because almost every mistake in method represents a variation on it. The false argument ran, "Factor A is present, therefore only factor A is present, therefore factor B is absent". No-one, of course, would normally fall into this error except in dealing with rather complex issues. If someone says, "I enjoyed the egg I ate for breakfast" and his friend replies, "What a pity you didn't have a cup of tea"—"But I did have a cup of tea" —"But I thought you said you had an egg! How can you have had an egg for breakfast when it was a cup of tea you had for breakfast?" . . . one would suspect that the friend was mad; and, if we allowed the fallacies current amongst learned people to become current in our everyday lives, we should all go mad as well.

Call the fallacy what you will, so long as you recognize it for what it is. Some have called it the "nothing-but" fallacy, and they could produce a beautifully neat justification for their title by a quotation from Freud, "Psycho-analytic investigations of the individual teach with especial emphasis that god is in every case modelled after the father . . . so that god is at bottom nothing but an exalted father".[6] Not often does one encounter the fallacy so naked.

For several reasons, however, it is more convenient to think of the mistake as a confusion between the whole and the part, because thinking of it in this way makes it very easy to detect. When a doctor announces (as doctors readily announced some time ago), "I am going to remove your appendix because it is useless to you", one may be fairly certain that his reasoning ran thus: "I know how the body functions; I do not know any useful function performed by the appendix; therefore the appendix is useless". Stated in terms of whole and part, his reasoning ran, "I know partly how the body functions; I know how the body functions [N.B. the switch from part to whole]; since I, who know the whole of the body's functions, do not know any function for the appendix, the appendix has no function". He proceeds to remove an organ of which he does not know the function. Another imaginary illustration. A dietician tells you that you need 3,000 calories per day in your food; obeying his instructions you achieve an intake of 3,000 calories per day, but gradually you become ill and eventually die of malnutrition. After a time in Purgatory you meet St. Peter and decide to find out why you died of malnutrition when you had been so faithful to the dietician's instructions. St. Peter explains, "The dietician knew you needed 3,000 calories per day [i.e. he knew part of what you needed]; and so he assumed that he knew what you needed [i.e. the whole of what you needed]; but man does not live by calories alone, he also has to have sufficient vitamins. That, my dear friend, is why you died of malnutrition, through a confusion between the whole and the part."

Because our confused friend knows a part, he assumes that he knows the whole, of a subject; because someone else is ignorant of part of a subject our friend assumes that he is ignorant of the whole of the subject. These confusions should be easy to detect. Perhaps more subtly deceptive, one often finds oneself assuming that similarity in one respect implies similarity in every respect. As stated so baldly, one cannot magine anyone falling into this confusion, yet the very saints have been covered with scorn on account of it. For many psychologists, St. Teresa of Avila has to be regarded as nothing but a hysterical woman. They notice that her mystical trances seem similar to the trances into which hysterical women often fall, from which they conclude ("similar in one respect, therefore similar in all") that St. Teresa was *nothing but* a case of hysteria. A genuine psychologist, of course, would not be content with such limited comparisons; he would, amongst other things, compile graphs of the number of Carmelite convents founded by the hysterical women of his entourage—then he would realize that similarity in one respect does not involve similarity in all.

The assumption that similarity in one respect will lead to similarity in all respects has perhaps produced its most cramping effects in the discussions centring around the very subject of this book, i.e. science (or knowledge, *scientia*). One often hears it said, for example, that "history is not a science" or that "sociology is not a science", and the same has been said at one time or another of psychology, ethics or theology. But what exactly are people trying to say when they make such statements? Surely they mean that these studies (history, sociology, etc.) do not conform in observations, methods, and aims, to the pattern of science which they themselves have accepted as the one true pattern—and that because these studies are not similar in all respects to their "science", therefore they are not "scientific".

Nowadays, since most people's minds have been conditioned by the observations, methods and aims of physics, the term "scientific" is taken to describe knowledge obtained by similar processes to that of this dominant science of physics. But before allowing this norm for what is scientific or unscientific to pass unquestioned we would do well to consider the immense harm caused by this very restrictive habit in the past.

For instance, in the thirteenth century the question arose as to whether theology is a science. Since, at that time, the title of "master of those that know" was accorded to Aristotle, the theologians of that age were in fact asking whether their discipline conformed to the norm of science laid down by Aristotle. According to him, science is universal and necessary knowledge of the essence of things through their causes—broadly speaking it employs a classificatory, deductive method. Was theology, therefore, a science? Some theologians said it did not conform to this pattern, adding "so much the worse

B

for science." Others, wishing to maintain the dignity of their discipline, said that it was a science. Victory, on the whole, went to the second party, but there is reason to believe that their victory did occasionally prove harmful, and prevent theology from developing its own proper method.[7]

The physical sciences themselves had to face the same prejudice when they first became a central interest in the later Middle Ages. The keen minds of Nicholas of Oresme, Buridan and others of the Paris school were hampered by their inability to break loose from Aristotelian methods. Not until Galileo firmly insisted that the physical sciences *were* actually bringing knowledge—even if it was by un-Aristotelian methods—did the physical sciences acquire confidence in themselves and freedom of experiment. The wheel has now come full circle, and it is the physical sciences which provide the standard for what is regarded as "scientific"—with equally disastrous results very often. For it leads to the wrong question being asked. The question should not run, "Is history (or sociology, psychology, etc.) scientific?" (i.e. does it use the methods of physical science?); one should say, "*in fact*, history (sociology, psychology, etc.) do bring us knowledge. *How* do they do so? By what methods? What are the methods proper to these studies?". Because then we would have a more comprehensive and exact idea of what is scientific.

Clearly there has been a change over the centuries in our view of scientific method. There has also, however, been a more subtle change in our very view of knowledge itself and what it involves. This change is best brought out by a brief comparison between the medieval and the modern attitude towards knowledge.

For the orthodox medieval thinker knowledge was a good in itself which blossomed out as the ultimate fulfilment of man's nature in the contemplation, the knowledge and enjoyment of the three Persons of the Blessed Trinity. Knowledge brought its own fruition, the union of the knower and the known, the lover united with the beloved in the ecstasy of communion. Consequently it was believed that the contemplative life was the highest form of life, and that the active life was meritorious only in so far as it served to bring men to contemplation. It was superfluous to ask what was the *use* of this contemplation, what *end* it was meant to serve, for in contemplation we arrive at the fruition, the enjoyment, the end towards which all our activities, our useful works are ordered.

And at the centre of this view of the world was God, the source and the end of all human longings.

With the "Copernican revolution" many throughout Europe ceased to hold this view of the world and of man's place in it. It is commonly stated that Copernicus, by proving that the earth is not the centre of the universe, made men realize that man is not the centre of the universe either, and so taught him to accept a humbler attitude towards his own status. But this common opinion states the very opposite of the truth. It is in modern times rather than the Middle Ages that man has come to regard himself as the centre of Creation. In the Middle Ages such representative thinkers as Dante and St. Thomas Aquinas knew very well that man had been created by God as one being in the scale of being; for them, God is the centre and circumference of all things, upholding all creatures in the scale of being, and man's place is a little lower than that of the angels, a little higher than that of the brute creatures.

In fact the immediate effect of Copernicus' discovery alone was probably not very great. It was because Copernicus' discovery coincided with new theological teachings (in Calvin and Luther), which stressed man's isolation and his need to fear the wrath of God, that we can truly speak of a revolution in man's world view at that time. For men began to see themselves as separate from the rest of creation, cut off from the brutes through their intellectual capacity, cut off from God by his wrath, and having no companionship with other intellectual beings such as the angels or the saints. And a great fear came upon men when they realized their dreadful isolation (cf. pp. 225-6).

It was this overwhelming fear which changed their attitude towards knowledge. As everyone knows, the reverse side of fear is the desire for domination; a person full of fear always

tries to work it off by acts of violence, by snatching at whatever he fears he is missing. Such a person cannot rest contem-
platively in the enjoyment of anything but attempts to
dominate all things, all things whatsoever being further objects
of fear—to be dominated.

Not surprisingly, therefore, the acknowledged apostle of
modernity, Francis Bacon, re-defined knowledge. "Knowledge", he said, "is power"; and by power he meant the
power to dominate nature, to make things serve man's
purposes.[8] Knowledge, from the seventeenth century onwards,
is regarded as a means of changing the face of the earth,
wresting nature's secrets from her by violence, cutting down
virgin forests and splitting the atom. "Knowledge is power",
said Francis Bacon, and his words have been echoed by one
thinker after another until we come to Marx's classical statement that hitherto philosophers had interpreted the world but
from now on they would *change* it. "In the beginning", said
Engels, "was the deed"—not, be it noticed, the Word, the
Logos, the rational principle, but the deed. Action must
determine theory; knowledge is measured in terms of its use
for man's purposes. This is the last stage in the process of
man's idolizing his own knowledge; nothing is beyond the
reach of his power, since, as Marx's official interpreter says,
"our knowledge of the laws of nature is completely reliable
. . . there is nothing unknowable in the world" (Stalin).

Whereas Bacon thought that knowledge was a means of
dominating nature, and whereas Marx, Engels and Stalin see
it as their task to change nature by technical discoveries, St.
Thomas thinks of knowledge as the process of graciously
receiving from nature, and so from God, the light which we
could never manufacture for ourselves. For Bacon and the
Marxists, then, it is obvious that the active life is the highest,
the contemplative life unproductive: "The virgin consecrated
to God", as Bacon drily remarks, "brings forth nothing".
To St. Thomas the contemplative life is the highest life, and
ultimately the most fruitful for everyone—not only for those
living it, since, as he would have pointed out, the virgin
consecrated to God is the mother of many, who by her prayers

and sufferings brings to birth in Christ so many souls that were dead.

Perhaps the following pages will enable the reader to judge the issues that are at stake in our attitude towards knowledge, and help him to decide whether the desire to change the world does not need to be integrated into a contemplative vision, if change is to mean rebuilding and not destruction.

Finally, a few words about the kind of reader for whom the book is meant. It is meant for the general reader, and has been written in the knowledge that many of the books addressed to the general reader never reach him. Time and again I have found very intelligent men, postmen, trade unionists, school-teachers, miners and undergraduates, abandoning books not because their content was beyond their grasp (as they modestly assumed) but simply because the books demanded a command of language such as few of these men possess. As far as possible, therefore, I have tried to explain the meaning of any alarming terms that cannot be avoided. Which explains why the sections on Phenomenology, Existentialism and Logical Positivism have so few notes to them—if I had quoted directly from the authors discussed there I should have had to explain their terms so minutely that we should never have come to an end, especially in the Logical Positivism section which may even now prove too complicated. I am aware that this has led to unsatisfactory accounts of some thinkers—it struck me in reading through the typescript, to take one instance, that Freud's "super-ego" is a far more important concept than I have been able to indicate. But all I have hoped to do, in any case, is to make my friends, the postmen, the miners, the undergraduates, etc., feel at home in these remote houses of learning. Once they get over their feelings of awkwardness in the face of learned men they can begin to make their own judgements.

NOTES

[1] According to the *Index Medicus* over 1,000 works on pulmonary tuberculosis appeared in 1945–46!

[2] Polanyi (*The Logic of Liberty*, Kegan Paul, 1951, pp. 14–15) describes the irrational opposition to hypnosis, and concludes, "The hatred

against the discoverers of a phenomenon which threatened to undo the
cherished beliefs of science was as bitter and inexorable as that of the
religious persecutors two centuries before. It was, in fact, of the same
character."

  ³ Quoted by G. Ardley in *Aquinas and Kant*, Longmans, 1950, p. 26.
  ⁴ WILLIAM JAMES, *The Will to Believe*, pp. 10–11.
  ⁵ cf. J. S. CAMMACK, S. J., *Moral Problems of Mental Defect*, Burns Oates &
Washbourne, 1938, pp. 47–52.
  ⁶ SIGMUND FREUD, *Totem and Taboo*, Pelican Edition, p. 196.
  ⁷ cf. R. GUELLUY, *Philosophie et Théologie chez Guillaume d'Ockham*,
Paris, J. Vrin, 1947.
  ⁸ That this is the drift of Bacon's thought can be seen from *The
Philosophy of Francis Bacon* by F. H. Anderson (Chicago, 1948).

I

MODERN PHILOSOPHY

PHILOSOPHERS, FOR the average man, are an object of fun. It is as well that they should remain so on the whole, since the days when philosophers could be regarded as mankind's guides towards wisdom seem to be past. A Socrates, a Plato or an Aristotle might have attracted to himself the young men and the questioning minds of his day, but nowadays no-one would be more surprised than the Professor of Philosophy himself if his pupils began to come to him for advice upon how to run their lives. To give such advice is not his task; he simply expounds Plato or Kant or Carnap. Any suggestion that he might arrive at some conclusion which would involve a change in his way of life or anyone else's would prove shocking to him.

Philosophy has become a game, out of which not even the philosophers get much fun, since they do not play it—they simply draw up the rules and spend their lives revising them. Each generation of philosophers leaves behind it a fresh deposit of rules, so that their successors have more and more rules to revise and occupy themselves with during their lectures. When Descartes, for instance, said, "I think, therefore I am", he provided professional philosophers with a source for endless volumes of commentary which they are still producing. It would be impossible for most people to read through a fraction of these commentaries, and at first sight it would seem pointless, no man in his senses ever having doubted that he exists. Doubting about whether one exists is such a bad habit that we are well advised not to fall into it. Then why occupy ourselves with philosophy at all if it deals with such remote doubts? Why not refuse to adopt bad habits so as to save oneself the trouble of correcting them?

33

There are two main reasons: the first being that one cannot avoid these bad habits, because the philosophers, or their popularizers, make them part of our tradition; and what begins in the philosopher's study as a possibility very often ends up in the morning newspaper as an authorized view of the world. Some years ago, for instance, philosophers began to talk about the philosophical implications behind Einstein's theory of relativity, and before you could ask them what they thought they were doing the general public began to talk glibly of everything being relative: "Time is not real, it is only relative", "Morality is not an absolute; it is only relative", or, "I was not really responsible since my responsibility is only relative"; these and similar statements were heard on all sides, because the philosopher's surmises had become the current nonsense. So for this reason alone the study of philosophy has its value, in making us aware of the bad habits that are current and teaching us either to avoid them or to get out of them.

A more positive value arises from the insight into our lives which emerges from some philosophical investigations. Even Descartes' "I think, therefore I am" was intended to show, by rigorous reasoning, that you cannot doubt everything; and though most people know obscurely that you cannot do so, there are considerable advantages in knowing this truth clearly and in knowing why you cannot do so. Philosophy, when it is valuable, therefore, is clarified commonsense. So in the rest of this section on philosophy only those ideas will be considered which are not obviously silly.

A question which has not occupied the philosophers as much as it ought should be asked here at the very beginning; what are we trying to do when we philosophize? Because they have assumed that they knew perfectly well what questions they were trying to answer, philosophers have sometimes fallen into despair at the differences in their answers. It is humbly suggested that these differences are very often due to their asking different questions; hence it is not surprising that they have given different answers.

On the whole philosophers can be divided into two groups, those who want a quick, simple answer using as few explanatory

terms as possible, and those who move more slowly trying to
devise as many terms as possible to do justice to the complexity
of the situation. Suppose a representative from each of these
groups is faced with the same observation, namely that the
presence of Josephine makes Napoleon bored. How would they
account for this observation in philosophical terms? The representative of the first group would probably say that men are
bored by whatever does not excite them, that Josephine has
lost her power of excitement and therefore Napoleon is bored.
Immediately this philosopher has reduced the question to a few
simple terms, to "the power of excitement", "boredom", and
the fact that Napoleon belongs to the class "man".

The representative of the second group would probably move
more slowly. He would point out that Napoleon's "boredom"
in the presence of Josephine cannot be so quickly reduced to
the absence of excitement, since Napoleon often betrays excitement when Josephine is there, and has a tendency, for instance,
to swear at her in his excitement. Furthermore he is often
"bored" when he is excited; he is excited by the presence of
Mlle. X, but knows very well that he is also bored by her.
Again, is it true to say that Josephine has lost her power of
excitement? for there are many men who become excited in
her presence. Clearly it is no sufficient explanation that
Napoleon belongs to the class "man". This philosopher has
immediately begun to distinguish between various shades of
boredom and excitement, and to point out that there is a good
deal more to Napoleon than the mere fact that he belongs to
the class "man".

Both methods of dealing with this observation have their
advantage from the philosophical standpoint. The first has the
advantage that by reducing explanations to a few simple terms
it can be clearly stated. Consequently it makes it easier to
arrive at generalizations; because the few simple terms are
general and abstract; for instance, the abstract notions of
"power of excitement", or "boredom", or "man", can be
readily applied to men in general in very many situations.
Again, it will be a convenient method for the physical scientist,
who, for example, when dealing with the stars, is interested in

their quantities, their mass, their size and their position, but is not particularly interested in their qualities, such as redness or brightness, except in so far as they can be measured on a frequency scale. And, of course, the method will become less valuable the more complex the subject being dealt with; a star may be easily dealt with in quantitative terms, but a new factor enters in when one is dealing with living things, such as trees, even more when one is dealing with animals; whilst the method, on its own, becomes most inadequate when dealing with complex subjects such as human beings, whose quantitative aspects are very much less important than their qualities.

Above all this method will be the one most congenial to the logician, since the subject of the logician's studies is the relationship between abstract terms, terms such as "man" or "class" or "relation"; the fewer of them he has to keep in his head at one time the more easily he can see the relationships between them. Therefore, from the very beginning he will try to reduce a situation to as few terms as possible; complexity is his enemy.

Those studies which are best dealt with by the first method are the ones least amenable to the second method and vice-versa. For whereas the second method would only confuse the logician or the physical scientist by drawing attention to such details as the fact that Napoleon is a particular man with peculiar qualities and cannot just be called "a man", or by drawing attention to the peculiarly beautiful colouring of certain leaves of a tree in the evening sunlight, it is the second method which is most likely to do justice to the study of living things, to questions of morality and artistic appreciation which are all complicated by the wealth of relationships which they involve. For instance, in discussing how a soldier should behave towards a prisoner, which is an ethical question, one cannot reduce the situation to the simple fact of "one man having power over another man" and discussing how he should use that power. Here the first of our methods would be totally inadequate and we should have to use the second method, asking whether the soldier himself was endangering his own life and that of his comrades by keeping the prisoner alive, asking whether the military situation at that particular time demanded urgent action or whether a decision could be delayed, asking how many times this same prisoner had escaped already, and so on.

The first method is the way of abstraction, leaving out of account as many of the relationships involved as possible; the second method is the way of insight, trying to see things in that uniqueness which is due to their complex relationships. The first method is a preparation for action; for the physical scientist, wishing to act upon the world by his experiments, has no time to consider all the factors involved—whether, for instance, his atomic experiments might eventually be used for atomic bombs; similarly, the soldier faced with his prisoner can scarcely sit down and subject his prisoner to psycho-analysis to discover whether the prisoner's dreams reveal a trustworthy or an untrustworthy nature. If the first method is a preparation for action the second method is a means of meditation, of seizing a situation in all its complexity and omitting none of the relevant factors. The ethical theorist, for example, who is considering the soldier's behaviour towards his prisoner must at all costs avoid the precipitate decision which the soldier has to take; his is the way of meditation.

So far we have been outlining the two methods without naming the philosophical schools which employ one or the other —of course the methods are not exclusive, since the man of action does think occasionally and the meditative man can scarcely avoid some action, but philosophical schools do favour one method or the other. Those who employ the first method are described as *positivist* in inclination, those who employ the second are of a *phenomenological* turn (phenomenology, derived from " phenomena" ; phenomenologists are concerned above all with the complexity of phenomena).

At the end of the thirteenth century lived a Franciscan philosopher who used the phenomenological method with the utmost skill, Duns Scotus. Ever aware of the complexity of the world and the infinite relationships in which even such a simple creature as a particular tree was involved, Scotus always attempted to see the uniqueness of things, to grasp their individuality here-and-now, this tree in this place at this time. His philosophical motto might well have been: Refrain from reducing the number of your terms in case you should neglect the complexity of the world. Clearly this way of approaching the world was bound to produce reactions of impatience in people who want to get down to things more quickly, and the generation after Scotus produced a philosopher whose motto might well have been: refrain from multiplying the number of your terms unless it is absolutely necessary. This philosopher, William of Ockham, had thereby provided a method and a programme for physical scientists; and so it is not surprising that the great Paris school of physical scientists in the fourteenth century were Ockhamists rather than Scotists.

This reaction of the positivist Ockham from the phenomenological Scotus has taken place in reverse in our own day; an overdose of positivism led to an outbreak of phenomenology. The positivists of the nineteenth century had so reduced the many-sidedness and infinite shadings of the world in favour of their simple terms from physical science, such as "matter" and "motion", that a reaction was bound to come. No-one could go on living permanently in such a dehydrated world! The reaction led to the formation of a phenomenological school under Edmund Husserl and his pupils, Heidegger, Scheler, von Hildebrand, Pfänder, etc. The fact that Germans have taken the lead in this reaction is not surprising, since they were the first to suffer violently from the abuse of physical science and its appropriate philosophy. Likewise the reaction's failure to affect Britain may partly be attributed to the comfort and ease which the British have continued to derive from the use and abuse of physical science. At the same time one Briton, that sensitive soul, A. N. Whitehead, has formulated the phenomenologist viewpoint in his own way in these words: "The misconception which has haunted philosophic literature throughout the centuries is the notion of 'independent' existence. There is no such mode of existence; every entity is only to be understood in terms of the way in which it is interwoven with the rest of the universe". In other words, Whitehead is a phenomenologist, distrustful of the abstraction which ignores relations, ever attempting to achieve a vision of the unique and concrete.

From our discussion of what philosophy is about we have learnt to ask philosophers what they think they are doing. Before giving accounts of modern philosophies one should also ask the philosophers what are the observations which they begin with and take as the material for their philosophizing. So many of their quarrels are to be explained through their arriving at different places by beginning from different places.

For example, what struck Aristotle about the world was the existence of *things*, of rocks and trees and men, etc. No matter what changes take place they take place in *things;* rocks, trees and men may change but some *thing* persists throughout these changes. After many years we may come back to some spot and see that a certain rock has changed, nevertheless we describe it as the same rock; the thing "rock" has persisted throughout the years. Again we may meet a person whom we have not seen since we were at school together; he will have changed, his head become bald perhaps and his teeth false. But we should not say that he has been destroyed on that account; the changes are accidental but the substance, that which makes him what he is, remains over the years. Therefore *substances* subject to change were the starting-point of Aristotle's philosophy; it was from this preliminary observation that all his other key-terms such as "causality", "accident", "potentiality" and "act", "quality" and "quantity", were derived.

It is worth while pointing out that most men begin their observation of the world in the same way as Aristotle. They notice *things* which endure in time. Therefore the average person has always been inclined to accept Aristotle's philosophy; it begins and ends in common sense, and so can never be entirely antiquated—or not, at least, until men lose their common sense. Which explains also why the modern philosophers who stick most closely to Aristotle, the Thomists, are not reluctant to describe their thought as the philosophy of common sense.

Now once we start our thinking with these initial Aristotelian terms as a basis it is inevitable that the structure which we build up from them should take a certain shape; the relationships between the various terms, or parts of the structure, are limited by the limitation of the terms. Clearly, if one began with different initial terms one would eventually arrive at a different structure. This, in fact, has been done on several occasions in modern times although the people doing it have not always been aware that they were beginning from different initial observations; the result has been that they became angry with Aristotle for having erected a different structure, not realizing that he had in fact used different basic terms.

For instance, after the discoveries of Copernicus, Galileo and Newton had made physical science fashionable, the philosophers no longer saw the world directly, as Aristotle had seen it. Locke and Hume, to name two, saw the world in terms of the facts which physical science had made universally known. Since modern physical science does not interest itself in the *natures* of things (of men, rocks, trees, etc.) but in the laws by which it attempts to order "facts", the philosophers under their influence did likewise. For instance, whereas an Aristotelian philosopher, or the average man, would describe a reunion with an old friend by saying, say, "I met old Shackleton again for the first time since 1920", a Lockean or Humian would say, "I remember the fact that I met a person named Shackleton in 1920; I remember the fact that I met a person named Shackleton recently; it is also a fact that I associate these two facts. By what law (comparable to the laws enunciated by Newton) can I account for all these facts?" Obviously there is a world of difference between taking "facts" (i.e. the statement, "the fact that . . .") as one's initial term, and taking "things" as one's initial terms.

If Hume and Locke and many another had realized the world of difference between beginning with "things" and beginning with "facts" (i.e. the *statement*, "the fact that . . .") they would not have spent so much time showing the uselessness of Aristotle's "substance", because they would have realized that they themselves had excluded "things" by starting from the "facts". For the truth of the matter is that "facts" are not given to us at the beginning of our normal experience in the direct way that men and trees and other *things* are given to us. "Facts" are what we ascertain as a result of testing or experi-

ment; they are the content of the statements which we have
been testing. Whereas "things" are directly given to us through
seeing, hearing and so forth, "facts" are only given to us
indirectly through a screen of mental testing; therefore strictly
speaking we should not say that Hume, Locke, etc. begin with
"facts" but with statements such as "it is a fact that . . .".

Once we realize this difference between the initial terms of
Aristotle and Hume or Locke *we* have no difficulty in seeing
Hume's difficulty about "substance". "Substance" belongs to
the existing world outside our minds, to the world of men,
apples and gooseberry-bushes; Aristotle's world is a substantial
world, the one in which we live and are jostled and step on
each other's toes. "The fact that . . ." immediately takes us
away from this substantial world into the realm of statements
—which are the results of *mental* processes, and not primarily
of processes in the external world. Therefore once he had
taken "the fact that . . ." as the start for his philosophizing
no wonder Hume could not cram substances into his system!
It was, quite literally, just as impossible as to cram chairs,
trees and other *things* into his own head!

Therefore the quarrel about "substance" between Aristotelians and Humians should never have arisen: when they used
the word "substance" each side meant something different.

In the same way they should never have quarrelled about
causality; that is, Hume ought not to have attacked a notion
the very possibility of which he had excluded by taking "the
fact that . . ." as his initial material for philosophizing.
Whereas, in other words, an Aristotelian can rightly say, "My
child caused my papers to fall to the floor by blowing them",
because his original terms are things (child, papers, etc.), a
Humian would have to record this as, "The fact that my child
blew my papers was followed by the fact that my papers fell on
to the floor". The Humian could not say "the fact that my
child blew my papers *caused* the fact that my papers fell onto
the floor"—one fact cannot *cause* another fact, though one fact
may be followed by another fact. Perhaps this becomes clearer
if one points out that "facts are the contents of statements we
have been testing", and therefore always relate to the state-

ments or propositions which contain them. Now one could
never say that statement A *caused* statement B; one might say
that statement B was associated in one's mind with statement
A; one might even say that statement A implied statement B
either according to the laws of logic or according to the laws of
physical science. But one could never say statement A *caused*
statement B in the same way as my little girl, Mary Dominica,
caused my papers to fall to the floor.

Therefore the Humian should not have been surprised at
failing to discover the causal relationship within his system, for
his initial terms had excluded it. Causality is a relationship
between *things*, not between "facts"; the relationship between
"facts" is that simply of succession.

These distinctions between the initial terms of Aristotle and
of Hume are particularly valuable when we are comparing
their modern followers, the Thomists on one side and the positivists on the other—Carnap, Wittgenstein, Russell. All of
the arguments between these two schools would be greatly
clarified if those taking part realized that each side *begins* from
a different place.

And the same is true of the other types of philosophy we
shall be discussing. The material, as it were, of Marx's philosophizing is neither things nor facts but *society*; from this initial
term spring all his characteristic notions, such as "class-
warfare", "dialectic", "withering of the state" and other
seemingly odd notions. Since Marxism begins with this highly
abstract and confusing notion of society it is not surprising that
other philosophers, such as Thomists and positivists, find
Marxism difficult to understand; they should remember with
sympathy that a person whose attention is immediately caught
by "society" finds it almost as difficult to understand those
who start off from things or from "it is a fact that. . . ."

The existentialist takes a different starting-point; he concen-
trates upon specifically *human* experiences such as dread,
anxiety, hope, the flux of time and so on; consequently he
develops a philosophy which seems very strange to those of
another tradition, but which is less strange, perhaps, once we
recognize that the existentialist has chosen a very particular—

although not necessarily odd—starting point, i.e. specifically *human* experience.

As we shall see later, when we are discussing logic, each of these schools of philosophy has its own "logic"; there is an Aristotelian "logic", a positivist "logic", a Marxist "logic" and (since Jasper's book on "Truth") an existentialist "logic". The explanation of the quotation-marks round "logic" is that logicians are such a sharp-tongued breed of men that we should hate to appear to be judging the validity of any of these "logics", and thus incur their wrath. For an Aristotelian has been known to say that the description of Marxist "logic" as "logic" was "an abuse of words"; the positivist would agree with the Aristotelian on this point but would maintain, with the Marxist, that the Aristotelian "logic" is "scholastic, grammar-ridden nonsense". And so the compliments would be passed around, like the Indian's pipe of peace, with that icy politeness cultivated by logicians.

But before exposing ourselves to that iciness, before discussing logic, let us try to explain the main points of Marxism, phenomenology, existentialism and logical positivism. We shall do so, for the most part, in our own language, because the special languages of these various philosophies take years to learn. This course would seem to have the disadvantage that we are liable to misrepresent the thinkers being discussed. As a matter of fact this is not a disadvantage so much as a pre-supposition, for many modern thinkers take it as an insult when someone claims to have understood what they are talking about. "Only one person has understood me", said Hegel, "and he misunderstood"—a statement which modern philosophers are apt to make triumphantly rather than sorrowfully. And so each of these sections should be prefaced by such a phrase as not "What Marx (or Husserl, etc.) really meant", but "What I think Marx (or Husserl, etc.) is driving at". Each of these men would protest that I have misunderstood him; for they demand of their readers a lifetime's study before they can be understood. So do I; so do we all; meantime we've all got other things to do with our lives.

MARXISM

IN PHILOSOPHY we have always to begin with the philosopher who comes one before the philosopher we are going to discuss. To discuss Marx (1818–1883) we must begin with Hegel (1770–1831); because Marx, as the saying goes, turned Hegel on his head. That is to say, whereas Hegel treats world history as the dialectic of the Idea Marx treats it as the dialectic of Matter.

What did Hegel mean by saying that world history was a process of realization of the Idea? He himself thought that he was stating in philosophical terminology (i.e. in a purified form), what the Christian Church had traditionally taught, that history displays the workings of God in the world. But Hegel maintained that Christianity had hitherto presented its content, i.e. absolute truth, in the form of pictorial and sensuous imagery; in his philosophy, though he was presenting the identical content, i.e. absolute truth, he was now presenting it in the absolute form, the form of pure thought liberated from pictorial and sensuous images. Thus Hegel claimed that God, as such, is the Idea, which is threefold. As universal he is God, the Father, producing out of itself the particular, God, the Son, which returns into the universal as the individual, God, the Holy Spirit; and therefore whoever has understood the Idea as expounded in Hegel's *History of the World* has understood the Trinity.

A Christian, confronted with this view of Hegel's, would maintain, on the contrary, that anyone who claims to have *understood* the Trinity in all its workings has thereby shown himself to have misunderstood the first thing about the Trinity: that it is a mystery. A mystery of faith does present us with intelligible truth, but our intellects can never exhaust the riches of this truth; consequently anyone who claims to have done so, as Hegel did, has fallen into grave error. Not surprisingly, this intellectual error even produced disastrous results in the practical order, for Hegel believed that the Idea was now realized in its purity in the Prussian state. The dialectic of the Idea had achieved its realization in history in the Prussian state; not unnaturally, given his viewpoint, Hegel proceeded to treat this state as though it were God.

In a similar fashion Hegel's follower, Marx, treats world history as the dialectic, not this time of the Idea, but of Matter.

The way in which this dialectic of Matter operates in history, according to Marx, is as follows. Matter at a certain period of time has taken various forms such as the hand-mill, barons and serfs, and the medieval priesthood. All these various forms are simply reflections of the dialectical movement of Matter at the stage of feudalism. But this movement of the dialectic known as feudalism, "with the inexorability of a natural law" [1] produces a negation of itself—capitalism. Capitalism is the second phase of the dialectical movement, and in its turn gives birth to its own negation—communism. Feudalism, capitalism and communism are known respectively as the thesis, antithesis and synthesis of the dialectical movement of matter. That, in a nutshell, is the materialist interpretation of history. [2]

Without question the importance which Marx attaches to material factors in shaping world events has given historians tremendously valuable insights into those events. No competent historian nowadays would even dream of describing a past society without first of all establishing the economic framework of that society, and this has meant giving a new assessment to whole stretches of the past. When Macaulay,[3] for instance, wrote of the seventeenth-century struggle in England he wrote as though the parliamentarians were fighting for individual rights and majority rule against royalists defending the king's absolute right to govern as he deemed best. But nowadays, largely as a result of Marx's influence, historians would agree that the parliamentarians in general were rising to political power through their recently acquired economic power whilst the royalists came from traditional families trying to retain political control of the country at a time when their economic control had been broken. Consequently historians are no longer content to take the seventeenth-century man's pamphlets, books and declarations of his religious convictions as adequate causes for his actions; his ledgers, his commercial interests, and changing techniques of production must also be taken into account if we are to understand him. For example, the foreign policy of Oliver Cromwell cannot be properly accounted for unless we realize how much it was determined by Britain's commercial rivalry with the Dutch, and by financiers such as Martin Noell. Nor can Shaftesbury's opposition to Charles II be understood entirely as a political struggle—the economiç interests of the Whig aristocracy played a considerable part in it. And one could illustrate these new assessments of history due to historical materialism indefinitely.

Unfortunately the neglected factor in history which Marx brought to light, i.e. the material means of production, was treated by him as if it were ultimately the one determining factor.[4] Marx in his later life probably did come to see this to be an error[5] (the "nothing-but" fallacy as we have previously named it); yet it has so generally been taken as true Marxist doctrine that its false logic needs to be exposed. The doctrine was most concisely stated by Engels, in a speech delivered at Marx's grave-side, when he said that Marx "had discovered the law of evolution in human history; he discovered the simple fact, hitherto concealed by an overgrowth of ideology, that mankind must first of all eat and drink, have shelter and clothing, before it can pursue position, science, religion, art, etc.; and that therefore the production of the immediate means of subsistence and consequently the degree of economic development attained by a given people or during a given epoch, form the foundations upon which the state institutions, the legal conceptions, the art and even the religious ideas of the people concerned have been evolved, and in the light of which these things must therefore be explained, instead of vice versa as has hitherto been the case".[6]

Leaving aside the confusion Engels causes by speaking of the "law of evolution in human history",[7] it simply does not follow that "politics, science, religion, art, etc. . . . must be explained in the light of the production of the immediate material means of subsistence" on the ground that we have to eat and drink, etc. before we can engage in these pursuits. Apart from anything else, before we can even eat and drink we have to be begotten and conceived, but who would therefore claim that all our subsequent activities are to be explained in the light of this process of begetting and conceiving? Some Freudians almost do so, it is true (which perhaps explains why Freud is taboo to Marxists—because he goes one further than they do—beyond the stomach, to the womb), but they are reasoning wrongly. In other words, to be born, to eat and breathe, etc. are *conditions* which have to be fulfilled if I am to do anything at all, but they are not therefore the *cause* of everything I do and think. Just as, for instance, my writing these lines is *conditional* upon my having pencil and paper but is not *caused* by my pencil and paper. The pencil and paper are only two of a countless number of conditions for my writing, such as having read Karl Marx, residing on this planet rather than another, etc. But, if one were to describe all these conditions as the *cause* of what I am doing, then one would have to say that the cause of any event was the total condition of the universe immediately before it happened. Obviously anyone is free to use the word "cause" in this sense, if he chooses, but to do so would make it impossible to attribute any definite meaning to the word.

And so when a Marxist "explains" politics, science, art, religion, etc. in the light of "immediate material means of subsistence" he is confusing a condition with a cause.[8]

One is strongly inclined to suspect that Marx himself would never have allowed this confusion to persist if only he could really have freed himself (as indeed he believed he had) from the mystification of the Hegelian dialectic. For in later life he spoke most scornfully of those people who, as he said, "metamorphose my historical sketch of the genesis of capitalism in Western Europe into an historico-philosophic theory of the *marche-générale* imposed by fate upon every people", a theory "the supreme virtue of which consists in being super-historical".[9] Similarly, when certain dialectical Marxists maintained that the movement of the dialectic would demand in Russia the emergence of a capitalist-dominated proletariat before the communist synthesis could be achieved, he more or less told them not to be so silly. "The chapter on primitive accumulation does not pretend to do any more than trace the path by which, in Western Europe, the capitalist order of economy emerged from the feudal order of economy".[10] He points out that there is no compelling necessity for Russian society to go through the same process, and he thereby as good as jettisons his earlier notion that the dialectic could be taken as an explanation of all history.

In fact, Marx analysed modern Western society in terms of the economic conflict between feudalism and capitalism, and then declared those terms to be the ultimate ones for the interpretation of all human history.[11] A similar illegitimate transference took place when he declared that "the history of all hitherto existing society is the history of class warfare";[12] he noticed the class warfare in Victorian England, saw Victorian society as nothing but class warfare, and then used this notion to explain all hitherto existing society. It seems as though his habit of making illegitimate transferences became thoroughly ingrained, since he even said of Darwin's *Evolution of Species*, "Darwin's book is very important and serves me as a basis in natural science for the class struggle in history".[13] Obviously Darwin's book did nothing of the sort unless human and animal behaviour are to be identified. And in that case Kropotkin's well-documented description of co-operation in the animal kingdom,[14] which reversed Darwin's one-sided viewpoint, should have led Marx to reverse his view of history. If we equate animal and human behaviour we might equally well declare, on the basis of Kropotkin's work, that "the history of all existing society is the history of human co-operation". The truth of the matter is that history exhibits both conflict and co-operation, and it is a mistake to neglect either.

When the reader turns from Marx's interpretation of history to his specifically philosophical teaching he realizes that the deficiencies of the former are largely due to the crudity of Marx's philosophical conceptions. Accustomed as the reader is to careful distinctions of terms and methods of exact analysis,

he finds in Marxism a view of the world such as he can find
nowhere else in the European tradition, unless he goes back
to the philosophers before Socrates. Marxism, in its technical
philosophical terminology, does not rise above the pre-
Socratic level. Pre-Socratic philosophers there are who
"explain" the world in terms of matter, water, air or fire, in
the same way that Marx "explains" the world in terms of
matter, but not since Socrates applied his sharp mind to these
problems has any recognized philosopher other than Marx
been content with such crudities.

Indeed, so vague (and abstract) is the notion of "matter"
that one scarcely knows how to begin dealing with it. The
notion is described in this way: "The world in its very nature
is *material*, and the manifold phenomena in the world represent
different forms of self-moving matter".[15] Let us examine this
statement more closely. All the phenomena, the appearances,
which we encounter in the world (tables, chairs, mountains,
trees, men and women) are all "material". If by "material"
we mean "whatsoever is seen, touched, heard, tasted or
smelt", then to describe phenomena (i.e. whatever is seen,
touched, heard, tasted or smelt) as "material" is equivalent
to saying, "Grass is grass" or "White is white". It is not
untrue, but it just does not tell us anything we did not already
know.

This point has to be dwelt upon because there are others
besides the Marxists under the illusion that they have seen or
felt or smelt or touched or tasted "matter", and who seem
never to have realized that the word "matter" signifies an
abstraction. In fact, no-one has ever seen (or smelt, etc.)
"matter". What we see (smell, etc.) are tables, chairs, men
and women and so forth—individual *things*, which are material
(i.e. which are seen, touched, etc.). It is not that we see a
table or a man, and then *see* the "matter" of which the table
and the man are made; no-one has ever *seen* "matter"—the
word signifies an abstraction which we use to summarize
material things. All that we see are individual *things* such as
tables, men, etc.

We have pointed out that the Marxist quotation is a truism,

if "material" means "what is seen, touched, heard, etc.".
But if the quotation means that the world in its very nature is
nothing but material, then the statement, without further
arguments to clarify it, is clearly a statement of faith and not
of fact. Furthermore it is a very improbable statement. Apart
from the enormous difficulty of explaining what moves
material things if there is nothing but "matter" in the
universe, there can obviously be no *evidence* that there are not
other beings in the universe—beings, for instance, which can
know each other without the need for seeing, touching, etc.

Therefore this statement of Marxist faith (that everything is
matter in one form or another) must be regarded as a very
crude attempt to "explain" the world. It simply throws out
the word "matter" as a cover for everything—without even
suggesting *how* "matter" acquires the capacity for producing
life and performing all the wonderful feats daily performed by
birds, bats and dogs—much less how one form of "matter"
(the reader of these lines) manages to understand another form
of "matter" (the author of them).[16]

One could continue indefinitely, but without much profit,
illustrating the primitive nature of Marx's basic concepts. And
again one suspects that Marx himself was beginning to realize
this towards the end of his life; for although he had for many
years been using the word "class" it was only towards the end
that he tried to work out what precisely he meant by the
word, "and it seems significant that of the chapter [of his
unfinished manuscript] called *The Classes* he should have
written only a page and a half. Marx dropped the analysis of
society at the moment when he was approaching its real
difficulties".[17] The explanation of why he took so long to see
the ambiguities in his favourite terms such as "dialectic",
"matter", "class", etc. seems to be that he had not been so
successful as he imagined in uprooting the ingrained preference
for the abstract over the concrete which Hegel had instilled
into him. Hegel, even when stood upon his head, remains an
idealist.

How difficult it is for thinkers to stick to the concrete we
have already seen in reference to Marx's substitution of the

abstraction "matter" for material things. We see it again
even when he is deliberately trying to avoid abstractness, as
when he says, "The people is not the real State. The State is
an abstraction. The people alone is concrete".[18] But is "the
people alone" concrete? Surely the only concrete existents
are individual things and persons? When we speak of certain
individuals as "the people" we have already begun to abstract
from them as individuals; and however legitimate that may
be, it still prohibits us from saying that "the people alone is
concrete". It is this confusion between abstract and concrete
which leads Marx, for instance, to say of Christianity (the
religion of the concrete Word-made-flesh): "For a society of
this type, Christianity, with its cult of the abstract human
being, is the most suitable religion".[19] It is no wonder, then,
that Marx should often have quoted approvingly Hegel's
dictum: "Even the criminal thought of a scoundrel is grander
and more sublime than the wonders of the heavens";[20] or
that he can speak of "capital" (an abstraction) as though it
were a living being. "No matter how long may be the series
of periodical reproductions and antecedent accumulations
through which the capital now functioning may have passed,
it always retains its primal virginity".[21]

So much stress upon Marx's confusion of abstract ideas and
concrete things would have been out of place here if the
confusion did not also obscure his deepest, most original and
valuable contribution to contemporary thought; this was his
insight into the social nature of man. His insistence that man
is not simply an isolated individual but a social creature has
proved of enormous value in reversing a misleading and
dangerous current of thought in political philosophy. Representatives of this current (such as Hobbes, Locke, Rousseau, etc.)
had posed themselves the following problem: on one side you
have the individual, on the other side you have society, or the
state; where does one draw the demarcation line between the
individual's rights and society's rights? Does each individual,
upon reaching maturity, enter into a contract with society as
to mutual rights? Or was there originally such a primitive
contract in the early days of society, which each individual

either ratifies or rejects? Questions which give rise to endless unprofitable discussions, either leading to the glorification of the state (as in Hobbes' *Leviathan* and Rousseau's "General Will") or else to a negative view of society (as in Locke and the nineteenth-century liberals). The questions were unprofitable because they posited one abstraction, "the individual", beside another abstraction, "society" (or "the state") and then tried to relate them. The relationship which they derived was inevitably abstract! That is, it expressed the mental relations of two ideas rather than the real relationship of men towards each other.

The Marxists have put an end to all that airy philosophizing. Employing the method of phenomenology, the Marxist says that since phenomena are bound together, "no single happening in the world can be understood when taken in isolation".[22] Applying this principle to political life he points out that men are born into a society and are dependent upon these societies for their material means of subsistence, their education, and so forth. It is a waste of time, then, for sociologists to begin by considering the individual outside of all social relationships and then try to work out what those social relationships should be! Men do not live in isolation, but amongst other men, therefore why not study them as they do live—together?

Studying men in their social relationships was exactly what Marx set out to do, and in so doing practically founded the modern science of sociology. It was on the basis of Marx's works that the Fabian Socialists, such as the Webbs, built their monumental sociological enquiries. Marx was also an inspiration to such thinkers as R. H. Tawney, Ernest Bonner and Dr. Temple, who have used his insights in order to show the positive rôle played by society and the state in forming individuals. Education, unemployment relief, health insurance, social regulations of all kinds have been introduced since Marx's day, all reflecting the truth that men are born into society with civic obligations towards each other, all vindicating the teaching that man is a social creature.

Innumerable volumes have already been written in which the subject of this present book (i.e. learning and the nature of knowledge) is dealt with in terms of prevalent social structures. Under Marx's influence the "sociologists of knowledge" (e.g. Scheler, Mannheim, etc.) have raised many such vital questions. It may have struck the reader of these pages as curious, for instance, that Marx and Darwin begin to see the human and the animal kingdom as battle-grounds at about the same date. Was there any essential connection leading to this occurring simultaneously? Having asked himself that question the scholar notices that other thinkers of that time were also concentrating on the warlike aspects of nature— Wallace and Malthus, for instance. Why was this? Was it simply because Darwin and Marx both happened to read Malthus at the same time? Whatever the answer to these particular questions it is obvious that the sociology of knowledge owes a great debt to Marx if only through his having raised such questions.

As always, however, there is confusion of the abstract and the concrete. Sociology itself would become a menace if its professors followed Marx in his teaching that "the essence of man is no abstraction inherent in each separate individual. In reality it is the *ensemble* (aggregate) of social relations".[23] True, the essence of man is no abstraction, but if the essence of man were the *ensemble* of social relations, there would simply be no men and no social relations—you cannot have social relations unless there are existing men to have them, and no ensembling of social relations will ever give man an essence unless men already have essences.

As always, there is the nothing-but assumption. The truth that "human thought is a social phenomenon and cannot be understood apart from the history of society"[24] is taken to mean, quite falsely, that human thought is nothing but a social phenomenon—denying the originality of which individual human beings are capable. Thus Marx is led to speak as if a social need were itself sufficient to call forth knowledge on the part of society. Christianity he explains as due to the needs of the oppressed classes in the ancient world, Egyptian astronomy as a response to the need for predicting the Nile floods, and seventeenth-century inventions as products of capitalism. But he leaves unmentioned the rôle, for instance, of Jesus Christ; he seems to be unaware that it required great intelligence on the part of some individual Egyptian to work out the astronomy; nor does he tell us, for example, what particular social need Galileo's pendulum experiments were meant to answer. Thank God that contemporary doctors searching for cures for cancer and tuberculosis do not accept Marx's belief in social needs giving the answer, but devote their individual energies to finding it.[25]

Using what has been said so far it should be possible for any reader to take up Marx's writings, his great *Capital* first of all, and read them with his eyes open for the main fallacies. But the reader has so far been given little reason to see why Marxism has gripped the minds not only of the half-educated millions but also of highly-educated professors in many famous universities. Is there anything in Marxist philosophy, as opposed, say, to its economic teaching, which can account for the almost unbelievable rapidity with which this philosophy has spread throughout the world?

Clearly, I think, there is. When Marx said "Hitherto philosophers have only *interpreted* the world differently; the point is, to change it", he was putting forward a programme, and people are always more ready to act on a programme than to think out principles. "A true but complicated idea has always less chance of succeeding than one which is false but simple", as de Tocqueville wisely remarked. And Marx's ideas are fundamentally very simple; in place, for example, of the delicate distinctions drawn by traditional philosophers in dealing with the process of knowing, Marx flatly declares that "the ideal is nothing but the material when it has been transposed and translated inside the human head".[26] There is something engaging for men of action in this downrightness with which Marx dismisses traditional problems of philosophy, as there is in such statements as "the question of whether human thought can achieve objective truth is not a question of theory but a practical question. In practice Man must prove the truth, i.e. the reality, power and this-sidedness of his thought. The dispute over the reality or unreality of thought which is isolated from practice is a purely *scholastic* question . . ." [27] And, of course, once a man accepts this criterion of truth he necessarily becomes fanatical—because he must *prove* himself right by achieving power and compelling society to behave in accordance with Marxist theory. If society were *not* to behave in accordance with his theories that would be a practical disproof of them. Consequently, in order to prove that money is unnecessary Lenin was prepared to allow millions of people to starve;[28] consequently, the German communists in 1932 were prepared to help Hitler to power— he would not last long, because the dialectic would not allow it;[29] equally consistently, the communists of Eastern Europe murder Christians, because according to Marxist theory there ought not to be any Christians once the economic structure has changed. In the same way the Marxist can maintain that there is no exploitation in the Soviet Union; and what appears to be exploitation by technocrats is an illusion, since Marx has said that the exploiting class is the class which owns the means of production—the technocrats may control those means, but they do not own them—therefore it is impossible by definition for the technocrats to be doing any exploiting!

All this criticism is true enough, and yet we have still not probed to the depths at which Marx's philosophy touched the needs of so many people. A hint of these depths is found in Marx's statement that "philosophy cannot translate itself into reality without a rising of the proletariat, the proletariat cannot rise without philosophy becoming a reality".[30] In other words, for generations philosophers had sat comfortably in their studies, blandly spinning out their abstract thoughts, themselves untouched by everyday life and their thought failing to touch the needs of human beings. Now Marx ends all that; once more he relates philosophy to human suffering, to the inarticulate suffering of the oppressed proletariat. Human suffering had again found a voice in the person of Karl Marx—that suffering was to realize itself in Marx's philosophy, and philosophy could once more become a reality.

Who, after reading Marx's impassioned writings, can doubt that this is the secret of his influence? Man is sick; man is alienated from himself; "all the means for developing production . . . mutilate the worker into a fragment of a human being . . . and drag his wife and children beneath the Juggernaut wheels of capital's car".[31] That is the point of Marx's diagnosis; men are made inhuman; they are "alienated" from their very selves. This theme of the worker's alienation from himself sounds like a ground swell throughout all the work of Marx—the worker's "own labour has been alienated from himself, has been appropriated by the capitalist and incorporated into capital".[32] Nor is the worker's alienation from the work of his own hands merely a technical problem; it includes the "moral factor".[33]

For man's present miserable condition (the capitalist's no less than the worker's, since he too is "alienated") is due to sin—"Original sin is everywhere at work. With the development of the capitalist method of production, of accumulation, and of wealth, the capitalist ceases to be the mere incarnation of capital. He has a fellow-feeling for his own Adam . . . whilst the archetypal capitalist stigmatizes individual consumption as a sin against his function, the modernised capitalist is able to regard accumulation as 'renunciation' of his impulse towards enjoyment. Alas, two souls dwell within his breast, and one seeks divorce from the other".[34]

What was this original sin? It was the division of labour, since "to subdivide a man is to execute him, if he deserves the sentence; to assassinate him, if he does not. . . . The subdivision of labour is the assassination of a people".[35]

What was the condition of man before this sin was committed? It was that of "primitive communism . . . a primal form, which can be shown to have existed among the Romans, the Teutons, and the Celts".[36]

Is there any hope that man will overcome the effects of this original sin and once more achieve a communist society? There certainly is, for there will inevitably come a "communist society, where nobody has one exclusive sphere of activity but each can become accomplished in any branch he wishes, society regulates the general production and thus makes it possible for me to do one thing to-day and another tomorrow, to hunt in the morning, fish in the afternoon, rear cattle in the evening, criticize after dinner, just as I have a mind, without ever becoming hunter, fisherman, shepherd or critic".[37]

There remains one question: who is to accomplish this "re-integration of man, his return to himself, the abolition of his self-alienation"?[38] Can anyone, after reading Marx's life, doubt that it is Karl Marx who, Prometheus-like, will snatch happiness for humanity from the gods, as Prometheus himself snatched the secret of fire? The myth of Prometheus fascinated Marx throughout his life, and there is every evidence that he tried to fulfil it in his own person.[39]

Thus the pattern of his thought is an ancient one. In the beginning there was a communist paradise;[40] then there was a fall which alienated man from himself; a saviour comes and re-establishes man in his paradisial condition, elevating him to a higher form of human nature.

If anyone should object that the above pattern treats as essential religious categories which are accidental to Marx's thought, then they might do well to remember what Marx himself said: "The criticism of religion is the foundation of all criticism".[41] From the days of his association with Bruno Bauer and his discussions with Feuerbach Marx had wrestled with religious themes; they became part of him, the very categories of his own thinking.

In view of the fact that Marxism falls so naturally into religious categories it may seem surprising that few attempts have been made to assimilate Marxism into traditional religions. Certainly the similarities between traditional Christian teaching and Marxism are very striking. Let the reader consider the following parallels and work them out for himself. Firstly, Christians and Marxists each see life, not as the bourgeois sees it, in terms of his own enjoyment, but as a battle—a warfare against the powers of darkness in the case of the Christian, a warfare against the evils of capitalism in the case of the Marxist. Secondly, both attach tremendous significance to the body: Christians believe in the resurrection of the body; the Church's liturgy speaks of departed souls as imperfect until they are joined again to their bodies; for St. Thomas Aquinas the soul is the body-in-act, and his teaching has even been described as "Christian materialism":[42] Marxists insist that man must first of all be fed,[43] his material needs satisfied, and the distribution of material goods regulated according to each man's needs. Thirdly, they each have a holy dread of empty words: faith without works is dead, says the Christian—if anyone claims to have faith but allows his brother and sister to go naked or unfed his faith is vain; says the Marxist, "The question of whether human thought can achieve objective truth is not a question of theory but a practical question. In practice Man must prove the truth, i.e. the reality, power and this-sidedness of his thought. The dispute over the reality or unreality of thought which is isolated from practice is a purely *scholastic* question".[44] Fourthly, Marxists and Christians alike are faced with the task of reconciling necessity and free-will in their philosophies; for it is often forgotten that Marxists violently repudiate the suggestion that they are plain materialists—on the contrary, they are *dialectical* materialists who maintain that there is room for human free will within the operation of the dialectic. Just as Christians believe that not a sparrow falls without the will of the Father whilst still believing themselves free to do as they will.

Besides these very evident approximations there are others calculated to engage the metaphysically minded, who might consider whether Engels was not reaching backward to the forgotten Aristotelian notion of *substance* when he tried to clarify what he meant by *motion* : "Modern natural science has had to take over from philosophy the principle of the indestructibility of motion; it cannot any longer exist without this principle".[45] But most interesting of all would be a detailed comparison between Marx's teaching on property and that of St. Thomas. Certainly one cannot find in St. Thomas the simple statement, "Property is theft",[46] but the practical application of St. Thomas' teaching ("It is robbery to spend more than is necessary"[47]) in the mid-nineteenth century might easily have led one to judge that a great deal of mid-nineteenth-century "property" was theft. And any of the starving masses who at that time "stole" what was necessary for their lives could have justified their actions from St. Thomas' teaching.[48] Clearly St. Thomas' teaching on property is much closer to Marx's than most commentators have suggested. Property is an expression of a man, and if he is *alienated* from his labour, as the members of the proletariat are, then he is mutilated, as Marx says; he does not possess what is proper to him, as St. Thomas says. The justification of property in St. Thomas' eyes, lies in the social use which it allows a man to serve. Is this the form of property envisaged by Marx, in one of his more sober moments? When he said,

"The capitalist method of appropriation proceeding out of the capitalist method of production, and consequently capitalist private property, is the first negation of individual private property based upon individual labour. But with the inexorability of a law of nature, capitalist production begets its own negation. It is a negation of a negation. The second negation does not re-establish private property, but it does re-establish individual property upon the basis of the acquisitions of the capitalist era; i.e. on co-operation and the common ownership of the land and of the means of production (which labour itself produces).

"The transformation of scattered private property based upon individual labour into capitalist property is, of course, a far more protracted process, a far more violent and difficult process than the transformation of capitalist private property (already, in actual fact, based upon a social method of production) into social property. In the former case we are concerned with the expropriation of the mass of the people by a few usurpers; in the latter case we are concerned with the expropriation of a few usurpers by the mass of the people".[49]

Yet, in spite of these similarities between the letter of St. Thomas' writings and those of Marx, a modern follower of St. Thomas categorically declares that "dialectical materialism is more than an error; it is a sin", and that "the Christian must

c

regard it not as bad and false teaching but as truly Satanic".[50]
And he is right; since all the literal coincidences between
Christian and Marxist teaching cannot blind us to the totally
different spirit which animates each of them. At the centre of
the Christian's world is God who out of his gracious love takes
human nature upon himself, thus offering to human beings
that divine life which of their own strength they could never
hope to achieve. At the centre of the Marxist world stands a
Promethean figure, the future man of Marx's dreams, who by
violence will wrest from nature her secrets and so transform
himself into the lord of creation. The whispered, "Ye shall be
as gods" is for the Marxist the source and the realization of all
his ambitions; for the Christian it is the ultimate Satanic temptation leading inevitably to perdition.

Consequently the Christian is not surprised at the many
similarities between his own beliefs and the Marxist movement,
knowing as he does that Satan is the *simia Dei*, the ape of God;
Satan apes the Blessed Trinity with his threefold dialectic,
imitating God to deceive people, using "counterfeit signs and
wonders . . . so that they give credit to falsehood" (2 Thess.
ii. 10–11). The Christian knows that the Antichrist will be
a worldly power enjoying such control over the earth as no-
one has exercised before—"by these wonders, which it was
enabled to do in its master's presence, it deluded the inhabitants
of the world" (Apoc. xiii. 14). And he also knows that
by refusing these counterfeit gifts of the Antichrist, and
refusing to be deluded by its counterfeit wonders, he is pre-
served to receive freely that which shall never be taken away
from him—"Come, you who are thirsty, take, you who will, the
water of life; it is my free gift" (Apoc. xxii. 17).

NOTES

¹ *Capital*, Everyman Ed., p. 789.
² M. Bober (*Marx's Interpretation of History*, Harvard U.P., 1948)
deals with the subject exhaustively.
³ Marx's criticism of Macaulay, and the Whig historians in general, is
blistering (cf. *Capital*, p. 278. n.2.) and his strictures on the Reformation
sometimes read like those of a violent Catholic (cf. *Capital*, pp. 382,
715–16, 794–5).

⁴ He is constantly maintaining that this determination occurs with "the inexorability of a law of nature" (*Capital*, p. 789 and Preface to 2nd edition, p. 863).

⁵ The contradictions involved are brought out in Engel's letter to Bloch of the 21st September 1890 (*The Correspondence of Marx and Engels*, Lawrence & Wishart 1934, p. 475), where he maintains that he and Marx were themselves guilty of spreading this absurdity, denies that to be what they meant, but still goes on to maintain that each of us desires "what he is impelled to do by his physical, constitutional, external, and in the last resort, economic circumstances". Later (p. 510) he says that this misunderstanding is due to "the common undialectical conception of cause and effect". Engel's conception of cause and effect was different from the common one; it may be correct, but he nowhere shows that it is.

⁶ Engel's speech at Marx's graveside (*Karl Marx Selected Works*, Ed. C. P. Dutt, Lawrence & Wishart, 1942, Vol. I, p. 16).

⁷ It is an abuse of terms to transfer the concept of "evolution" from biology to human history. The absurdities to which it leads are illustrated by Marx's note on "evolution of machinery" (*Capital*, p. 367, n.2.). It should be noticed that in biology it is the *species*, not the individual, which evolves; consequently to apply "evolution" to human history is to treat human beings not as *individuals* but as representatives of a species. The neglect of the individual in Marx follows inevitably; it is as though he simply could not see human beings but only classes of them. Marx presumably would justify his view by his thesis that everything that has happened previously to communism was "pre-history"; *history* only begins with communism.

⁸ cf. Engel's rejection of the ordinary use of "cause". Note 5.

⁹ *Marx-Engels Correspondence*, p. 354.

¹⁰ ibid., p. 353.

¹¹ Although Marx himself never tried to apply these terms in detail to pre-capitalist periods, Engels (who, Marx said, "is always one step ahead of me") did so disastrously in his work *The Origin of the Family*.

¹² *Communist Manifesto*.

¹³ *Marx-Engels Correspondence*, p. 125.

¹⁴ R. KROPOTKIN, *Mutual Aid*, (1902), Pelican Books, 1939.

¹⁵ This is Stalin's summary of the teaching quoted by I. M. Bochenski. (*Diamat*, Bern, A. Francke AG. Verlag, 1950, p. 80).

¹⁶ "The dialectics of the brain is only the reflection of the forms of motion of the real world, both of nature and of history". (ENGELS, *Dialectics of Nature*, Lawrence & Wishart, 1941, p. 153).

¹⁷ EDMUND WILSON, *To the Finland Station*, Secker & Warburg, 1941, p. 300.

¹⁸ Marx in his Critique of Hegel's *Philosophy of Laws* quoted in *De Marx au Marxisme*, R. Aron, Paris, Editions du Flore, 1951.

¹⁹ *Capital*, p. 53.

²⁰ MARX, *Selected Works*, p. 87.

²¹ *Capital*, p. 645.

[22] Quoted BOCHENSKI, op. cit., p. 125.

[23] MARX, *Theses on Feuerbach*, Thesis VI. (*Selected Works*).

[24] BOCHENSKI, op. cit., p. 140.

[25] M. Bober (op. cit.) has some illuminating pages on Marxism and the process of invention.

[26] Foreword to 2nd ed. of *Capital*.

[27] MARX, *Theses on Feuerbach*, II.

[28] cf. POLANYI, *The Logic of Liberty*, p. 131–2.

[29] cf. THEIMER, *Der Marxismus*, Bern., A. Francke AG. Verlag, 1950, pp. 54–55.

[30] Marx on Hegel's *Philosophy of Laws*.

[31] Quoted from *Capital* by E. Wilson, op. cit., p. 314.

[32] *Capital*, pp. 162, 385, 386.

[33] *Capital*, p. 159.

[34] *Capital*, p. 652.

[35] Marx quoting Urquhart. *Capital*, p. 385.

[36] *Capital*, p. 51, n.

[37] ENGELS, *The German Ideology*, Lawrence & Wishart, 1938, p. 72.

[38] "Ce communisme se sait déjà réintegration ou retour de l'homme a lui-même, abolition de l'aliénation d'avec lui-même". Marx, quoted in *De Marx au Marxisme*.

[39] cf. EDMUND WILSON, op. cit., p. 116.

[40] cf. ENGELS, *The Origin of the Family*, Lawrence & Wishart, 1940, pp. 106–7.

[41] *Communist Manifesto*.

[42] VICTOR WHITE, O.P., *Dominican Studies*, Vol. I, p. 33.

[43] So does St. Thomas Aquinas.

[44] MARX, *Second Thesis on Feuerbach*.

[45] ENGELS, *Dialectics of Nature*, p. 21.

[46] The one remark of Proudhon's which Marx thought intelligent.

[47] *Summa Theologica*, II–II Q. 66 Art. II ad 3.

[48] For St. Thomas' teaching on property cf. the Question quoted in previous note.

[49] *Capital*, 846–7.

[50] BOCHENSKI, op. cit., p. 166.

PHENOMENOLOGY

IF EVERYONE has heard of Marxism few have heard of phenomenology, which is in a sense the philosopher's philosophy.
Moreover it is the philosophy of German philosophers whose
works have not been translated or else have been badly translated. And since even phenomenologists quarrel constantly
about the meaning of the master phenomenologist, Husserl
(1859-1938), it will be obvious that this section will be very
general—unashamedly so, for life is not long enough to master
all the voluminous complicated texts (many still unpublished)
in which Husserl sets down his thoughts.

Husserl's phenomenological school included some of Germany's most outstanding thinkers, whose very divergent views
and careers show how impossible they found it to co-ordinate
his teaching. Max Scheler, for instance, became known at one
time as "the Catholic Nietzsche", but ended his life as an
unbeliever. Martin Heidegger began his life as a pupil of the
Jesuits, abandoned his faith, became a member of the Nazi
party and is the fountainhead of atheistic existentialism, though
he himself is not an atheist. Edith Stein became a Carmelite
nun and was murdered by the Nazis. Hering is a Protestant
professor, Dietrich von Hildebrand a Catholic one; Koyré
seems to be sympathetic to both sides.

The most convenient way of seeing through this tangle of
lives to the philosophy which inspired them would seem to be
by saying what Husserl's phenomenology was a reaction against.

Primarily it was a reaction against any attempt to reduce
knowledge to the psychological accompaniments of the act of
knowing, such attempts as had been made by Husserl's *bêtes-
noires*, Locke, Hume, and their followers. An example of such
a reduction would be the following. I say, "All men are equal
in the sight of God". A Humian would reduce this thought to
the psychological processes through which I go when thinking
it. He would say that an idea has come into my mind which
I have associated with the words "all men", another idea has

come along with the "equal", and another one with "in the sight of God"; he would then go on to say that what I call my thought was nothing but the association of these ideas. Granted that, he would then point out that there was no *necessary* connection between these ideas, but that they had become associated in my mind by custom or habit. If we wish to study thought, then, we must study the customary association of ideas. In other words, the study of thought is a branch of psychology, and thinking can be reduced to the customary processes through which the mind goes as it thinks. Such a view is called "psychologism" and represents one more addition to our collection of "nothing-but" fallacies.

For if we accept this psychologism it is obvious that the question of whether my thought is true becomes meaningless; we can only discuss the process by which I arrived at it—or it arrived at me, to be precise. Any discussion of objective truth becomes impossible, and even such pursuits as logic or mathematics lose their objectivity—they are nothing but associations of ideas.

How does a phenomenologist deal with such an account of knowing? He points out, in the first place, that the Humian has failed to draw a distinction between thought and the images which accompany thought (by using the word "idea" to cover both). For instance, suppose I think of Winston Churchill. Many different images may come into my mind on the different occasions that I think of him; on one occasion I may have an image of the printed words "Winston Churchill" before my mind, on another occasion I may think of a cigar, or at another time of a microphone with a robust figure before it. The images through which I think, or which accompany my thought, may be different on each occasion but on each occasion it is Winston Churchill of whom I am thinking. In other words, my thought cannot be reduced to the images with the aid of which I think. Again, suppose I am confronted with a statement about equality. I may once more have an image of the printed sign " = " or the word "equate", or I may think of two candlesticks of equal size, but in no case is my thought tied down to any particular one of these images. A human being cannot think *without* some accompanying images, but to conclude from this that images are thoughts would be just as misguided as to conclude that eating is breathing because breathing always accompanies eating.

Once this radical criticism of Humian theory had been carried out by the phenomenologists it became possible again to deal with questions of thought precisely as questions of thought. So that when I say, "All men are equal in the sight of God" the question of what processes accompanied this thought is abandoned to psychology and its content, *what* it says, falls rightly within philosophy. We can ask whether it is true; and the discussion takes place on an objective intellectual level.

Another service rendered by phenomenologists, in vindication of our intellectual capacity, and in opposition to attempts to reduce this capacity to mere feeling or imagination, lies in their criticism of the Humian account of universals. For a Humian, when I use the word "dog" I am simply emitting a sound to express the image which has been built up in my mind by constantly encountering some object to which the sound "dog" has been applied. The universal "dog", therefore, is arrived at as a result of comparing many sensations of what is called "dog"—and it is no more than a convenient label; it does not express any essence by which a dog is a dog and not a cat. In reply to which the phenomenologist replies that unless I could recognize the essence of a dog when I encountered one, then I could never compare my different sensations in order to build up a convenient image, or label (which is what the Humian says I do). Unless I know *what* they have in common I should never know *that* they have anything in common. Therefore the idea "dog" is not arrived at as a result of many comparisons but is achieved in one immediate insight. One observation of one dog is sufficient for my mind to grasp the essence of the dog. In knowing, therefore, I know the *essences* of the objects around me. Knowing is not just a process of attaching convenient labels, since the universal expresses something in reality.

This theory, that our intellects see the essences of things, is once more a vindication of our intellectual powers and is strikingly similar to the medieval scholastic theory of universals. The orthodox medieval scholastic would say that we require only one observation in order to know the *metaphysical* universal, i.e. the essence of some existing thing. The *logical* universal, he would admit, is only arrived at by comparisons, because logic deals not directly with *what* we know (this is the province of metaphysics) but with the *words* we use to signify things. In which case, obviously, the *logical* universal is much more what is meant by Locke and Hume; and this explains why they disbelieved in metaphysics—that they confused the tasks of logic and metaphysics; their universal did not deal with the *essences of things* because it was the *logical* universal, which deals with *words*.

Seeing essences is a practice remote from Humian habits, but it is a practice which the phenomenologists have skilfully defended in destroying the Humian illusion that our experience is limited to the experience of our senses. No illusion has produced more baneful effects on modern thought than that which maintains all our experience to be sense-experience. The reason for this limitation is not far to seek; it arose from the prestige given by philosophers to seventeenth-century physical science. Having noted the success of this science, which successfully used instruments in order to record impressions of the world, they tried to build up a picture of the world from the sort of impressions which are recorded on instruments. They tried to turn themselves into instruments receiving "impressions" (which an instrument, by the way, does not do), in order to work out what the world would look like if they themselves were instruments and not human beings. For this reason the Humians talk interminably about sense-data, as though sense-data were the original material upon which human beings have to work in order to construct a picture of the world. Obviously this is a quite incorrect statement of how we do in fact perceive objects.

At this present moment I am not perceiving a scattered series of blue, white, yellow and green surfaces against a mahogany surface; I am perceiving a series of blue, white, yellow and green books on a mahogany table—my original, primitive experience is an experience of *things*. If the Humian likes to

analyse my perception and say that my senses have contributed
something to this perception, and that my intellect has contributed something else, I would agree with him. But I would also
point out that this division into sense-data and intellectual
operation is itself the result of subsequent reflection, and that
it does not describe my original, primitive experience. The
term "sense-data" is itself an abstraction *from* my primitive,
original experience, which was an experience of *things*. "Sense-
data" is a term used to describe what the Humian imagines my
experience would be like if I were an instrument and not a
human being. Therefore it is an imaginative abstraction. The
Humian then goes on to build up a picture of the world on the
basis of this abstraction plus what he imagines an instrument
would do if it had an intellect superimposed on it. The result,
not unnaturally, is highly abstract and imaginative—it could
scarcely be anything else! And it is not surprising that the
picture of the world presented by Hume (and his positivist
successors) is not one which human beings recognize as the one
in which they live.

In fact, this example illustrates that the empiricist school
founded by Hume does not faithfully record our primitive experiences but imposes upon our experience the limitations of a
highly abstract theory about how we know. It limits our
experience to sense-experience. The mistake is quite understandable since our knowledge does come to us by way of the
senses. But the senses are the *medium*, they are not the *object* of
knowledge.

When I look at Edinburgh castle from the north side, for
example, the impressions I receive through my senses (my
"sense-data") are different from the impressions gained by
looking at it from the west, and different again from the sense-
data on the south side. But *what* I perceive in each case is
Edinburgh castle; the *object* of my perception is precisely
Edinburgh castle—not my "sense-data" which are the medium
and not the object of my perception. If I observe my "sense-
data" at all it is by subsequently reflecting on my original
experience and observing the image which I retain in my mind,
which I have abstracted from my original experience.

It will be obvious, therefore, that the empiricists are in fact admitting that we have experience other than sense-experience (despite their theories) when they speak of their experience of "sense-data", i.e. the mental image abstracted from primitive experience. Once it is fully recognized that the word "experience" is legitimately applied to our experience of our own thoughts or of the beauty that we perceive, or of the values that we experience in our lives, the way is cleared of prejudice against the phenomenological method.

Before explaining the phenomenological method, however, let us just glance at the tremendous liberation of the intellect which Husserl has carried out. He has put materialism out of court along with idealism and empiricism. In other words he has shown that man's intellectual faculty enables him to see the *essence* of things. This view is very similar to the theory of knowing taught by the medieval schoolmen; and, no doubt, Husserl derived it from Franz Brentano (an ex-Dominican, who continued, however, to apply the principles of medieval philosophy in his teaching).

The schoolmen taught that the knower intends, or goes out towards, the object in order to apprehend it. There takes place a process of assimilation. Clearly this process cannot be altogether, or even essentially, material, since, if it were material, the subject and the object would change each other in the same way that two material objects change each other on contact. In which case there would simply be a reaction; whereas if knowing means anything at all it means grasping something without altering it, grasping it as it is. The way in which two material objects encounter each other results in external contact. The way in which a subject goes out to the object is immaterial, in virtue of which it is able to know the object in its essence and not to alter it upon impact.

Such an account of knowing is hardly to be found amongst European philosophers between the time of the schoolmen and the time of Husserl. In the meantime philosophers had asked themselves, not, "*What* do we know?" but "How *can* we know?" thus immediately transferring discussion from the philosophical level to the psychological level, discussing the faculties by which we can know rather than the objects which we do in fact know. And not unnaturally these psychological discussions could go on indefinitely, because we never know definitely what we *can* do until we have, in fact, done it; and we could go on for ever unless we brought the discussion down to earth by reference to *what* we know or do, to the *object* of our faculties.

By transferring attention to the objects of knowledge (to essences, to beauty, to goodness) Husserl brought European philosophy around to saner mental habits than philosophers had enjoyed for some time. He did this by using what is his best-known contribution to philosophy, his phenomenological method, which we have tried to illustrate. Unfortunately it is the fate of those who develop an original method to find their followers over-enthusiastically claiming that it will solve all the problems which have hitherto worried humanity; and Husserl's followers have sometimes been guilty of such over-enthusiasm. In reaction against such excessive claims certain philosophers have been inclined to say that the phenomenological method is not at all original—that it simply represents an attempt to persuade German philosophical students to look at the world for once, instead of gazing for ever at their own ideas about it. There is a good deal of sound sense in this summary judgement, for it is undoubtedly true that German philosophers have very often been so caught up with their own ideas that they scarcely bothered to look at the world. But all philosophers, except the very greatest, have been caught in the same snare—even the empiricists and materialists. For, as we have seen, the empiricists present us with a theoretical picture of a world such as no sane man has ever lived in. And the materialists talk about "matter" as though they had actually seen it, when "matter" is simply the word which they choose to refer to the idea by which they hope to "explain" the world. Therefore even if the phenomenological method is not so very original, at least its rediscovery was extremely salutary for European thinkers, and a short account of it may prove equally valuable.

Husserl begins by saying that instead of concentrating upon our mental constructions (such as "the fact that . . .", or "matter", or "mind") we should direct our attention towards the things themselves (*an die Sache selbst*). Tired of all the philosophical systems which obscured men's vision so that they could no longer see straight, Husserl wanted to approach the world with an entirely fresh mind; he wanted in this way to found a "first philosophy" without any presuppositions whatsoever about what sort of world he was going to encounter. In virtue of his phenomenological method he hoped that this "first philosophy" would be a "strict science", but maintained that in order to realize this aim he would have to preserve it free from the methods of the other sciences (which are not "first philosophies" but involve innumerable presuppositions).

Clearly his general aim has much to commend it, as we have already suggested (pp. 36–8). It is a meditative approach, "neither inductive nor deductive, but reflexive", and aims not so much at drawing inferences *from* the object one is observing as at penetrating more deeply into the object itself. Some notion of this approach may be gathered from an anecdote about the poet, Gerard Manley Hopkins (who, as a Scotist, was a natural phenomenologist). One day Hopkins was walking down a garden pathway when he suddenly stopped, and looking towards a spot on the ground, began to turn round on his heel. After he had been doing this for some time an alarmed gardener, thinking him slightly queer, asked him what he was doing; to which Hopkins replied that he was trying to get the "inscape" of one single piece of gravel which was caught in the sun's rays, and which he was trying to see from all angles. Hopkins did not try to "elucidate" the piece of gravel by placing it into the category of "small stones" and then saying that it was one of many such "small stones"; on the contrary he was meditating upon it, and the result of his meditations was not a proposition but a better vision of that particular piece of gravel—he was penetrating more deeply into it. And that is the aim of all good phenomenologists—as it were to let the appearances, what is actually given to us in experience, sink into our consciousness without our minds continually decreeing what has to appear.

Of course, the best test for the value of a method is to see what results it produces, to see its application, rather than enter into endless discussions as to how it *could* be applied. Husserl's own most valuable application of it seems to have been in his criticism of empiricist, idealist and materialist theories of knowledge; but in general the subjects where the phenomenological method has best proved itself are ethics, psychology and aesthetics. Nor is this surprising, since these studies deal with those parts of our experience, with goodness, beauty and emotions, which had been neglected since all our experience came to be regarded as sense-experience.

True to their method the phenomenologists do not study ethics, for instance, by asking "What is goodness?" or "What is duty?" because such questions are abstract, are full of pre-suppositions, and can scarcely lead to anything more than definitions of words. Since the phenomenologist is trying primarily to achieve an insight into values, rather than to define words, he begins by taking a concrete situation and describing it, so as to bring out the values it embodies. The values are there, they are objective, they can be experienced; it is only a question of achieving an insight into them by adequate pheno-menological analysis. For example, whereas the abstract ethical philosopher asks himself, "What is contrition?" and gives himself the verbal answer "Contrition means being sorry for one's sins", the phenomenologist goes deeper than this. He examines the actions of a contrite person and points out that even when the contrite person has reversed all the effects of the action which he deplores he has still not satisfied himself; his con-trition demands something more. This is because he is sorry not so much for his *action* as for being the kind of person who could perform such an action. And therefore it is not enough to say with the abstract philosopher that "contrition means sorrow for one's sins". It means much more; it involves sorrow over oneself for being *that kind of person*. From this illustration it will be obvious that the phenomenologist's method of taking a concrete case does enable him to achieve a deeper insight into the values which lay there, as it were, unsuspected.

Bergson, for example, examines the behaviour of a criminal who tries to return to the scene of his crime. In the past it has more or less been assumed that there was some "psychological"

reason for this, and the word "psychological" has been treated
as if it were an explanation—in fact, it is simply a word thrown
at the situation. But Bergson points out that not only does the
criminal endanger his own safety by returning to the scene, he
also usually endangers his safety by seeking someone to whom
he can confess his crime. Why? The reason why he does so
is because his crime has cut him off from society and what he
fears is not only, not even primarily, the punishment which
faces him; he fears his isolation from his fellows; and by going
back to the scene or by making a confession he is actually
trying to *wipe out* his crime and reintegrate himself into the
community. He dreads the prospect of being a closed soul, shut
in upon himself. In this case of the criminal Bergson sees the
essence of immoral and moral action, evil being characteristic
of a "closed" soul and goodness showing itself in "open" souls;
so that those who achieve the highest goodness, the saints, are
those who are completely open to the world and their fellows,
their hearts as wide as the sand on the sea shore. From his
phenomenological analysis of a criminal Bergson achieves an
insight into the essence of goodness, even to the essence of holiness.[1]

Another very able phenomenologist is Dietrich von Hildebrand, whose examination of purity contains so many fruitful
observations. He points out, for example, that many people
are assumed to be pure who are simply insensitive to sexual
attractions, and that this is a mistaken notion of purity—purity
is something positive achieved through sensitiveness to sex, for
insensibility is in itself a defect. "It would therefore be absurd
offhand to declare sexual insensibility a desirable condition, let
alone to regard it as the culmination of purity."[2]

One could fill volumes with these very penetrating observations on ethical questions which we owe to the phenomenologists. The greatest name amongst them, undoubtedly, is that
of Max Scheler (1874–1928). Scheler's lasting achievement is
to have shown that values are objective, they are not simply
relative, nor do we make them up as we go along. We have
inborn within our souls the same ability to recognize goodness
when we meet it as our eyes have to recognize colours when we

see them; there is no question of our having to learn to impose values on the world, since they are there in the world and our souls are endowed with the ability to recognize them. Equally valuable are those analyses in which he shows that our actions are not directed towards pleasure but towards values; if they seem to be directed towards pleasure that is because we have mistakenly identified the emotional state which accompanies our striving for value with the value itself. The culmination of Scheler's ethical work lay in his theory of love and his descriptions of the uniqueness of each person. He begins by tearing the nineteenth-century notion of love to pieces; the nineteenth century thought that altruism was the same as love, although it is actually a form of sentiment, a form of *ressentiment* adopted by those who hate the higher values—the love which they cannot reach. Love, on the contrary, is not essentially a matter of sympathy or feeling; nor is it even love for a value as such— one cannot just love "the good". Love is always directed towards the person, and persons are always something more than the sum of values which they embody, because it is the *person* who is the supreme reality. Furthermore one only sees the values which they embody when one first loves them; it is in our loving that persons and values are revealed to us.

And yet, when the worth of this phenomenological method as used by Scheler, Hildebrand, etc. has been acknowledged it must be confessed that its limitations need to be pointed out. One obvious limitation is that it provides no indication of where the description of phenomena comes to an end and the properly "scientific" work of discovering causal relationships between the various phenomena begins. Without some such indication there is no guarantee that the description will not become sheer poetry. By what standard, for instance, does one distinguish the description of the skylark by Shelley in his "Ode to the Skylark" from the description of the skylark by an ornithologist? Both are no doubt "true" in some sense, but it is the philosopher's task to explain in *what* sense each of them is true. Because the phenomenological method does not provide us with any sure means of distinguishing in what sense they are true, it has rightly been described as "pre-philosophic".

Since the phenomenologist employs a method which is "pre-philosophic" it would perhaps be more enlightening to say that phenomenologists are advocating a certain *attitude* towards the world, a certain spirit in which one approaches philosophical problems, rather than that they are providing a specifically philosophical technique. And by calling attention to the importance of one's attitude before one ever reaches the conscious level of philosophical reasoning, or any other kind of reasoning, they have brought to light a much neglected truth. The attitude, for example, in which someone such as the late H. G. Wells even approached the study of history was characterized by a lack of reverence; his pre-conscious attitude reflected itself in every judgement of his conscious mind upon historical events. G. K. Chesterton, on the other hand, was essentially reverent in everything he did, and this also reflected itself in all his works. Or, to take a more everyday case, the farmer whose pre-conscious attitude towards the land he cultivates is reverent will produce very different results from the farmer who lacks this reverence, no matter how much their farming techniques may have in common. In so far as phenomenologists have persuaded philosophers to adopt an attitude of openness towards the world and not to impose their own preconceptions upon it they are to be followed. Where one cannot follow them is when they carry their desire for presuppositionless thought into the properly philosophical domain, when they pass from the pre-conscious to the conscious.

This is what Husserl did when he developed his theory of what he calls *epoche*. This famous Husserlian *epoche* has sometimes been compared to Descartes' doubt as meaning that one should doubt all statements in order to sift the true from the false. But, although this comparison contains some truth, the *epoche* means more precisely that suspension of judgement which allows us to see the essence of a thing without our minds making any judgement upon its existence or its causal relations with other things. As soon as we begin to judge we begin, also, to some extent, to falsify, and therefore Husserl recommends philosophers to use his *epoche* technique, the suspension of judgement; in this way one should eventually arrive at a "pure phenomenology".

But human beings can never arrive at a "pure phenomenology". This is the fatal weakness in Husserl's thought, that
he tries to do something which a creature simply cannot do.
A creature simply cannot view the world without some presuppositions, nor can a creature arrive at the truth except by
making judgements. It is also a fact that every judgement by
a creature falls short of the whole truth, but that is just part of
our creaturely imperfection; it cannot be avoided any more than
a creature can avoid imperfection in his every act. But to
abandon judgements because they involve us in error would be
like refusing to act in life because action involves us in some
measure of sin. There are errors on the way of judgement and
sins on the road of life, but in no other way and by no other
road can we eventually arrive at the truth which lies at the
end of judging and living.

Phenomenology, therefore, when it moves from the pre-
conscious to the conscious, philosophical level, is vitiated by
the same denial of creatureliness as vitiates Marxism. Husserl's
aim, according to one of his pupils, was to achieve "a knowledge
which was absolutely one with its object and therefore guaran-
teed against every error. It is quite clear from the standpoint
of St. Thomas, that this end cannot be considered attainable.
Such an ideal of knowledge is realized in God's knowledge: for
Him being and knowledge are one, but for us they are separate".[3] God does not have to make judgements in order to
arrive at the truth because his vision is the vision of truth, but
we who are creatures upon the road of life do have to make
judgements, we have to relate knowing and being by making
judgements; if we did not have to do so we would no longer
be creatures, and our every thought would be creative in the
same way that God's thought is creative. In fact one phenomenologist has led himself to believe that he, the thinker, is no
longer a creature, for Martin Heidegger declares that "the
thinker utters Being".[4]

The proper method, then, for a philosopher does not consist
in suspending judgement but precisely in making judgements,
judging that A is the cause of B or that it is untrue to say that
"the thinker utters Being". Such judgements belong to what is

traditionally known as "metaphysics", and in this sense metaphysics must act as the phenomenologists' sheet-anchor. Without metaphysics the phenomenological method leads to sheer chaos, as we have observed it in the development of phenomenologists themselves. Heidegger became a member of the Nazi party, and Max Scheler wrote *Die Stellung des Menschen im Kosmos* in which he repudiates almost everything he had defended in *Vom Ewigen im Menschen*. Perhaps the trajectory of Husserl's own thought is the most revealing of all, for he began by attacking all forms of subjectivism but by the end of his days was defending a position which is very hard to distinguish from subjectivism.

Some phenomenologists have managed to retain their balance, but always, it would seem, in virtue of their metaphysics, or those presuppositions which they eventually accepted after testing their validity. Edith Stein, for instance, schooled herself in the metaphysics of St. Thomas and continued to use the phenomenological method within the framework of Thomist metaphysics. The results are embodied in such works as *St. Thomas and Husserl, Eternal and Finite Being* and *The Science of the Cross*. Her presuppositions she tested by sacrificing her life during the Nazi tyranny over Europe. And in the end she may well prove to have been the greatest glory of the phenomenological school.

NOTES

[1] BERGSON, *Two Moralities*, Macmillan and Co., 1935, pp. 10–11.
[2] HILDEBRAND, *In Defence of Purity*, English ed., Sheed and Ward, 1945, p. 59.
[3] EDITH STEIN, "Husserl und Skt. Thomas" *Jahrbuch für Philosophie und phänomenologische Forschung. Ergänzungsband*, Halle, 1929 Max Niemeyer Verlag.
[4] HEIDEGGER, *Existence and Being*, Vision Press, 1949, p. 391.

EXISTENTIALISM

"WHAT IS existentialism?" must have been one of the most frequently asked questions of recent years; and the nearest approach to a satisfactory answer was, perhaps, that given by Nicolaus Berdyaev, who replied, "Existentialism?   *I* am existentialism." The question is an unprofitable one because the title of existentialist has been repudiated by many (such as Heidegger and Marcel) on the ground that they do not hold the views described by other people as "existentialist". Therefore the most sensible method seems to be to ask, *who* are the people generally recognized as existentialists? and what have they in common which has led people to describe them by the same name?

The list of "existentialists" discovered since existentialism became fashionable is a very lengthy one indeed. Some would say that God on Mount Sinai was the first existentialist, since when Moses asked him his name he replied, "I am who am" —in other words, God's existence can only be explained in virtue of God's existence and cannot be enclosed in human names or ideas. Others would claim Socrates as an existentialist since he left a question-mark at the end of all his discussions to show that existence lies outside the limits of human speech; by his death he showed that such questions are to be answered not by words but by a life laid down for the truth. Another "existentialist" is St. Augustine who saw in the thrust of a trembling glance that God is he who is. Of recent years St. Thomas Aquinas has been included in the list, as well as Duns Scotus. Pascal is counted amongst their number by almost everyone competent to judge. These are the more venerable names. During the last century the list begins with the modern initiator of the movement, Søren Kierkegaard (1813–1855), the Danish man of letters; Dostoevsky, the Russian novelist; Nicolaus Berdyaev and Leo Chestov, Russian thinkers; Martin Buber, the Jewish philosopher, Rilke, the poet, and Kafka, the novelist; Karl Barth, the Protestant theologian;

Peter Wust, the Catholic philosopher; Ferdinand Ebner, an Austrian Catholic schoolmaster; Gabriel Marcel, a French convert to Catholicism; the atheist J. P. Sartre; Karl Jaspers, professor of philosophy at Basel, who was originally a psychiatrist; Martin Heidegger, professor of philosophy at Freiburg; Albert Camus, the young French novelist and Georges Bataille, his literary compatriot.

With such a formidable list of candidates for consideration one may be excused for pointing out that almost certainly no-one on earth ever has, or ever will, read all the works of all the thinkers listed here. Nor is it necessary to read them all in order to acquire a fairly firm grasp of what distinguishes existentialists from other kinds of thinkers. And since we are expressly interested in habits of mind, let us begin by examining the existentialist's way of looking at the world. After which some pages on Kierkegaard, Heidegger and Marcel will help us to make an assessment of the movement, and its value for us.

The starting-point of existentialist philosophers is their concentration upon unique, specifically *human* experience. Whereas the Aristotelian begins with *things*, and the Humian with *facts*, or the phenomenologist with "essences", the existentialist begins with specifically *human* experiences, the experiences of dread, or hope or existence. And it is not surprising that the leading existentialists should have appeared when they did, because they belong to a period when everyone was becoming more conscious that the philosophers had left man out of their picture of the world; the Humians had turned us into instruments recording sense-data. With his phenomenological method Husserl broadened the scope of experience for philosophical consideration, and included the intellect amongst the faculties by which we directly experience reality. Some of his pupils (Max Scheler and Heidegger, for instance) have gone beyond intellectual experience; they have taken all human experience as the point of departure for their philosophy, and have placed the human person at the centre of their philosophizing.

To place modern existentialists in their line of succession from Husserl is useful because it explains why they all use the phenomenological method (though in a way which would horrify him). It also explains why the chief of the existentialists, Kierkegaard, did not become well-known until almost a century after his death; Kierkegaard was not a professional philosopher and therefore did not feel obliged previously to work out a method in order to justify his concentration upon the person as the highest reality; he simply went straight to the heart of human experience whereas the philosophers had to wait until Husserl had unchained them before they felt free to do so. And it is interesting to notice that Marcel had worked out his own "existentialism" before he had ever heard of Kierkegaard, and years before the world became such rich soil for Kierkegaard's ideas.

Seeing the existentialists in their context also makes it obvious that existentialism represents a reaction against the bad mental habits to which philosophers had succumbed; it is nature's way of teaching philosophers that they are neither disembodied intellects nor glorified instruments, but human beings. An incident between two philosophers best sums up the need for such a reaction. After Gabriel Marcel had once outlined his views at a philosophical meeting Julien Benda, a representative of the idealism which the existentialist abhors, rose and announced that he did not consider such themes to be properly philosophical, saying "The death of Julien Benda is far less important to Julien Benda than is the death of Gabriel Marcel to M. Marcel". Which, of course, is sheer play-acting; Julien Benda is just shutting his eyes and living in the world of his imagination if he believes that the one thing of which he can be certain, his own death, is of no great importance to him.

However, since most human beings have never pretended that their own deaths were of little importance, most human beings do not need to take such a drastic "existentialist cure" as the philosophers have to take in order to start living in the real world rather than in the world of their imaginations. Therefore it is unfortunate that the general public, through the popularizing of existentialism, has been subjected to a cure for the disease of philosophers. The general public has come out in spots in consequence.

On this account we do not intend to develop the attacks upon idealist philosophy in which the existentialists engage. Instead let us isolate the unique human experience upon which the existentialists have concentrated.

Suddenly, at some odd moment, I become aware of my existence. The day-to-day round has been going on, eating and working and talking, when suddenly everything around me takes on an unaccustomed appearance. Here am I, at this moment, in this particular place, with two hands and a headache—and over there are chairs, brown and shining in the light of the lamp. How utterly strange and unfamiliar it seems. Why should I, or anything, exist at all?

For the first time, I realize that I exist and that other things exist. What am I doing here at all? Somehow I must try to penetrate the mystery of it. Whether I like it or not, here I am, and I have no choice about it; I *must* try to make something of it all. As the existentialists are fond of saying, I have no choice but to choose. Even if I try to avoid penetrating the mystery I am still choosing to avoid doing so. Wherever I turn I have to choose. It is because they have woken up to their own existence and the choice to which this commits them that existentialist philosophers lay so much stress on *decision* as a means of interpreting the mystery. It is a difficult means to handle—but it is the indispensable one. There are, of course, many aspects of experience connected with each of our decisions, experiences of anguish, of hope, of boredom, etc. By analyzing these experiences in phenomenological fashion the existentialist hopes to find in them some clue to the riddle of existence, to elucidate his own existence through these, his most intimate experiences. What he decides for may become clearer, what he hopes for, what he fears—what he is.

The first person to ask himself these questions so insistently in modern times was Søren Kierkegaard.

Kierkegaard (1813–1855)

Søren Kierkegaard was the son of a most curious father, and his father was to be the dominating influence in his life. When

Søren was a boy he would sometimes ask his father to take him out for a walk. Instead of actually going out with his son, Michael Pederson Kierkegaard would walk with him up and down the room describing the streets and shops that they would have been passing through if they had been out walking; after they would talk about God. This is but one instance of what Kierkegaard later rightly described as a "crazy education". No wonder he became a most singular person.

At the same time the elder Kierkegaard was a very religious person, something of an Old Testament patriarch, and if Kierkegaard's sanity was nearly destroyed by his father it was probably his relationship with his father which helped him to retain his sanity. For an insane person is *aliéné*, out of contact with the world—all relationships are broken. The ultimate madness is suicide, by which all relationships are brought to an end; and at one stage of his life Kierkegaard nearly did commit suicide. It was at a time when his reaction against his father's stern religious ideas had reached a climax and he wanted to shoot himself. Realizing that he had been faced with the sin of despair he saw that he "must repent himself back into the family, into the clan, into the race, back to God". Kierkegaard as a youngster had at least established *some* relationship with his father, and along that thread he was able to climb back to God; his reconciliation with his father which occurred at this time was also his reconciliation with God, the Father. Returning home, for Kierkegaard, meant returning to Christianity. Of his father he says, "From him I learned what father-love is, and I got a conception of the divine father-love, the one unshakeable thing in life, the true archimedean point".

But the family is not only the father any more than God is one Person, the Father. The mother has her place there just as the Trinity of Persons, God, has its feminine principle.[1] Consequently the fact that Kierkegaard never established any relationship with his mother meant that he never *wholly* re-integrated himself into the family, into Christianity (symbolized for him by home) or into God. For Kierkegaard's mother seems to have played no part in his life—she was too simple, too homely and everyday, altogether too ordinary to awaken any spark in Kierkegaard. By allowing the relationship with his feminine side to be cut off in this way Kierkegaard distorted his whole life, for the acceptance of it is a condition of *receiving*. One receives one's daily bread from God, the Father, it is true, but *through* mother earth; one receives one's very life from one's mother. To deny these receiving-relationships is to go unnourished, and Kierkegaard is the type of the un-nourished soul.

Besides relationships with his father and mother there was a third relationship in his life which he never accepted. In 1836 he fell in love with Regine Olsen and became engaged to her; and there seemed to be nothing whatsoever to prevent their marriage except Kierkegaard's refusal to accept the relation-ship. In 1841 he broke off the engagement. We may reason-ably suppose that this was due to his opinion "that there are men whose destiny it is to be sacrificed in one way or another for others in order to bring the idea out—and that I with my peculiar cross was one of them". Whether that was true or not, and whether it makes sense for a Christian to talk of a "peculiar cross" when there is only *one* Cross for all Christians, it is certainly true that this broken engagement betokened a refusal to receive. "My engagement to her and the breaking of it is really my relationship to God, my engagement to God, if I dare say so." He does not seem to have drawn the conclusion that by breaking off the relationship he was once more refusing to receive a gift from God, thus leaving his soul unnourished.

Not unconnected with his failure to establish a relationship with his mother and with Regine was Kierkegaard's failure to establish contact with that other channel through which he should have accepted maternal solicitude, i.e. the society in which he lived. For a second firm conviction he held was, "that I should never be tried by having to work for my living —partly because I thought that I should die very young, and partly because I thought that in consideration of my peculiar cross God would spare me this suffering and problem". Whether it was God or his imagination which decided that he would never have to earn his living is not for us to say. One must, however, point out that he failed to achieve relationship with society, first of all when he frittered away his time and never completed his university studies, and secondly, later in life, when he allowed his fear of possible scandal to prevent him from serving the community as a country parson. Instead he continued to live a materially comfortable life on the annuities left by his father. When these annuities ran out in 1855 Kierkegaard died. Whether God's work in him had been completed or whether it was because his imagination once more refused to face the reality of a place in society where he would have to earn his living, and he therefore died of a neurosis,[2] we cannot judge.

It is necessary to go into these personal relationships of Kierkegaard's before referring to his thought for two reasons. First that existentialists, being committed to specifically human experience as their starting-point, are always talking about themselves, whether explicitly or implicitly, and therefore they are as it were giving a running commentary on their own lives. Secondly, because Kierkegaard has been acclaimed as a Christian teacher, and the very fact that he talks so brilliantly about Christianity, that his style is so convincing, carries the reader of his works away with him. Since, however, Christians are to be known by their fruits, not their words, some notion of Kierkegaard's limitations in life helps to bring his teaching into perspective. His living relationship to Christ has to be indicated.

Kierkegaard himself, on June 1, 1835, unmistakably showed his realization of this when he wrote, "What I really need is to become clear in my own mind *what I must do*, not what I must know—except in so far as a knowing must precede every action. The important thing is to understand what I am destined for, to perceive what the Deity wants *me* to do; the point is to find the truth which is true *for me*, to find *the idea for which I am ready to live and die*". In other words, he saw that the highest grace which a Christian can ask for is the grace of martyrdom. How clearly he saw the truth that the Christian Church is first and foremost the Church of the martyrs! Witness the scorn and ridicule which he poured out in 1854 upon the description of the dead Bishop Mynster as a "witness to the truth" ("martyr" is the Greek word for "witness"). Bishop Mynster had been head of the Danish State Church and stood for Kierkegaard as a symbol of Protestant deadness and conformity. When the newspapers described him as a martyr they offended Kierkegaard's deep awareness that the conception of martyrdom had been shamefully diluted.

What Kierkegaard does not seem to have realized was that he himself remained a victim of this Lutheran pietist tradition which had substituted "confessors" for "martyrs". The notion of confessor had been substituted for that of martyr since the very first days of Protestantism; Protestants might acclaim Luther as a "confessor" for his appearance at the Diet of Worms—never could they describe him as a "martyr". Martyrdom, the glory of the Christian Church since its very foundation, had never received recognition within the Lutheran tradition. It is possible that Kierkegaard was trying to escape from this tradition, as some have maintained; Georg Brandes asserted that if Kierkegaard had lived longer he would have had to choose either "to make a leap into the black abyss of Catholicism, or over to the headland of freedom"; Erich Przywara, the Jesuit, maintains that Kierkegaard's life has to be seen as a longing for the motherhood of Mary and the motherhood of the Catholic Church.[3]   Be that as it may, Kierkegaard saw clearly that the foundation of a Church, the bones and blood of martyrs, was lacking in Danish Protestantism. But he did nothing to remedy the lack by his own life; he himself continued to live as a comfortable bourgeois citizen of Copenhagen whilst tirading against the like of Bishop Mynster.

Why was this? Surely it was that he followed the neurotic pattern of substituting the thought for the deed. Constantly, throughout his life, one is aware of this contradiction between his thought and his behaviour. Perhaps his father had started it by taking him for imaginary walks instead of real ones. The richness of his religious vision only confirms the Christian belief that such insights as he enjoyed may be granted to people although these insights are of less external worth than the unsublimated sexuality and extraversion which obscure them—so long as the sexuality and activity are exercised in the service of charity.[4]   Like the neurotic, Kierkegaard is continually aware of his condition but unable to do anything about it.   For instance, in Holy Week 1848 he wrote, "My whole nature is changed.   My close reserve, my *introversion* is broken—I must speak".   But deeds, not words, are the sign of the Christian martyr.

These limitations having been pointed out, it is now possible to give a balanced summary of Kierkegaard's leading themes.

Like Marx, Kierkegaard developed his thought in reaction from Hegel's teaching, but in a very different fashion.   To Kierkegaard it seemed that Hegel had the universe far too tidily organized—inside his own head.   The real is rational, said Hegel, and went on to assume that his reason could enclose everything real in the universe within his philosophical system.   We have already seen how he transformed the Christian mystery of the Trinity into the dialectic of the Idea as the universal, the particular, the individual.   If that was the way in which he subjected the supernatural world to the dictates of his own ideas one is not surprised to find him treating the natural world in an equally cavalier fashion. Without bothering to make any experiments he defined "heat" in the following manner: "Heat is the self-restoration of matter in its formlessness, its liquidity the triumph of its abstract homogeneity over specific definiteness, its abstract, purely self-existing continuity as negation of negation, is here set as activity".[5]   Once he had given a definition Hegel thought that he knew the essence of what he had defined.   It was this cock-sure attitude towards the universe, the universe as a kind of pale reflection of the thinker's ideas, which led Kierkegaard to renounce Hegel's system, and every philosophical system, for ever.   As he himself says, he walked out of the system into *existence*.

Modern existentialism may be dated from the moment when Søren Kierkegaard walked out of the Hegelian system into existence.   Unfortunately he brought a little of the system with him.   He retained the false notion of reason which Hegel had taught him.   Consequently when he chose to exist, rather than to petrify in Hegel's system, he thought that he must also reject and despise reason—unaware apparently of a legitimate conception of reason quite distinct from Hegel's (cf. pp. 8–9). Having identified Hegelian idealism with reason, and having come to abhor Hegel's idealism, he presented himself with the first of those alternatives for which he is famous—either reason or faith. "Either/or is the key to heaven. Both-and is the way to hell".

Such was the first of the either/or alternatives with which the history of existentialist thought is strewn. It inaugurates a style of violent thinking which may be necessary in times of urgent action but can scarcely act as a sound rule in general. With a revolver pressed against his temples the philosopher looks at some propositions about the world and says "Either A is true or B is true. If B is true then I will kill myself". Obviously all those philosophers who have survived from such violent thinking will have decided that A is true, and henceforward will be fanatical defenders of proposition A. Their fanaticism will prevent them from reconsidering their original "either/or"; otherwise, in a moment of sweet reasonableness, they might realize that A and B are both true, though neither states the whole truth.

Yet there was a good deal of justification for Kierkegaard's using his either/or method at that particular time and on the issue which confronted him. For the issue confronting him was "How to *become* a Christian"; the key-word here is "become" for it points to his fearless acknowledgement that he was no more Christian than the so-called "Christian" society around him. In order to be a Christian one has to *choose* to become a Christian. Most of the "Christian" society around him simply assumed that everyone was a Christian in the same way that they were born with two hands or two eyes. Christianity was a matter of sound common sense, like obeying the laws of the state or wearing the right kind of clothes when one went to dinner. The God whom most of Kierkegaard's fellow-citizens paid their respects to was not the God of Abraham, Isaac and Jacob, not God the Lord and giver of life whom we must worship, worship even by the sacrifice of one's first-born if the inflexible will of him who is Lord of life demands it; they did not worship at all—they maintained diplomatic relations with an absentee king who came to hold a court levee on a Sunday, a faint reflection of the constitutional monarch just then becoming fashionable in Europe.

To this comfortable society Kierkegaard directed his shattering either/or. Either God, or mammon; either the God of Abraham, Isaac and Jacob or the god of this world, the belly, the lusts, desire for gold; either the Cross or perdition. In order to be a Christian one has to make the choice between serving God and serving the Devil. There is no avoiding the decision. One has no choice but to choose.

Undoubtedly Kierkegaard was justified in confronting his contemporaries with the decision to be Christians. Between God and the Devil, between Heaven and Hell there is an absolute gulf; here the method of either/or is justified to the very utmost. But we are by now accustomed to seeing thinkers applying a method which is valid in one field of thought to another field where it is no longer valid, and this is exactly what Kierkegaard now began to do. Either reason or faith, he said; either God as an object or God as subject; either a hidden God or a God whom you can see; you must either become more and more inward in your Christian life or else destroy that life by being outward, like Bishop Mynster.

When he formulated these alternatives Kierkegaard was trying to bring out truths that had long been ignored, and we can learn much from him, so long as we remember that he is stating half-truths, and that half-truths become falsehoods when they are treated as if they were the whole truth.

It is a fact, for instance, that the theologians had for years been talking about God in an objective way. The formal object of their science being God, the theologians had treated God in much the same way as other scientists treat the objects of their sciences. The physicists conduct experiments on material things, the biologists toy about with living organisms, poking them and dissecting them and sending electric currents through them. It seemed to Kierkegaard that the theologians were dealing likewise with God; they had turned God into a thing or an object which had to behave according to the laws of the theologian's reasoning; if the theologians laid down laws according to which a man would be damned then it was as though no power in Heaven could save him. Like Pascal before him, Kierkegaard had seen God turned into the object of speculation. And like Pascal he turned away from the God of the philosophers towards the God of Abraham, Isaac and Jacob, not a God to whom one brightly says, "Come in" as he knocks on the study door, but a God who draws each man out to the desert places in fear and trembling and demands worship from the prostrate creature. Nowhere does Kierkegaard better illustrate his radical break with nineteenth-century conceptions than in his *Fear and Trembling*, of which he himself said that it "alone will give me the name of an immortal author . . . people will almost shudder at the frightful pathos of the book". In it he describes the journey of Abraham to Mount Horeb where he went to sacrifice his beloved son, his first-born, Isaac; the reader does indeed sweat with Abraham and endures the agony of faith.

There is so much to be learned from *Fear and Trembling*. Here God is no longer an object to be handled; God is "infinite subjectivity" with a will which transcends the petty laws drawn up in ethical systems, not a God to be argued with. God must be obeyed, as Kierkegaard pointed out when speaking of sceptics: "They would have us believe that objections against Christianity come from intellectual doubt, when they in fact come from insubordination, unwillingness to obey, rebellion against all authority. Therefore they have hitherto been beating the air against the objectors, because they have fought intellectually with doubt instead of ethically with rebellion . . . so it is not properly doubt but insubordination. In vain do they try to bring the machinery into action, for the ground is bog or quicksand."

The very decision to obey is itself the purificatory process which frees one from doubts because it thrusts deeper into one's personality than does the superficial consideration of ideas. Once a person decides to commit himself by faith he releases all those deep forces within himself which guide him to make the right decision. There can be no intellectual guarantee for this, because God demands the risk of faith, the leap into the absurd, and he cannot be treated as a heavenly insurance-bank: "Faith hopes by virtue of the absurd, not by virtue of the human understanding". Abraham receives Isaac back in virtue of his faith, his leap into the absurd.

But we come to see how misguided this view of faith really is when we learn that Kierkegaard wrote *Fear and Trembling* for Regine Olsen by way of indirect communication, and when we see it against the background of his life. He had made his own leap into the absurd by sacrificing Regine, as Abraham sacrificed Isaac, and he expected to receive her back, as Abraham received Isaac back. But he did not receive Regine back, at least in this life, for in the meantime she married Schlegel. And he himself realized obscurely how misguided he had been when he wrote later, "If I had had faith, I should have remained with Regine". Here is his admission that faith is not necessarily blind, and that the leap of faith needs to be preceded by the use of reason. For if he had used his practical reason upon the situation he would have gone outwards towards Regine in love, in an act of reasoned faith, and received her. Instead he tried to turn Regine inwards into himself, to make her a part of his religion of "hidden inward-ness"; instead of giving himself to her he tried to take her into himself by an act which he called "faith" or "leap into the absurd" but which was, in fact, the work of his imagination undisciplined by reason.

It would be unfair to take *Fear and Trembling* as though it contained the whole of Kierkegaard's views on faith, for he later came to a somewhat more sweetly contemplative and reasonable view of Christianity. But *Fear and Trembling* is worth special consideration by anyone seeking to understand Kierkegaard, because it expresses so violently the false alterna-tives with which he faced himself and others. This work is another example of "nothing-but" philosophizing, of isolating certain factors or truths and treating them as though they were the only factors, or the whole truth. For God is not only the hidden God of the Old Testament; he revealed himself in his own Son. God is not only pure spirit; he became flesh and dwelt amongst us. God is not only the God of Abraham, Isaac and Joseph inexorably demanding blind sacrifice; he is the Lamb who sacrifices himself for us, himself the light of the world. Nor is faith merely a blind leap into the absurd, for it is illuminated by the light of hope. And Christianity is something more than an expression of faith alone, of inwardness; it insists that men should do good works and turn their vision outwards towards the widows and the fatherless.

Of course, if Søren Kierkegaard had done nothing more than we have suggested in these few pages it would be difficult to explain the tremendous impact produced by his works upon subsequent thinkers. In fact his self-revelation in his voluminous works will always remain a rich quarry for psychologists, theologians, and historians, in search of the deep motivations of human beings. But for our present purpose it is enough to have pointed out that he has directed philosophers' attention towards human experience and has presented them with the either/or method of arriving at truth.

NOTES

[1] In *Life of the Spirit*, Nov. 1950, Fr. Victor White O.P. writes of "the deep mystery of the 'Motherhood of God' . . . . God himself is the ultimate and eternal prototype of Motherhood, Womanhood—even materiality" . . . "As Christ, ascending to heaven, leads the way to God our Eternal Father, perhaps Mary, assumed into the same heaven, will lead us to deeper knowledge and love of God our Eternal Mother". St. Ephraim the Syrian, proclaimed a Doctor of the Church in 1920, speaks of the Holy Spirit as "Mother in God", the "eternal Woman in God".

[2] As is maintained by A. Kunzli. *Die Angst als abendländische Krankheit*, Zürich, Rascher Verlag, 1948.

[3] PRZYWARA, *Das Geheimnis Kierkegaards*, München und Berlin, Verlag von R. Oldenbourg, 1929. Cornelio Fabro, ("Foi et raison dans l'oeuvre de Kierkegaard" *Recherches de Sciences Philosophiques et Théologiques*, Paris J. Vrin, 1948) also points out that *some* of Kierkegaard's thoughts on faith may be given an orthodox Catholic interpretation.

[4] cf. VICTOR WHITE, O.P. "St. Thomas' Conception of Revelation", *Dominican Studies*, Jan. 1948, p. 33.

[5] Quoted by B. Bavink, *The Anatomy of Modern Science*, G. Bell & Sons, 1932, p. 30.

Martin Heidegger (1889–   )

Unlike most existentialists Martin Heidegger is of peasant stock—he was born at Messkirch in 1889. He seems to retain some of the telluric, almost demonic, power of the peasantry even in his most learned writings, for his early Jesuit training did not manage to smooth away his rough-hewn qualities.

It is interesting to notice that Heidegger's first large work was a study of Duns Scotus (whom we have already described as the ablest exponent of the phenomenological method), because there are many illuminating parallels to be drawn between Scotus and Heidegger. To begin with, they both enjoy a very sharp insight into the uniqueness of each existent, an almost painful sense of the unrepeatable here-and-now, the moment which is slipping away from us at the very instant we begin to think of it. Scotus, for instance, describes the human person as "incommunicable existence" as "ultimate loneliness", for there is a fine point of the person whose privacy God himself respects. This gift of seeing things in their uniqueness is essential for the philosopher no less than for the poet, but proves to be an extremely awkward gift for the philosopher, who has not only to portray the richness of the world but also to find unifying concepts by which he can account for its variety and richness. There is an obvious danger that the philosopher will get lost in the poet; and it is no accident either that Heidegger should have lately become a poetical philosopher, or that the truest of Scotists, Gerard Manley Hopkins, should have been a poet. It further explains why all three of them use such a difficult vocabulary; their words seem to get twisted into ever subtler complications and more elusive refinements because their sense of uniqueness makes them almost reluctant to use the same word twice for some aspect of existence, because that aspect changes in a very short time—it is no longer exactly the same as it was ten seconds ago, and therefore cannot be described by exactly the same word as one used ten seconds ago. Through being so intensely aware of the quick shifting of "incommunicable

D

existence" Hopkins is led to use such expressions as "fire-feathering heaven" or "Miracle-in-Mary of flame", and Heidegger, more Teutonically, to speak of existence as "*Sich-schon-vorweg-in-der-Welt-Sein*" (literally, "self-already-before-hand-in-the-world-Being").

The danger, of course, for all three of these writers lies in their impatience that the richness of language *about* existence does not come anywhere near to the richness of existence itself; consequently they are tempted to invent new words without being able to show clearly what each word signifies. For instance, Scotus speaks of the "horseness" of horses, that which makes them what they are; Heidegger speaks of "this essential element of the essence" on one occasion, and, at another time, even of the "disessence".[1] Clearly this way of using words is in danger of assuming that there is something corresponding to every word whatsoever. Which is not the case, for if we attempted to put the world into writing "I do not think the world itself would contain the books which would have to be written".[2] One becomes caught in an infinite regress by trying to produce a complete correspondence between reality and language about reality, for even if I were only to try to describe this single room under its every aspect I could never complete the task—apart from anything else, the room includes myself, and my latest description of the room would not include a description of my latest description.

This danger of confusing words with things, a particular danger in the German language, seems to have been responsible for the curious doctrine of "nothingness" which Heidegger puts forward in *Being and Time*, his weightiest work. Here Heidegger shows himself acutely aware that the method of phenomenology should lead one on to the very ground of the being one is describing. He points out that the central existential experience is one of anxiety—not of fear. The distinction is of the utmost importance, for whereas fear has a definite, limited object, it is the essence of anxiety that we cannot put our finger on any object. When we fear we always fear some thing, a certain man or beast or some future event; we can always put our finger on it; but when we ask ourselves what

is the object of our anxiety we can only answer, "Nothing".
Moreover, this "nothingness" is corroding, it spreads out over
all our lives; Heidegger avoids the contradiction of saying
that "nothingness *is* real" by saying that "nothingness itself
'produces' nothingness" ("*das Nichts selbst nichtet*"). From this
fundamental experience of "nothingness" he goes on to attempt
to elucidate existence in terms of "nothingness" and the care,
the being-in-the-world, which is existence.

Some philosophers, when confronted with this analysis, have
simply laughed and maintained that Heidegger is turning the
peculiarities of the German language into a philosophy. This
accusation against Heidegger is certainly justified in many
cases—when he says, for instance, "Our ancient word '*war*'
[German equivalent of English "was"] means 'protection'.
We see this in '*wahrnehmen*', [English—"to perceive"] i.e. to
take into protection, as also in '*gewahren*' [English—"to
become aware of"] and '*verwahren*' [English—"to guard"]."[3]
Heidegger then goes on to relate "*war*" with the German for
truth (i.e. *Wahrheit*) and to elucidate the search for truth in
terms of this derivation of a word—without even bothering,
however, to discuss whether this derivation is, in fact, correct
—which it is not! Even against his use of the word "nothingness" this accusation is to some extent justified, since the
absence, in anxiety, of any definite object upon which one can
put one's finger, does not imply that there is *no* such object,
but merely that we cannot name it definitely. The absence of
any particular knowable object does not mean the presence of
"nothingness". At the same time, everyone will agree that
Heidegger's distinction between fear and anxiety represents a
masterly piece of phenomenological analysis; and once he has
raised the question it is necessary for thinkers to work out what
it means for men to be in this condition of anxiety.

The same brilliant observation characterizes the whole of
his *Being and Time*. His main theme is that European men
have almost lost their very sense of "being". Especially since
Descartes they have confused the way in which objects which
we use *are present* and the way in which we humans *exist*. For
a human being is not just one usable object amongst other

usable objects; books, tables and cats are simply present, whereas human beings (except when they lose their sense of being) exist—*ex sistere* meaning that as human beings we *stand outside* ourselves, going out and comprehending these objects which are present. Because we have fallen into the habit of behaving like such objects and have forgotten what it means to *exist*. Heidegger is, so to speak, trying to shake us and shock us into a realization of the awe-fulness of our existence. Once that has happened to us we may be in a condition to approach the meaning of being at the same depth as Heidegger's favourite pre-Socratic philosophers approached it. Yet even Heidegger has not managed to reveal to us this lost philosophy of being; for *Being and Time* ends with a question, "What is being?". And the subsequent volume in which an answer was anticipated has not yet appeared, and probably never will.

However, the fact that *Being and Time* leaves us with a question is of minor importance compared with its devastating description of our human condition, a description which has captured the minds of men throughout the world. Mercilessly, Heidegger exposes the way in which we try to gloss over the awe-fulness of existence and the need to commit ourselves to existence, the way in which, for instance, we say, "One dies usually at three score and ten"—as if "one" ever existed, when it is *I* who exist and *I* who have to die. There is no "one" who can do it for me, and I am only trying to deceive myself by constantly speaking of "one", refusing the burden of existence and casting it on to "one". We are committed to death, heading all the time for death, which is the peak moment of *ex-sistence*, when we stand outside ourselves. Not that Heidegger therefore holds out promises of fuller existence after death. Apart from anything else such a life lies beyond the scope of a method which limits itself to what is given and experienced. But such promises, in any case, would only constitute another cheap way of blunting the sharpness and anguish of existence. We are cast off into a world where "man as such is guilty" and anguished; we have to endure this cast-offness, this guilt and this anguish in order to exist—and in the end this means existence-unto-death.

In Heidegger's later works there is a change of emphasis, although their atmosphere is still very much that of a philosophical nightmare of chaos and darkness. But by concentrating upon discovering what we mean by "truth" he has performed a valuable, if as yet incomplete, service. The point of his extremely complicated reflections seems to be that "truth" has too readily been accepted as the conformity of the mind to its object. But the essence of truth is something much deeper than this mere conformity of the mind to its object, for there is a sense in which it is not we who judge the truth, but the truth which reveals itself to us. The truth does not depend upon our judgements—it unveils itself almost spontaneously once we achieve existence.

Though Heidegger claims that his version of "truth" is original it does remind one of the scholastic theory which fixed the deep origin of all truths before all human judgement, in the truth of God's ideas. From this truth the many truths reached in human expressions are derived. If we can imagine the scholastic theory, minus God, we have some notion of what Heidegger is probing for. And in general there is much to be said for viewing Heidegger's philosophy as scholasticism without God (e.g. his view of the human person = Scotus' view, minus God).

NOTES

[1] *Existence and Being*, Vision Press, 1949, p. 294.
[2] John xxi. 25.
[3] *Holzwege*, Frankfurt a/M, Klostermann Verlag, 1949, p. 321.

Gabriel Marcel (1877–   )

As we have already pointed out, Gabriel Marcel thought himself round to an "existentialist" position well before he became acquainted with the works of Kierkegaard. Subsequently he took the step which Brandes believed was one alternative for Kierkegaard when, in 1929, he was received into the Catholic Church. Since then he has devoted himself to elaborating his Christian "existentialist" position mainly by indirect communication in the form of plays, which by their dramatic quality are obviously suited to express the dramatic features of existentialism.

Since Marcel's language avoids the more startling eccentricities of existentialist vocabulary he can be read by the general reader without too much difficulty, and so we intend here simply to pick out what seem to be his most valuable contributions to contemporary thought, leaving aside the niceties of his position.

Marcel, better than anyone else, has given us phenomenological descriptions of experience which show the falsity of restricting experience to sense-experience. He rightly points out that the Humian school have allowed their theories of experience to be dominated by a most misleading comparison. They compare existence to the impressing of a seal onto hot wax: human beings are, as it were, the hot wax receiving the seal of impressions from the external world. But human beings are not just passive instruments in this way; for a human being to receive impressions not only the senses but the whole person has to be engaged (including attention of the will and the intellect). It is not as though the senses receive something and then the intellect wakes up and records it. On the contrary, before even the senses can do their work properly, the person, at the pre-conscious level, has to be awake, attending. Everyone is aware of times when one person quite literally does not hear or see something which the person next to him does hear or see, because the first person is not *attending* at that particular time; he does not cease to have eyes or ears—it is simply that these organs are functions of a person and that the person is attending to something else at that time. For instance, when Charles Darwin visited the Fuegian islanders from his ship, the *Beagle*, the natives were excited by the sight of the small boats which took the landing party ashore, but failed to notice the ship itself lying at anchor in front of them.[1]

Because experience cannot be limited to the work of the senses nor treated simply as passive, Marcel prefers to use the term "responsiveness" to indicate our dealings with the world. A response, obviously, is not a mechanical reaction; it means welcoming experience, and therefore once more brings out the importance of that pre-conscious attitude which we have mentioned before.[2] So much depends upon the very dispositions with which one approaches the world. Marcel himself distinguishes this responsive attitude towards the world from the instrumental-reaction theory by pointing out that it involves one in an "I-Thou" relationship. The universe is not a *thing* to be handled and manipulated for the satisfaction of man, as our modern technicians seem to think. Such a technical way of approaching the universe not only turns the universe into a mere object for consumption, it even degrades man himself to being a mere consumer; it establishes an impersonal relationship between one impersonal "it", which is the universe, and another impersonal "it", which is the instrument-like man. The "I-Thou" relationship, however, is the response which I make as a person to another person—I say "thou", and immediately there is established an intimate relationship, a relationship of communion. It establishes also an atmosphere of reverence and gratitude which is immediately dissipated as soon as we become technicians again and treat the universe and our fellow-creatures as "its".

Applications of this "I-Thou" theory in every field of our personal and social life can be made with great fruitfulness. Each of us is aware that the surest way of destroying a friendship is to treat our friends, not as "thous" but as "its", using them instead of revering them—in fact (for that is what it amounts to) betraying them. There is inevitable alienation. And this process of alienation is exactly what has happened to modern man, who feels himself a stranger in the world; he has used nature as an instrument for his own satisfaction as if this were within his rights and power. Consequently he has broken the "I-Thou" relationship; he has lost his communion with other things in the universe- -he has excommunicated himself. He needs to go down on his knees, to say "I confess to thee", and to be received once more into the communion of the "I-Thou" relationship.

From the "I-Thou" relationship as expounded by Marcel one passes to the most characteristic part of his philosophizing wherein he points out the difference between a mystery and a problem, for one might say that all "I-Thou" relationships involve us in a mystery whereas problems are impersonal concerns. One confronts a problem, but we are ourselves involved in mysteries. For instance M. Julien Benda (p. 79) has perverted the mystery of his own dying into the problem of death. Once he has begun to speak of death as though it were an object which he could observe in the same way that one observes a *Times* Crossword Puzzle, then he begins to speak of his own death with the detachment of a person solving the crossword puzzle. But whereas M. Benda might be able to give a cut-and-dried lecture on how he solves crossword puzzles, not even M. Benda will be able to give us a lecture on his experience of dying. Death, like everything else that matters a great deal to us, involves us in a mystery, for we are ourselves at stake. I call to "Brother Death" to receive me; I welcome Brother Death; I call him "thou". My death will be unique for me—no man can die my death—and no-one else can elucidate it for me, as they might explain a crossword puzzle to me. For since I, myself, am one of the factors in this mystery I only come to understand anything of it by knowing myself, which no man can do for me.

Whereas I can be the spectator when confronted with a problem and can walk all around it, examining it from every angle, when I am involved in a mystery I myself am in action —I cannot pretend to be a spectator when my very self is at stake.

Such are some of the themes which Gabriel Marcel has put into philosophical circulation. They are not new themes—they are as old as humanity, but Marcel has treated them with a freshness and originality that command admiration.

NOTES

[1] Quoted from Polanyi, *The Logic of Liberty*, p. 19.

[2] Besides Marcel other philosophers who stress the importance of our pre-conscious attitudes are Berdyaev, Buber and Ferdinand Ebner, all of whom use the term "I-Thou" to express the relationship of a person to the world. Peter Wust also brings out the need for a welcoming, reverent, grateful, pre-conscious attitude towards the world.

Existentialism Assessed

Some of the positive values in the existentialist current have already been mentioned. Above all, attention has nowadays been concentrated upon a question which only an idiot would deny to be of importance to us, the question, "What is man? What is his destiny?", and it is this question which all existentialists seek to answer. It is interesting to notice, moreover, that their analysis of the human situation reveals man to be a broken creature living in a broken world. How he is to achieve wholeness or to realize his destiny they are not agreed, though all realize that he has somehow to get beyond himself; Heidegger says that he has to ex-sist, to stand outside himself, even if he only does so in dying; Jaspers believes that man has to achieve "transcendence", even though again he only does so in that moment of ultimate brokenness which is death—for we must sail into this ultimate wreckage of our lives with our eyes open, achieving transcendence by fearlessly facing it in all its stark reality. To a Christian this view seems to be a form of worshipping the Cross without Christ, but at least it has the merit of seeing that man is a religious animal, a "God-seeker", as Scheler puts it.

Perhaps the most permanently valuable contribution made by existentialists lies in their recovery of the "I-Thou" relationship, for without this call of an "I" to a "Thou" man would be entirely shut up in a world of his own, imprisoned in the appearances, able to say "This appears to be . . ." but never "This is". By moving from the level of appearances to what is we move from phenomenology to metaphysics. We do this by breaking out of ourselves and crying "Thou" to God, the ground of all that is. Moreover we speak as person to person; it is not merely that we make a rational judgement, "Thou art" but that we commit our whole persons, giving ourselves, acknowledging "Thou". It is true that we do later formulate this personal acknowledgement at the rational level, when we say, for instance, "I believe in God . . ."; but it actually takes place at a deeper level, not in a rational judgement but in an act of personal acknowledgement, the call of "I" to "Thou". The rational formulation is necessary, of course, if we are to express this act, and its formulation shows it to be not irrational, but without the original act there would be nothing to formulate.

It is the belief of Ludwig Landgrebe [1] that metaphysics was undermined in the European tradition when the rational formulation of this acknowledgement of "Thou" was substituted for the act itself. Once the rational formulation is made primary, "God" becomes no more than an *inference from* the appearances; he is the non-apparent inferred by reason from what is apparent. There results a split between science, which deals with what appears, and faith, which is a leap from the appearances to the non-apparent God. No basis remains for metaphysics to deal with what *appears* in terms of what *is*. There is only a basis for metaphysics when we cry "Thou" to God, acknowledging the ground of being, seeing God *in* appearances—not inferring his existence *from* appearances. We no more infer the existence of God than we infer our own existence; we *acknowledge* our own existence and God's existence in the same act, for he is the ground of our existence. If we refuse to cry "Thou" to God we break the "I-Thou" relationship, we cut ourselves off from the source of being and we render impossible the science of being which is metaphysics.

By suggesting that the recovery of the "I-Thou" relationship will lead to a new respect for the despised discipline of metaphysics we are not suggesting, of course, that existentialists have all realized the implications of the "I-Thou" relationship as Landgrebe has. In fact, their failure to proceed beyond description to acknowledgement and judgement, beyond phenomenology to metaphysics, is a convenient point at which to indicate the deficiencies of existentialist thought.

The first difficulty arises from their inadequate description of the specifically human experience which is their starting-point. For although all our experience is human experience it is all experience *of* some thing, of cats and tables or men and women. Faced with the task of elucidating this experience we do right to ask *who* enjoys the experience, because that is

obviously one of the most important factors in it. But we also
need to ask ourselves *what* it is that we experience, for the object
of our experience is just as relevant a factor as we ourselves,
who are the subjects of it. Indeed, awareness of ourselves comes
to us as secondary, when we reflect upon experience; the
primary experience *is* thoroughly human, but we only become
conscious of the fact that it is human by a secondary reflection
upon it. Therefore if the existentialist is to give us a full
account of human experience he must begin by telling us *what*
it is that we experience (i.e. he must outline his metaphysics).
Only then can he properly describe the human factor in the
experience (i.e. what the human being was aiming at in directing his attention towards the objects in question—this would
mean describing man's condition, and what man is trying to
do about his condition, i.e. his ethical position). In the order
of formulation, therefore, metaphysics must come first and
ethics second.

Now this order is precisely the order which we find St.
Thomas Aquinas following. St. Thomas begins his *Summa
Theologica* by an account of what *is*, of being in general; he
then goes on to discuss *human* being, describing man's condition and the way he must act if he is to achieve harmony
with what *is*. Human being is set into the framework of being
in general; and therefore although St. Thomas does not in any
way minimize the singularity of human existence, neither does
he isolate human beings from the being of the universe in
general. We each have our individuality, but we are not unrelated to the universe.

How unsatisfactory it is to try to work out a metaphysics in
terms of secondary reflection upon our human condition is
obvious enough if we turn to Heidegger's attempt to do so.
He asks, what is the object of anxiety? and replies "Nothing";
from which he proceeds to develop a philosophy of "nothingness". But the reply should surely be that anxiety does not
have an object, that "anxiety" refers to a condition of a human
being. One cannot ask what is the *object* of a condition. One
can only ask, how did it come about? or, how is it going to be
removed? Answers to these questions can be attempted by

metaphysics, which offers a theory of the universe and man's position in it, but they can only be given with certainty by someone who knows whence man came and what he is destined for. Only the author of the universe could know that, and therefore it is a question of faith.

This illustration brings out the complete chaos which the existentialists cause by asking such unintelligible questions as, what is the object of an emotional condition? Knowing has an object and willing has an object, but emotional states are simply accompaniments—often very influential, admittedly— of these objective activities, and therefore to ask what is the object of an emotional state is to pose a meaningless question.

Because they lack and even despise objectivity, existentialists provide no standard by which we can judge the truth of either their own or anyone else's expressions. However, this lack of objectivity does not worry them because they have come to associate objectivity with that narrow conception of reason and the intellect which was part of the tradition against which they are reacting so violently. Of course, if reason were no more than the mechanical faculty by which we proceed from one point to another point without any judgement of where we are proceeding or why, they would be largely justified. But, as we have explained (pp. 8–9), reason is something much deeper, and to reject false objectivity does not mean to reject objectivity altogether. In all our knowing and willing we establish a relationship between ourselves as subjects and some object; the fact that people had fallen into the habit of ignoring the subject is no good reason for ignoring the object, for rejecting object-ivity. For the practical consequences of concentrating ex-clusively upon the conditions and emotional states of the subject are disastrous. To say, for example, that a person has faith means very little unless we know in *what* he has faith. Kierke-gaard had faith, and Adolph Hitler had faith, and St. Francis of Assisi had faith, but what distinguished these three persons was the object of their faith. And only by having some standard by which to judge the object of faith can one hope to distinguish between the rightness or wrongness of these three men.

To say "either objectivity or subjectivity" is to face oneself

with a false alternative. And the existentialist is facing us with
a further false alternative when he says that "existence" cannot
be expressed in words, that one cannot define existence.
Obviously this is true in the sense that the order of reality is
infinitely richer than the order of speech describing reality, but
it is untrue if taken to mean that we can say nothing intelligible
about "existence". St. John was right when he said that if
all of Jesus' doings were put into writing all the books in the
world would not contain it—but he never doubted that he
had expressed *some* of these doings in his own gospel. Similarly,
even when the existentialist says that "existence is indefinable"
he is saying something intelligible about existence, he is in a
negative way expressing the richness of existence. We need
not despair because we do not understand the whole of
existence and only know in part, for that is our creaturely lot.

But according to our assessment this is precisely what the
typical modern man, as expressed in existentialism, refuses to
acknowledge. He will not recognize that he is a creature;
therefore he has to assume the rôle of God; this he cannot do,
and therefore he falls into despair. Those who have not
recognized their subjection as creatures, says André Gide,
"are 'the salt of the earth', and are responsible for God. For
I am convinced that God is not, and that we must make him
real".[2] "Man is basically a desire to be a God"; "Man is
nothing else but what he makes of himself"; "My liberty is
choice of being God"[3] as Sartre puts it. No wonder Sartre is
full of anguish, since he considers himself responsible for the
whole world; he is "a passion to be God" but "a useless
passion" because he can never realize what he desires to be.

It is no use pointing out to Sartre that his position of
desiring to be God but knowing that he cannot be, is absurd,
because that is exactly what Sartre himself says—he begins by
assuming that it is absurd to exist. Confronted with such an
initial assumption one cannot argue, because the assumption
is made at a pre-conscious level and argument takes place at
the conscious level. The most profitable course is to try to
understand why European man has fallen into the habit of
assuming that existence is absurd, or that he is not a creature,

for the two seem to go together. In the Middle Ages, for instance, the pre-conscious assumption was that being and goodness were identical; men questioned all kinds of assumptions, but they never questioned the goodness and rationality of existence. Taking their lead from the Mother of God they received the gift of being as she received the angel of the Annunciation, in humility and joy, "Be it done unto me according to thy Word"; it was the reply of utter humility, acceptance of creaturehood, a cry of joy for the gift of being.

Much has happened to European man since the Middle Ages. He is no longer a Catholic but a lapsed Catholic, and he has developed habits of pride. One writer said that he would rather hug his own misery than be fed,[4] for it is easier to give up one's joy than to give up one's pride. At least the denial of creatureliness and refusal to accept the joy of being is understandable if it is true that existentialism represents an expression of lapsed Catholicism. When Heidegger, for instance, says that his primary experience is of anxiety and nothingness, that "man as such is guilty", is "cast-off", he is confirming Edith Stein's view that "Heidegger's philosophy is the philosophy of a bad conscience". Nor is Heidegger an exception. However much they may proclaim "the death of God" the existentialists do not seem to be able to stop talking about theological issues, and even a Christian must occasionally feel that they have religion on the brain.

Indeed, the unmistakably "religious" atmosphere of existentialism has convinced some Christians that existentialism conceals a fundamental desire for life in Christ. These Christians point out, for instance, that Heidegger speaks of the "holiness" of the poet's vocation, that he often speaks of sacrifice ("Sacrifice is rooted in the nature of the event through which Being claims man for the truth of Being")[5], that he is not a materialist. All of which is no doubt true, but a religious aura does not make a man a Christian. There is a religious atmosphere about the Devil; the Devil is not a materialist but pure spirit, and sacrifice has often been made to false gods. Whether or not existentialism is proposing homage to false gods is hard to decide; even the possibility, however, brings out the urgent need for thinkers who have the gift of discerning spirits, of revealing the wolf in sheep's clothing.

Obviously there are other feasible interpretations of existentialism. Some have held that the "guilt", "anguish" and "nothingness" are symptoms of our modern way of life. In contemporary life, they say, there is no natural way of easing the tension which the modern world produces. Tension was resolved by primitive man in the form of action. Constantly faced by peril from the elements and brute beasts his organism naturally went into a state of tension as a defence-measure (his medulla began to release adrenalin). By fighting the elements and the brute beasts this tension was resolved in the form of action (that nervous and muscular activity for which adrenalin is released). Modern men live in a state of perpetual tension produced through insecurity, imminent war and incessant noise; they have no natural way of releasing this tension, and so they seek distractions for it; there are some men, especially introverts, who cannot find distraction from the tension, and so they try to give a name to it, to explain it. Whether they call it *nausée* with Sartre or *Angst* with Heidegger makes little difference, the tension goes unrelieved.

To the psychologist this, no doubt, is the most convenient explanation of the movement. He has every opportunity to document his explanation. Kierkegaard is an obvious case; he refuses to marry and take his place in society and is subject to suicidal thoughts. Franz Kafka's life shows a similar trajectory; his ambition was "to plough a field, to plant a tree, to father a child" but he refused his opportunities to act upon these ideas, and he also dwelt upon suicide. Ferdinand Ebner's life for a time fell into almost exactly the same pattern. There is no end to the evidence upon which a psychologist could draw. Nor need we regard the theological and psychological interpretations as mutually exclusive; they are complementary, for sanctity and sanity are intimately connected; a failure in charity and a bad conscience lead almost inevitably to bad nerves.

If it is objected that these reflections betray an attempt to reduce philosophy to a study of philosopher's psychology we can only reply that philosophers who concentrate so exclusively upon emotional states leave one no choice about this. One cannot ask whether an emotional state is *true*, one can only ask how it was brought about and how it may come to an end. We suggest that this particular state will be ended, when men acknowledge themselves to be creatures.

NOTES

[1] LUDWIG LANDGREBE, *Phänomenologie und Metaphysik*, Hamburg, Marion von Schroder Verlag, 1949, pp. 154–155.

[2] ANDRÉ GIDE, *Journal* 1942–49, Paris, Librairie Gallimard, 1950, p. 252.

[3] SARTRE, *L'être et le Néant*, Paris, Librairie Gallimard, 1943.

[4] P-R RÉGAMEY, O.P., *Poverty*, trans. R. Sheed, Sheed & Ward, 1949, p. 46.

[5] HEIDEGGER, *Existence and Being*, p. 390.

LOGICAL POSITIVISM

THE STARTING-POINT for the philosopher who is broadly to be described as a logical positivist has already been mentioned, for all logical positivists are the logical children of Hume. They first came into prominence as philosophers attempting to provide some theory which would account for the successful experiments of the physical scientists. The physical scientists were now beginning to state general laws of which their observations were the particular instances; not the natures of *things*, as with Aristotle, but certain observed *events* were their prime concern. Consequently the philosophers who followed in their wake set themselves the task of justifying inferences from one event to another event. Simplest of all instances: I know that day has dawned at regular intervals throughout the whole of my life, but on what grounds do I hold that it will dawn again within another few hours? Of course, I do hold that it will; but what theoretical justification can I claim for my opinion?

One should point out immediately that it is not the physical scientists who ask themselves this kind of question, but the philosophers who follow after them. For if a physical scientist were once to become a thorough positivist and try to formulate a justification for all his experiments before he carried them out he would obviously never carry them out; if he knew so much that he could formulate the justification successfully there would, moreover, be no need at all for him even to make experiments. This difference between the physical scientists and their philosophical followers needs to be borne in mind because it means that the positivist philosopher takes as *his* starting-point not the event (the concern of the physical scientist in his laboratory, etc.) but the statements *about* the event made by the physical scientists and later considered in his study by the philosopher. The physical scientist lives in a world of events, the positivist in a world of *statements* about events; the difference is often, and fatally, ignored by positivists who say that they are talking about "facts" when they are actually talking about statements which signify "facts" (or, better, events).

Once this close connection between physical scientists and positivists has been noted, it will be obvious that crises in the physical sciences tend to stimulate activity amongst the positivists. In recent times the crisis in physical science is to be dated at about the turn of the nineteenth century, when Max Planck and Einstein, amongst others, radically changed the world-picture that physical scientists had contented themselves with. Both the physicists and the mathematicians now began to ask themselves what on earth they were supposed to be doing when they pursued their physics or their mathematics. Since Newton's physics and Euclid's mathematics had been shown to be woefully limited, how could they themselves hope to be working on any firmer basis? This crisis gave the theorists their opportunity, and the story of modern positivism is more or less the story of how they have exploited that opportunity. It was then that Aristotle's logic became a casualty[1] and was consigned to the same rubbish-heap as Newton's physics and Euclid's mathematics by Bertrand Russell (who, in collaboration with A. N. Whitehead, wrote *Principia Mathematica* (1910)).

Amongst the most valuable effects of this exciting period was the renewed interest in the history of science, because the history of science enables us to see the methods and principles employed in previous ages and to check up on contemporary methods by comparison of the two. Émile Meyerson inspired many researchers in this field; and Pierre Duhem's masterly volumes showed that medieval philosophers were not unacquainted with these problems. Duhem particularly stressed the hypothetical character of "laws" relating to physical phenomena, pointing out, for instance, that St. Thomas Aquinas did not believe Ptolemy's astronomy was the last word on the subject—Ptolemy's astronomy was a useful hypothesis which more or less accounted for current astronomical observation but might well be replaced by any other hypothesis which would give a more complete account of the phenomena in question.[2] The tentative quality of physicists' hypotheses, and the limitations in our methods of investigation are points which naturally commended themselves to Catholics such as Duhem.

But the main centre of positivism for many years was Vienna, the home of a group of philosophers known as "the Vienna Circle", which included Schlick, Frank, Neurath, Wittgenstein and Carnap. Since many of these thinkers were Jews they sought refuge either in Great Britain or in the U.S.A. when the Nazis came to power. This exodus has produced a most striking geographical division of philosophical groups; professional philosophers in the U.S.A. and Great Britain remain under the influence of positivism whereas on the Continent positivism has become a much weaker force. In general this may be accounted for by the way in which Continentals have had to make so many life-and-death decisions during recent years and have "gone existentialist;" meanwhile the U.S.A. and Great Britain have provided a calm refuge in which it has not seemed entirely pointless to discuss detailed questions and fine points of philosophical language.

Certain general characteristics of the logical positivist movement are worth remembering when one is discussing it, because they help us to find our way through a mass of very complicated literature.

In the first place most positivists' views change so quickly that anyone formulating an objection to them is bound to be accused of criticizing views which are no longer held. A classical illustration of a positivist career comes to us in the story of Bertrand Russell's opinions; Russell has been a Meinongian Realist, Neutral Monist, Behaviourist at different times—his position changes from year to year. Just as difficult to follow is Carnap who began by declaring war upon every suggestion of "metaphysics;" but now he describes thinking as a "finding of entities", and it becomes very difficult to see how this "finding of entities" differs from the "metaphysics" of traditional philosophy.

Secondly, logical positivist literature carries with it an atmosphere of bitter controversy which has usually in the past been associated with theological disputes; the whole movement is sectarian in its fierceness and enmities. Amongst the "Viennese", Neurath was noted for his ceaseless war upon metaphysics and his eagerness to accept any programme which favoured materialism.

3. Thirdly, the logicians amongst the positivists have invented a "logic" which differs from the traditional Aristotelian "logic" and which, they believe, renders Aristotelian "logic" out of date. It is interesting to notice, however, that their "logic" cannot be considered so original as they once claimed; it has the same characteristics as all those logics which attempt to justify a certain theory of physical science. The physical science of the Stoics, for instance, was based upon the division of time and space into discontinuous points; the Stoic logicians therefore took sentences from physical science as their primary logical unit and treated sentences as if they were discontinuous units, linguistic atoms. For the Stoic logician, therefore, the main task was to describe how we can make inferences from one sentence to another sentence, how we can move from one discontinuous atom to another discontinuous atom. This effort led him to a theory of how one sentence implies another which differed considerably from the Aristotelian theory of implication. Aristotle, in his physics, did not divide the world up into discontinuous points, nor did he take sentences as units of implication; implication was possible, in Aristotle's view, because nature is continuous and one can make inferences from the nature of some things to the nature of other things. Therefore when he spoke of "implication" he meant something different from what the Stoics meant.

In the Middle Ages William of Ockham saw the physical world in a way similar to that of the Stoics; the universe is composed of atoms. Not surprisingly, Ockham the logician took sentences as his basic logical units and, in describing how difficult it was to move from one unit to another unit, stated logical rules which have endeared him to modern logicians of the positivist school.

Following in the footsteps of the Stoics and Ockham a positivist such as Wittgenstein based his *Tractatus Logico-*

Philosophicus upon the assumption that there are "logical simples", basic atomic units of language which directly represent the basic atoms of the physical world. Without such units of language, he maintains, one could go on dividing sentences *ad infinitum* and never getting any nearer to reality —there would be no link between language and the world which language describes. Obviously Wittgenstein's view is only justified if the world is, in fact, divided into discontinuous atoms. He has to assume so for purposes of his logic and positivism. The result is that he lands himself in all the difficulties which have always faced those who divide space and time up into separate points. On the basis of that division, it will be remembered, it becomes impossible to see how Achilles could ever catch the tortoise, because by the time he has reached any point which the tortoise was occupying at a previous instant the tortoise has already moved on to some other point. And so Achilles could never catch the tortoise. This desperate situation of Achilles in the atomic physical world is reflected in the logic which attempts to justify the atomic view of the physical world. Bertrand Russell has confessed that logical analysis of this sort inevitably leads to a combination of scepticism and blind faith: "As a general rule, the effect of logical analysis is to show the mutual independence of propositions which had been thought to be logically connected. As logic improves, less and less can be proved. The result, if we regard logical analysis as a game, is an insincere scepticism. But if we are unwilling to profess disbelief that we are in fact incapable of entertaining, the result of logical analysis is to increase the number of independent premisses that we accept in our analysis of knowledge".[3] In other words, we all know that Achilles can catch the tortoise; we also know that he could not do so if space and time were divided into separate points; it seems reasonable to assume, therefore, that space and time are not divided in this way. Any logic (whether Stoic, Wittgensteinian or Russellian) which proposes such a division inevitably results in baseless scepticism.

The fourth general characteristic of logical positivists is their habit of destroying the old gods of metaphysics with the aid of their new tool, i.e. language-analysis, and then bowing down before this new tool which has brought them such great victories, worshipping language-analysis as the one metaphysical god. They turn their method into a metaphysics. From a psychological standpoint it is easy to understand how philosophers fall into this habit. "The effort to grasp thought in itself causes the mind to cease observing external things, without succeeding in observing itself. It observes itself no longer as living, acting and producing ideas; it looks only at produced, expressible and expressed ideas. Consequently it turns away from itself and from every object, for it seeks only thought. But as thought does not arise in the mind except from the presence of an object or of its sign, it follows that the custom of artificial reflection which turns the mind away from objects carries it towards words. Giving up the world of things, and of itself, the mind busies itself in the realm of words and shuts itself up in a logical existence".[4] When the logical positivist has been brought to this condition his relationship towards words is similar to Cardinal Newman's relationship towards God. Newman said that from childhood he was aware of two self-evident things, his own existence and the existence of God. The logical positivist, similarly, accepts his own existence but the second thing for him is not God, but words. If he sometimes confuses the attributes of words with God's attributes, that is understandable.

Yet one may well sympathize with the positivist attack on metaphysics if one bears in mind that these positivists originated in Austria, where "metaphysics" meant the kind of cloudy speculations indulged in by the German followers of Hegel. Hegel, for instance, tells us that "pure being and pure nothing are the same;" a statement which, according to Carnap, can be shown to be nonsense once the grammatical errors it involves are eliminated. Carnap is right, no doubt, in saying that Hegelian "metaphysics" can be largely shown to be nonsense once Hegel's grammatical errors are revealed. But he is clearly unjustified in then going on to say that all the statements which have been called metaphysical statements are nonsense, that metaphysical problems are shown to be pseudo-problems as soon as grammatical errors are avoided. Obviously Carnap's own statement is a metaphysical statement in so far as he maintains that all metaphysics can be reduced to grammatical errors. If he had restricted himself to saying that, having found all Hegel's philosophical problems to rest upon such errors he was then going to examine every statement ever made in the name of metaphysics in order to show that they all rest upon similar errors, his thesis would be less objectionable. (Though even then he would still have to answer the query as to his standard of judgement for correct grammar). But in that case he would simply be recommending a philosophical programme. In fact, of course, he has turned his programme into a judgement; he has made a metaphysics of his method.

Obviously the most sensible thing for the Viennese Circle to have done, once they had issued a programme, was to carry it out; they should have shown that *every* statement traditionally accepted as "metaphysical" did, in fact, involve a grammatical error; instead, they declared that *all* such statements, by their very nature (in virtue of being "metaphysical") *do* embody some grammatical error. They became defenders of a creed, turning their programme into an -ism; they became the defenders of logical positivism. Under the pressure of this mood logical positivists made such truculent declarations as their famous verification statement: that before a statement could be accepted as meaningful it must be capable of verification by sense-experience. This dogmatic declaration, not unnaturally, called forth unanswerable rejoinders. It was immediately pointed out that the verification statement itself cannot be verified by sense-experience—the positivists had cut off the branch on which they were attempting to sit.

Furthermore the statement makes the curious assumption that we verify by sense-experience alone, whereas we in fact verify a proposition by means of our senses and our *intellects* in order to judge whether it is true or not. And the question of how our intellects and senses manage to perform this complicated operation raises all the traditional metaphysical problems.

It is worth noting, however, that the verification statement does not say that metaphysical propositions are false; it says they are meaningless. This distinction is worth bearing in mind because positivists are often accused of being atheists or agnostics on the ground that they find metaphysical propositions about God to be meaningless. However, as Hume pointed out long ago, scepticism on the subject of metaphysics may simply diminish our trust in reason and widen the area of faith; and not a few positivists, such as Wittgenstein, have combined metaphysical scepticism with religious faith.

Once we have become acquainted with these general characteristics of the movement we can turn towards the problems it has raised in the field of logic. Its innovations were first explicitly stated, and Aristotelian logic jettisoned, when Bertrand Russell confronted himself with the "paradoxes". He eventually suggested a logical answer to them in the *Principia Mathematica*. Instances of the paradoxes are the following. Suppose a person says, "What I am saying is false"; then if what he says is true, he is lying; but if what he says is false, he is telling the truth. "There is a barber in a village where the men who do not shave themselves are shaved by the barber; if the barber does not shave himself he is one of those who are shaved by the barber, i.e. by himself; but if the barber does shave himself then he is one of those not shaved by the barber; therefore he does not shave himself."

On a somewhat higher plane, in the mathematical consideration of classes, where the paradoxes were first taken seriously: "Let w be the class of all those classes which are not members of themselves. Then whatever class x may be, 'x is a w' is equivalent to 'x is not an x'. Hence, giving to x the value of w, 'w is a w' is equivalent to 'w is not a w'."[5]

Confronted with these confusing paradoxes the general reader may be forgiven for thinking that he knows intuitively why they occur. For instance, the class of classes which contain themselves as members does not exist, and therefore to divide classes up into those which do, and those which do not, contain themselves, is equivalent to dividing beings up into those which exist and those which do not exist. Handling these non-existent beings or non-existent classes lands the positivists in precisely the same mess as they accuse Hegel of creating when he says, "Pure being and pure nothing are the same". Of the barber paradox the general reader would say that the fact that it defines a class of men by no means implies that such a class exists (or that the definition is free from contradiction). And in face of the gentleman who declares "What I am saying is false" he would realize that the sentence has confused what a word means and what it stands for; he would remember, for instance that the word "mile" is not a mile long, and that the word "green" is not green. He would then point out that if the word "what" means "what I have just said" then there is no vicious circle, whereas if the word "what" stands for itself as a word then the statement is just nonsense, because *words* cannot be described as either true or false (they have first to be contained in a sentence or judgement).

And perhaps the general reader would also get to the very root of the difficulty by pointing out that each of the paradoxes is based upon the fallacy of attributing to words or sentences a power which belongs only to minds: the power of reflexion, of referring to itself. I can refer to myself, for example, because of my mind's power of reflexion; but any *statement* which I make about my mind and its operations must necessarily be incomplete because my statement would not include my statement itself (which, presumably, reflects some fresh activity of my mind). By trying to make words perform the function proper to a mind one is trying to put one's own existence into words—where it will not go. It is like trying to find a box which will contain all boxes—an impossible quest, for such a box would contain itself, a box.

We have already encountered this difficulty in another form in the discussion of existentialism, where it was pointed out that a human being cannot pretend to contain the whole world because a human being is part of the world; we cannot pretend to be mere spectators at the drama of life for we are ourselves actors in it. If we do make these pretences we are trying to jump out of our creaturely skins, we are trying to be infinite, when we are, in fact, finite. Surely the fallacy of the paradoxes lies in their attempt to give sentences this power of stating the *whole* truth, when they cannot in fact be used to decide their own truth; when they cannot even be reflexive, as the human mind is.

Of course Russell and his followers, when acting as human beings, realize this common-sense viewpoint very well; he states the position clearly enough when he says "A proposition can never be about itself." But whereas the average man will be content at not finding any practical difficulties even in the paradoxes; whereas, that is to say, he will go on shaving himself, even though he is a barber in a village where the men who do not shave themselves are shaved by the barber, Russell wishes to clear up the paradoxes from a logical viewpoint. It was in working out the logic of them that he developed the discipline of symbolic logic which he claims has replaced Aristotelian logic. Since most positivists use symbolic logic as an instrument of their thought its main characteristics need to be summarized here (though very generally, because the issues raised by it are incredibly complicated).

An initial difficulty arises out of the elusive meaning of the word "logic", as was realized by St. Albert the Great when he said, "Some of the ancients used to maintain that logic is not a science, explaining that what is itself the mode of all science and doctrine [i.e. logic] cannot itself be a science." In other words, how can you have a science of the *way* in which one thinks correctly, when that science itself will need elaborating in the very *way* (or mode) which you are trying to describe scientifically? We seem to be involved in a vicious circle. In order to find out what logic is about you must proceed logically; but how do you know that you are proceeding logically, unless you already know what logic is?

It was, perhaps, their acute awareness of this difficulty which led Russell and the symbolic logicians to restrict the use of the word "logic" to the way, or form, of thought; because this affords at least a technical escape from the difficulty of relating the way one thinks to what one thinks, the mode to the object, the form to the matter. Traditional Aristotelian logic includes both the form and the matter, both formal and material logic. Possibly the quarrel between the new symbolic

logic and the ancient Aristotelian logic derives ultimately from
these different meanings of the word "logic"; and, as the
following paragraphs will suggest, the symbolic logicians have
only postponed the difficulty of relating form and matter by
restricting themselves to formal logic; the difficulty is repressed
only to recur again at another point.

Naturally the symbolic logicians are not the first to have
devoted their energy to formal logic, but it is true to say that
none has ever made such strenuous efforts as they to formalize
logic completely. And in this way they have brought out the
central problem of logic, one moreover which affects every
discipline, since they all use logic. It has been central in
European thought ever since Aristotle applied the distinction
between form and matter. Perhaps the most valuable service
rendered by the symbolic logicians may prove to have been
their unwitting demonstration of the limited application of this
ancient Aristotelian distinction. The question is this: what are
we doing when we formalize a discipline (such as thinking in
general, i.e. logic, or thinking about the stars, i.e. astronomy,
etc.)?

In order to see what logicians are trying to do when they
work out the rules of formal logic let us take an example from
a book which has recently enjoyed tremendous popularity. Mr.
Fred Hoyle points out in his *The Nature of the Universe* that he
knows a good deal more about the way stars move than did
the Hebrews of Biblical days. He then goes on to say, "Is it
in any way reasonable to suppose that it was given to the
Hebrews to understand mysteries far deeper than anything I
can comprehend when it is quite clear that they were completely ignorant of many matters that seem commonplace to
me?" [6] A logician, in order to test the validity of the argument
concealed in Mr. Hoyle's question, would re-cast the argument
in a *form* which would make it easier to see. The argument
can be stated thus: Mr. Hoyle knows more about subject A
(i.e. astronomy) than the ancient Hebrews about subject A;
therefore Mr. Hoyle knows more about subject B (i.e. how to
save souls) than the ancient Hebrews knew about subject B.
Once the argument has been formalized in that way its ab-

surdity begins to be obvious. The absurdity becomes even more glaring if we insert a different content, or matter, into the same form and say: Professor Jung knows more about subject A (i.e. in this case, psychology) than Mr. Hoyle knows about subject A; therefore Professor Jung knows more about subject B (i.e. astronomy) than Mr. Hoyle knows about subject B. By reducing statements to the same form in this way the formal logician is able to avoid many errors in thinking.

Actually this example is a very difficult one to reduce, and the sketch of a formalization which we have made is crude, but it brings out three limitations of formalization which are worth noticing. In the first place, Mr. Hoyle's argument is not so utterly absurd as we have made it sound; for when subject A and subject B are intimately related it is not unreasonable to suppose that a knowledge of the one will at least prepare us to acquire a knowledge of the other. For instance, a biologist will be in a better position to understand genetics than a mathematician; in actual fact, this is generally so but it is not so by logical necessity, i.e. the biologist may be incapable of doing the mathematics which modern genetics demands; and therefore, although the objects of his own science (living beings) are the same as the geneticist's, he is less fitted for understanding genetics than the mathematician who studies abstract numbers and relationships. However, it is clear that the actual relationship between the contents, or matter, of various disciplines does enter into any formal argument about them.

Secondly, the absurdity of the argument does not always become apparent immediately its form is brought out. For instance, "Mr. X knows more about a than Mr. Y knows about a: therefore Mr. X knows more about b than Mr. Y knows about b" does not intuitively appear absurd unless we either consciously or unconsciously attach some significance, or content, to a and b—or even to X and Y in certain cases. It only becomes so when we re-introduce some different content into the same form, when we bring in, say, knowledge of psychology to represent "a" and of astronomy to represent "b". Therefore, once more, we can see the limitations of considering the form of a statement as opposed to its matter.

Thirdly, reductions in formal logic only perform a negative function in relation to thought: they enable us to detect errors in thought, but do not themselves enable us to think. They act as efficient brakes, so to speak, but are no substitute for motor-power. Formal logic, therefore, in relation to thought, has a negative rôle to perform; the formal logician acts as custodian of the truth—when someone else has discovered it.

Modern symbolic logicians have rather side-stepped this difficulty of relating form and matter; they go ahead with their formalization, although the original issue of the paradoxes had brought the difficulty out clearly. In the paradoxes there is a contradiction between the form of the statement and its matter; perhaps this should be a warning to distrust the primitive distinction between form and matter. However, the symbolic logicians proceed undaunted. They take the various consti-tuents of a sentence, abstract from their meaning by using symbols (e.g. a, b, X, Y) and then operate with the symbols, ignoring their original meaning. In order that their procedure should have some meaning they have, of course, to re-interpret the symbols once more at the end of the operation.

Therefore the crucial question clearly is: what is the symbolic logician doing when he carries out his operations? He relates one symbol to another symbol; but what kind of relationship does he establish between the symbols? We know, for instance, that the relationship which a mathematician establishes be-tween his mathematical symbols is a quantitative relation. We know that the musician establishes the symbols on his score in a musical relation. Presumably the logician should establish a thought-relationship between his thought-symbols—but how can he do so if he has abstracted from their meaning?

The mathematician abstracts existing objects from their medium of existence and translates them into a mathematical medium. The musician takes sounds and translates them into a musical medium. The formal logician takes his thought-symbols and transfers them into another medium—but what medium is it? If it is another medium, then it is not the medium of thought. Since the alternative name for symbolic logic is mathe-matical logic, one may well believe that the symbolic logician is transferring his symbols into a mathematical medium; one's belief is strengthened when one remembers that Russell's early work attempted to show that logic is really a branch of mathematics. Later it was suggested that the reverse is true: that mathematics is a branch of logic. (The truth seems to be that one can impose almost any kind of relationship one likes on empty symbols and then fill them in another medium.) Thus one can take heaps of dry ink on paper and give them spatial relationships or even, if one is an artist, use them as the basis for certain artistic patterns—they have then been transferred into an artistic medium.

The problem, therefore, is: When you formalize a discipline you translate its *forms* into another medium where they now serve as the *matter* for a different discipline; but at the end of this operation are you still talking about your original discipline? Suppose, for instance, that you formalize biology by representing your discoveries in mathematical formulæ; are you then still acting as a biologist? Are you not stating *mathematical* relationships among living beings rather than *biological* relationships? And is formal logic still discussing thought-relationships when it has abstracted from the meaning of thought-symbols?

It is difficult to believe that symbolic logic has not abandoned the realm of thought when we consider some of the consequences flowing from the recent formalization of logic. They are mainly negative points, because however much one dislikes Poincaré's cheap jibe at the symbolic logicians—"since they have acquired wings, why don't they fly?"—it must be confessed that they have not revolutionized thought so much as they prophesied.

First of all, symbolic logic is philosophically neutral; it can be used by the philosophers of every school, though some philosophers are temperamentally averse from it. In the early days of symbolic logic this was not thought to be the case; because it was employed almost exclusively by positivists, people came to believe that one had to hold positivist views before one could use symbolic logic. But nowadays it is used by philosophers of very different schools, and even by Catholic theologians. Why is this? It may be that the methods of symbolic logic afford a sure means of arriving at the truth, that positivists and Catholic theologians can agree with its findings in so far as they are using this universal key to the truth. Or it may be that they can agree upon it for the reason that when they operate with their symbols they are simply going through a meaningless series of motions, and therefore have nothing to disagree about. If the operations have no meaning they can scarcely disagree about the meaning. If symbolic logic translates the forms of thought in general into a different medium (i.e. mathematical or musical) then the absence of disagreement is understandable —philosophers of different schools do not disagree on this issue because they are no longer discussing philosophy at all.

The second consequence of this recent attempt to formalize logic completely has been to throw logicians into confusion about the effectiveness of formalism. Since Gödel's famous essay on "formally undecidable statements" in 1931 the position has become critical. For Gödel did two things which have upset the logicians' apple cart. Firstly, he gave a *strict* proof that one can deduce a contradiction from any proof that it is impossible for contradictions to occur within a properly formalized system. This proves that purely formal systems are impossible, that they are not *formally* consistent. Secondly, he showed the essential incompleteness of any formal system when he proved that certain propositions within each class of systems can be seen to be true, *but*, that it is impossible to demonstrate their truth according to the rules of the system. Therefore, all formal systems are incomplete—nor is this merely because our knowledge is not sufficiently advanced; they are essentially incomplete, and will never be anything else.

Obviously these two Gödelian thunderbolts should have shaken the symbolic logicians so severely as to make them look for safer ground on which to stand. Some of them have done so, but on the whole there has not been sufficient re-examination of the basis upon which the whole system of symbolic logic has been built since the days of the *Principia Mathematica*.

Another consequence of this recent extreme formalization, which tends to show that it involves abandoning the realm of

3. strict thought, is that the symbolic logicians use the word "implication" in a new sense. For instance, when we say, in everyday language, that one proposition necessarily implies a second we are stating some connection between the subject-matter of the first proposition and the subject-matter of the second. When I say, for example, that if I love God then I love my neighbour I am asserting a connection between loving God and loving my neighbour. In everyday language, I am asserting an implication between the two. The symbolic logician, however, does not believe that "implication" involves a logical connection between the subject-matter of the first and second propositions. According to him the validity of an implication between the two does not depend upon anything but the truth or falsity of the two propositions considered *independently* (!)   For example, he says that the following are true implications, "If 2 and 2 = 4, then New York is a large city"; "if 2 and 2 = 5 then New York is a large city"; "if 2 and 2 = 5 then New York is a small city." But, "If 2 and 2 = 4 then New York is a small city" is false, although not meaningless.

The general reader confronted with these "implications" will conclude that they are only described as such by an abuse of everyday language. Furthermore he will have the consolation of knowing that a distinguished modern logician (C. I. Lewis)[7] tends to agree with him. Yet this curious use of the word "implication" had already been discussed in earlier days by the Stoics, and especially by Ockham.[8]   Once more, the connection between these three, the Stoics, Ockhamites and symbolic logicians, rests upon their dividing thought into logical simples, or atoms, to correspond to the physical atoms into which they believed the world was divided. Just as it becomes impossible to see how one atom affects other atoms if they are discontinuous, so it becomes impossible to see how one proposition affects another proposition (or implies another proposition) if propositions are regarded as discontinuous wholes.

Therefore the Aristotelian logician, confronted with the statement that "if 2 and 2 = 4 then New York is a large city," is a valid implication, would reply that it is not an implication at all. All the statement says is that this is the kind of world in which 2 and 2 = 4 and New York is a large city—there is no *logical* connection between the matter of the two propositions.

The reasons which have persuaded symbolic logicians to employ the word "implication" in this unusual sense are too complicated to go into here. So long as the reader who wishes to know more about the new logic realizes that he will have to cast off his everday assumptions about implication before doing so, these lines will have served their purpose. He will also have to learn to distinguish between what he has traditionally thought of as "logic" and what is nowadays termed "logic". The desire to make this distinction has arisen in recent times because of the attempts made to carry out a complete formalization of four different but related disciplines; semantics, mathematics, logic and physics.

In semantics Carnap has tried to present us with a formal language in which the meaning of the symbols is left out of account and they are operated with purely according to their form. When this is done the traditional laws of logic no longer apply within the formal language; for instance, it is no longer true to say that of two contradictory judgements one or the other must be true. The values "true" and "false" no longer have exhaustive application within the formal language. Since Aristotelian logic is based upon the assumption that of two contradictory judgements one or the other must be true, therefore, the inadequacy of Aristotelian logic is revealed. However, Carnap has to admit that in order to state the rules of his formal language he must use normal colloquial language over and above his formalized language. Therefore, the formalized language requires a *meta-language*.

In mathematics, a similar situation arose through the theories of the Dutch mathematician Brouwer, who has been called the "Bolshevik of mathematics". Brouwer maintains that before one can use mathematical concepts significantly one must be able actually to construct them; therefore it becomes impossible to speak significantly of *possible* numbers.

According to Brouwer, for example, if a box contains a *finite* (i.e. constructible) number of balls, therefore we can be certain

E

that the balls are either all white or they are not all white; *but*, in the case of an *infinite* (non-constructible) collection we cannot be certain that "all" are either white or not-white, because the word "all", applied to an infinite collection, is indeterminate. Thus the fact of proving that it is false that an infinite collection does not contain a certain member is not itself proof of its presence. Its presence could only be proved by directly constructing it, and not by deducing it from the denial of a negative. Consequently there may be actually constructible mathematical propositions whose contradictory we cannot construct. Since we cannot construct them we cannot speak significantly about them; we cannot answer the question of their truth or falsehood by "yes" or "no". Therefore, once more, the law that of two contradictory propositions one or the other must be true no longer applies universally. But, just as with semantics, the expression of this formalized, or actually constructible, mathematics has to be made in a language above this mathematics. One has to invoke *metamathematics*, expressed in colloquial language.

In logic the role of Carnap and Brouwer is fulfilled by the Polish thinker Lukasiewicz. With a proposition such as "Warsaw will be snow-covered in April 1960" it becomes impossible to apply the law of excluded middle; by considering how to formalize similar propositions, Lukasiewicz came to the conclusion that the values "true" and "false" were inadequate and required to be supplemented by a value such as "undecidable" (or even by an infinite scale of values). Therefore he developed a formalized three-valued logic (or one of infinite values). In order to operate this three-valued logic, however, he has to invoke certain *metalogical* rules. At this level again, the ancient two-valued logic is reinstated.

Physics has undergone the same formalization at the hands of Reichenbach. He has had to deal with the difficulty that modern physicists are unable to decide simultaneously both the speed and the position of an electron. This means that they are unable to give complete formulæ for the trajectory of an electron, which involves knowing both its speed and its position. Furthermore, they maintain that this inability is not due to their own inadequate knowledge but lies in the behaviour of the electron itself. This means to say that when they give the correct formula for the speed of the electron they cannot express its position exactly, and *vice versa*; yet it is the same electron which is in question in both cases. And so Reichenbach, formalizing this problem of physics, invokes a third value, besides "true" and "false", for propositions about the trajectory of electrons. Again, Reichenbach can only express the rules for this three-valued theory of physics in ordinary language, which uses two values. One might expect that he would follow Carnap, Brouwer and Lukasiewicz' example and describe this as *meta-physics*. But metaphysics is a word too redolent of Aristotelianism for Reichenbach to invoke, and so he avoids it. Nevertheless the problem which he is ultimately faced with is precisely the kind of problem that Aristotelians describe as metaphysical. It is precisely that of judging whether different words can be truly applied to the same thing (e.g. speed and position of the *same* electron. In what sense can we see that it is the same electron?).

Considering these results, and the need for a metalanguage, a metamathematics, a metalogic, and a metaphysics, it seems reasonable to assume that Aristotelian logic and metaphysics are not entirely outdated. When modern symbolic logicians use the words "logic" and "metalogic" they are referring to those same problems as Aristotle put under the heading of "logic". It is not surprising, therefore, that if they try to equate their logic with Aristotelian logic the two do not coincide. The modern equivalent of Aristotelian logic is "metalogic", where Aristotle's logical laws are valid.[9]

From the preceding sketch of the consequences of formalization we can see that the relationship between formal logic, which deals with forms of thought, and metaphysics, which deals with objects of thought, has not been satisfactorily worked out. Consequently it is not surprising that the confusion between logic and metaphysics occurs frequently. And when a group of thinkers, such as the positivists, begin by denying that metaphysical terms have any meaning it is almost inevitable that they should unwittingly pursue metaphysics under the impression that they are discussing formal logic.

Let us illustrate how this has occurred, since such illustrations will enable the general reader to separate the formal logic from the unacknowledged metaphysics when he is reading the logical positivists' works.

For instance Bertrand Russell confuses metaphysics and logic (or mathematics, with which he identifies it) when he rejects St. Thomas Aquinas' first proof for the existence of God. St. Thomas argues from the existence of beings which are caused and changed to the existence of a First Cause which is unchanged. Russell says that this argument rests on the assumption that every series must have a first term and that this assumption is false; for example, the series of proper fractions has no first term; "every mathematician knows" that "the series of negative integers ending with minus one" contradicts "the supposed impossibility of a series having no first term".[10] Here Russell is talking about mathematical (or logical) forms of thought, whereas St. Thomas is talking about metaphysical objects of thought. Russell is not talking about existents at all, and therefore it is possible for him to "think of" a series which has no first term; similarly I can "think of" a man with thirty-five heads—but that does not mean that there is an existing man with thirty-five heads. Those who confuse entities of thought with existents in this way would do well to remember Einstein's pronouncement about such entities " . . . in so far as mathematical statements refer to reality they are uncertain; and in so far as they are certain they do not refer to reality." Not often do we encounter this confusion so glaringly as in this passage from Bertrand Russell.

Russell also provides us with another illustration of this confusion when he says: " 'One' is a predicate of certain classes, e.g. 'satellite of the earth'; but when a class has only one member, it is nonsense to say that that member is one, unless the unit class was a class of classes—in which case it is generally false—'one' is a predicate of concepts, not of the things to which concepts are applicable; the predicate 'one' applies to 'satellite of the earth' but not to the moon."[11] How misguided it is to deny unity to the moon is obvious if we consider applying this thesis to the case of, say, dinosaurs. There was a time when there were a lot of dinosaurs; they are now extinct, but there must have been a last dinosaur which had lived for a period of its existence when other dinosaurs were alive. According to Russell's thesis it would have been correct to say that this dinosaur was "one" during the period when other dinosaurs were alive but incorrect to say so when all the other dinosaurs were dead. But the dinosaur itself does not cease to be a dinosaur because the other dinosaurs die; and therefore the predicate "one" does not cease to apply to it. Clearly our logical use of the word "one" ("one" is a predicate of classes) is founded upon our attributing unity to metaphysical objects; statements about forms of thought (i.e. formal logic) use the language by which we describe *what* we think about (i.e. metaphysics). Without metaphysical assumptions there can be no thought to formalize into formal logic; because he denies these assumptions but, in the nature of the case, cannot avoid making them, Russell substitutes formal logic for metaphysics. Since formal logic is no adequate substitute for metaphysics, the result is false metaphysics, leading him to deny the moon's unity.

Not unnaturally when the scope of formal logic has been extended to cover the scope of metaphysics the formal logician starts doing the metaphysician's job for him—without the metaphysician's tools, however. Previously formal logicians recognized that it was their job to analyse the modes of thought which are valid for all disciplines. But *modes* of thought found in *every* discipline obviously cannot serve as the *premises* for some separate, independent discipline. Therefore when modern formal logicians take these modes as premises for the deductive systems which they try to construct (e.g. *Principia Mathematica*) they are attempting the impossible. They are making forms of thought into substitutes for actual thinking; they are turning a method into a metaphysics. [12] And whilst it is true that the metaphysician uses logic, the reverse is not true, for formal logic presupposes metaphysics. Trying to make formal logic a substitute for metaphysics is like waiting for the tail to wag the horse. The results are disappointing.

Throughout these references to recent logical work use has been made of the distinction between "form" and "matter," or "content". Some of the benefits of this distinction have been shown (e.g. in assessing Mr. Hoyle's argument); but the disadvantages have also shown up. In order to overcome these disadvantages one would have to overhaul the many meanings of "form" and "matter" that have been current since Aristotle's day. Here (since we are particularly concerned with method and the danger of transforming a method of one discipline into that of another), it will be sufficient to point out that Aristotle originally made the distinction to apply to two objects. He said that the marble of a statue was its matter, its form being imposed by the sculptor. But this was less important in his mind than the second, the way in which living things (plants, for instance) impose their form upon the matter which they trans-form into organic parts of themselves.

Clearly there are differences between the use of the words "form" and "matter" in regard to a work of art and in living things. When this distinction is then applied to other disciplines, such as metaphysics or logic, we can expect some of the confusions we have discovered. Probably they could only be avoided, as we have said, by a thorough overhaul of the ambiguities involved; which is beyond our present aim.

A point worth noting about this use of the word "form", and the formalism which it leads to, is that it should not be made a measure of everything in our lives—a habit which formalists easily fall into. For instance, after describing the formal languages he has been constructing, Carnap says, "An alleged statement of the reality of the framework of entities is a pseudo-statement without cognitive content. To be sure, we have to face at this point one important question; it is a question of whether to accept the new linguistic forms. The acceptance cannot be judged as being either true or false because it is not an assertion. It can only be judged as being more or less expedient, fruitful, conducive to the aim for which language is intended."[13]

This is as if Hamlet, after listing the prospects of death, had then turned round and said, "I have at this point to face one important question—to be, or not to be." The question of whether to accept the new linguistic forms is not only one question; it is the whole question, in the sense that it decides every other question that follows—just as "to be, or not to be" decides everything that follows. And if we ask *why* we should accept the new linguistic forms, we are told by Carnap that any answer we give cannot be in terms of truth or falsehood, because it will not be an assertion. An assertion can be formalized, and therefore judged true or false according to the canons of the formalized system. But the actual decision to accept that formal system cannot be formalized within the system. Yet, although that decision cannot be described as true or false if we accept the canons of the formalized system, is there not a deeper sense of truth and falsehood applicable to the decision? After all, Carnap admits that the decision to accept his linguistic forms is determined by "the aim for which language is intended"; therefore, if there is an aim for which language is intended, there must be some person intending that aim. If a person has an aim in using language it can only be because that linguistic aim serves his deeper, personal aim. Now if he has an aim or purpose as a person that must be because he is in the world for some purpose—he has a destiny to fulfil. If he does not achieve that destiny it is because his decisions were not in accord with it—he was untrue to it; he chose falsehood. On the other hand, if he does achieve his destiny it is because his decisions were in accord with it—he was true to it; he chose truth.

Therefore if language has an aim, it is because the man using the language has an aim in life; and we *can* say that the decision to accept Carnap's linguistic forms is to be described as true or false, because the decision assumes an assertion about man's aim in life. Who makes this assertion? It cannot be the man himself; he cannot *give* his life a purpose, since he does not even give himself life—he receives it. Therefore he must also receive the assertion about his aim—from whoever gave him life. That is, from God. And the assertion (though it cannot be described as true or false in Carnap's formal language) is described as true or false according to the canons of God's language.

Questions of destiny, then (and even a decision about language falls within that larger question) cannot be decided

by the canons of humanly formalized systems. But since our
ultimate destiny decides what is worthwhile in life, questions
as to what is worthwhile (i.e. all values, goodness, truth,
beauty, etc.) are also outside the scope of these systems. For
this reason (cf. p. 36–7) those who fall victims to formal
analysis are unable to make much contribution to those
disciplines which deal with values (e.g. ethics, aesthetics,
sociology, etc.). And for the same reason it is fatal to allow
formal considerations to become our rule of life.

   At the same time the abuse of linguistic analysis should not
lead us to neglect its uses. Even if linguistic analysis cannot
tell us anything about our aim in life and how we can achieve
it, we can use this analysis in order to see precisely what is at
stake. If it does not provide us with grounds for our actions at
least it does clarify them, and brings out the points at issue.
And in so far as it serves this purpose the habit of linguistic
analysis should be cultivated by all of us. There are good
grounds for believing that its therapeutic value, its cure of
linguistic diseases, will prove a lasting service of logical
positivism. How helpful it can be we see in the following two
examples.

   Recently an American theologian said that, "The atomic
bomb, *in itself*, is no more immoral than a rifle or any other
weapon." Our habits of linguistic analysis prompt us immediately to fasten on the confusion in those two words, "in
itself." The subject of the sentence is not, "the atomic bomb,"
but "the atomic bomb, in itself,"—presumably there is some
distinction between the two. I myself cannot see the distinction,
but my mind becomes slightly confused because the use of the
"in itself" at least suggests that though the atomic bomb may
be immoral, the atomic bomb, in itself, is not immoral (if
other weapons are not). At a guess I should say that the
confusion arises because a quite clear thought has been con-
fusedly expressed. Clearly the "atomic bomb, in itself," is not
immoral—for the simple reason that the piece of matter in
question is neither immoral nor moral—it just exists; and
what does come under the judgement of morality is the action
of someone who uses it. Neither "the atomic bomb" nor "the

atomic bomb, in itself" is immoral—though persons who
touch one off may be.   Therefore, it would seem that the
theologian was trying to say something like this, "I can
imagine circumstances in which it would not be immoral for
a person to drop an atomic bomb."   If he had, in fact, said
that, we should be in a much better position to test the validity
of his statement, e.g. by finding out from him what these
imaginary circumstances were.

Another phrase from the theologians which has a whole
history of its own, and has had profound effects on world
history, is the phrase "justification by faith alone" coined by
Luther.   It is interesting to discover a Lutheran theologian,
Hans Asmussen, maintaining that some of the misunderstanding between Catholics and Lutherans over this phrase
arose because they were referring to different things.[14]   The
Catholics, he says, were referring to the whole process of
sanctification, in which, of course, man co-operates; but the
Lutherans were referring to the moment of decision at which
God pronounces the judgement, "Now you are on my side."
Whether Asmussen's view is historically correct or not, it is
interesting to speculate on how the course of events might have
been changed if Carnap had been there as linguistic adviser to
call attention to the operative word "alone".

Unfortunately Carnap was not available, but his advice is
now at hand, and it would be foolish in future to neglect the
good which all of us can derive from acquiring the logical
positivist's habit of minute linguistic analysis.

NOTES

[1] I should explain that by Aristotelian logic I mean what has traditionally been taken for Aristotelian logic. We are now assured by Prof.
Lukasiewicz in his brilliant *Aristotelian Syllogistic* (O.U.P., 1951) that this
traditional interpretation of Aristotle is false. He also proposes a radical
solution for those difficulties about "form" and "matter" which I have
tried to illustrate in this section; on p. 12 of this work he says,

" The expression ' form of thought ' is inexact and it seems to me
that this inexactitude arose from a wrong conception of logic. If you
believe indeed that logic is the science of the laws of thought, you will
be disposed to think that formal logic is an investigation of the forms
of thought.

It is not true, however, that logic is the science of the laws of thought. It is not the object of logic to investigate how we are thinking actually or how we ought to think. The first task belongs to psychology, the second to a practical art of a similar kind to mnemonics. Logic has no more to do with thinking than mathematics has."

Any reader who meditates upon these lines, and then goes to Prof. Lukasiewicz's book in order to find what modern formal logicians *are* trying to do, and what formal logic *is* about, will appreciate the tremendous difficulty of trying to explain these issues in everyday language.

² *Summa Theologica* I. Q. 32, art. 1 ad 2.

³ BERTRAND RUSSELL, *Library of Living Philosophers: Bertrand Russell.* Evanston, North Western University Press, 1944, p. 684.

⁴ GRATRY, *Logic*, La Salle Illinois, Open Court Publishing Company, 1944.

⁵ *Principia Mathematica*, p. 60. In "Existence and Coherence" (*Methodos*, 1950) Fr. Ivo Thomas O.P. has shown that the definition of "class" in the *Principia Mathematica* confuses logical "coherence" with actual "existence".

⁶ *Nature of the Universe*, Oxford, Basil Blackwell, 1950, p. 115.

⁷ LEWIS and LANGFORD, *Symbolic Logic*, The Century Company, 1932.

⁸ For a complete statement of this curious use of the word "implication" (generally known as "material implication") cf. J. Salamucha's "Die Aussagenlogik bei Wilhelm Ockham" in *Wilhelm Ockham* (1349–1949), Münster/Westf. Dietrich Coelds-Verlag, 1950.

⁹ We are well aware that these accounts of Carnap, Brouwer, Lukasiewicz and Reichenbach are highly schematized.

¹⁰ *History of Western Philosophy*, George Allen & Unwin, 1946, p. 484.

¹¹ *Revue Internationale de Philosophie*, Jan. 1950.

¹² "The question arises as to why analogy has penetrated to the domain of Formal Logic. The answer seems to be given by the theory of Prof. H. Scholz, who says that recent Formal Logic is nothing else than a part of classic Ontology. As a matter of fact, recent Formal Logic generally deals, not with rules, but with laws of being in its whole generality; most of the laws contained in the *Principia Mathematica*, e.g., as opposed to metalogical rules, are such laws. If this is so, it is not to be wondered at that some consideration must have been given to analogy, for 'being' is an analogical term and so are the names of all properties, relations, etc., belonging to being as such."—I. M. BOCHENSKI, O.P., *The Thomist*, Oct. 1948.

¹³ *Revue Internationale de Philosophie,* Jan. 1950.

¹⁴ HANS ASMUSSEN, *Warum noch Lutherische Kirche*, Stuttgart, Evangelisches Verlagswerk, 1949, pp. 74 et seq.

The Mutual Relationships of these Various Modern Philosophies

After surveying these modern philosophies it might be expected that we should sketch out a *true* philosophy. We shall not attempt to do so because it is to be hoped that the light of truth has been shed upon these different views as the discussion has proceeded. The light of truth is not something *which* one sees but something *by which* one sees. All the same, so as to avoid any suspicion that truth is here regarded as "relative" (i.e. not absolute), let us take the most crucial case and show how there is a correct form of relativism which does not exclude recognition of absolute truth. This crucial case is the case of logic, for if every science makes use of logic and there are incompatible logics, it would seem as though there are incompatible truths.

In fact, of course, as we have seen, these so-called incompatible logics differ because the philosophies which make use of these differing logics take different aspects of the world as their starting-points. Aristotelian philosophy begins with things and proceeds to draw implications about the property and behaviour of things; since each thing has a specific nature, according to Aristotle, and its actions are expressions of that nature, there is a continuity between the nature and the actions of the thing. Therefore Aristotelian logic maintains an implication between the nature and the actions or properties of things, in virtue of this continuity. Positivist philosophers take "events" (or, rather, statements about events such as, "it is a fact that . . ."), as their starting-point and since, on their own atomistic suppositions, there is no continuity between "events" other than that between the statements relating them, the positivist's logic does not permit him to maintain implications in the sense of Aristotelian logic; consequently positivist logic replaces the syllogism by a truth calculus (cf. p. 122) in which statements are considered independently of each other—apart from being brought together in the calculus.   Similarly Marxists begin with "society", and Marxist logic follows the dialectical movement of social classes.   And the latest philosophy, that of the existentialists, starts with the singularity and uniqueness of each experience; the only way in which you can move from one singular experience to another singular experience is neither by the syllogism (based upon things) nor by the positivist calculus (since singular experience escapes laws), but by an existentialist leap.   Therefore the existentialist logic is the logic of existence.

It is clear enough, then, that there are alternative logics because there are alternative starting-points for philosophizing. Perhaps the most interesting instance of a mode of thinking alternative to the one common in Western Europe is that of the Semitic mind.   For there is a constant tension in the European mentality between its Greek and its Semitic inheritance.   The Greek's logic, perfected in Aristotelianism, differs considerably from the Semitic way of thinking.   The Arabic theologian, for instance, objects to the Aristotelian syllogism because he does not see the world in terms of universals such as "dog", "man", or "horse", and the functioning of the syllogism depends upon the validity of the universal.   When I make a statement about "man" I cannot securely describe this term "man" as a universal because I cannot include in it all the characteristics that, say, men of the future might display.   And therefore the Arab does not think in universals; expressing his beliefs, for instance, he speaks in a manner which shocks the Aristotelian—he says, "There is no God, but Allah".   He uses a particular affirmative ("Allah") to transcend a universal negative ("there is no God"), thus declaring the irrelevance of universals.

An illustration of a similar way of thinking is given in the story of the meeting in Moscow addressed by an atheist.   The atheist spent an hour proving that it was impossible for there to be a God.   After his speech, he asked if anyone had any objections to his reasoning.   Whereupon an old man at the back of the audience stood up and cried "Christus voskres" ("Christ is risen"), a cry which was taken up by the rest of the audience. The old man had used a particular affirmative ("Christ is risen") to transcend a universal negative ("there is no God").

It is very difficult for us of another tradition to get into this way of *seeing* the world (which involves a different way of thinking). For the Arab does not use a universal as a means of tying two propositions into a syllogistic inference. He confronts us with two visions which (without any inference from them) flash off in us an awareness of something previously unknown. Sometimes this happens to us, for instance, when we see two aspects of the world simultaneously—and then, without any Aristotelian reasoning, we become aware of something else. We see the profile of someone we love against a clear blue sky; the face and the sky together awaken in us an intimation of the goodness deep down things or the quick passing of human life—or, we cannot say what precisely—but we *know*, we have deeper knowledge now. Such moments are most vividly described for us by the poets, and they only come to us when we are seeing the world in a certain way, when we are contemplating. If we are not contemplating—if, for instance, we are rushing to catch a bus when the beloved's profile and the clear blue sky come together, we may not receive this fresh knowledge—we are not seeing the world in a contemplative mode.

Now the logic of both the Aristotelian and the Arabic way of seeing the world is the appropriate one at different times, and it is this contrast between the two which allows us to see the proper function of Aristotelian logic. It also explains why Aristotelian logic will always continue to be used by men and preserve its validity—because men are committed to action, to making decisions; and the two-valued logic of Aristotle, its either/or, is an appropriate preparation for action.

Let us explain what we mean in saying that Aristotelian logic is the logic of decision, by contrasting it with its modern alternatives. We have already seen that modern logicians have worked out formal logics in which the law of excluded middle does not apply (cf. p. 123–5). In formalizing quantum physics, to take one example, they have developed a logic of three values which does not present us with the alternatives of "true or false" but adds a third value, "indeterminate". Nevertheless, in order to bring this logic out of an ideal world of mathematical relationships and apply it to the existing world one has to employ colloquial language in which the Aristotelian law of excluded middle is valid (cf. p. 125). When it comes to applying one's thought, making a decision, one has to decide for some course which excludes other courses, choosing the true and rejecting the false. Here, when a decision is in question, one has to operate with a two-valued logic.

Suppose that myself and a friend are considering what logic is valid in describing this desk. I might begin by saying that it is true that this desk is brown. My friend might then reply that this is an instance of the inadequacy of a two-valued logic, because, if it were valid, then we could say it is false that this desk is brown because there are certainly black streaks upon it. Therefore the two-valued logic does not apply. We might then reformulate my original statement, saying it is true that this desk is brown with black streaks upon it. But then, although we would have reformulated our original statement so as to bring it within the scope of a two-valued logic we should have sacrificed precision—"brown with black streaks upon it" being much less precise than just "brown"—though more exact. And even then it is a most unsatisfactory description of the desk, since we do not relate the area of brown to the area of black, or the length and shape of the black streaks, etc. In fact, if we were to do this perfectly, if we were to go on making our description more and more exact we should come to the point where the two-valued logic would be completely inapplicable. When we reached this point we should have a predicate ("brown with black streaks which are" etc., etc.!) so imprecise that we should not be able to construct its contradictory. That is to say we should come to a description of one portion of the table where the brown and black ran into each other, of which we might say that it is true it is brown but could not say that it is therefore false that it is not brown. We should have to introduce the third value of indeterminate.

Therefore the more exact our terms become, the less precise they become, and the more difficult we find it to apply a two-valued logic. It is this fact which has persuaded some logicians to hold that in order to give an exact and precise description of the shading of the world one has to have a logic of infinite values which correspond to the infinite shadings of the world. "1" might represent "true", "0" might represent "false", whilst in between would be an infinite range of fractions. Such a "logic of description" with an infinite range of values is all very well if human beings have nothing else to do with their lives but describe the world—though even then they are on an endless quest, a nonsensical one, because you cannot rationally pursue something which you know you will never reach. But one may very well question, in any case, whether there is any sense in speaking of a "logic of description" or a logic of infinite values, since the aim of logical thinking is to aid one to act rightly; and a logic which presents us with infinite values is one which gives us no aid whatsoever in our choice. A limited creature, such as man, is inevitably limited in his choices, and to persuade him that he has an infinite choice is to persuade him that he is not a limited, finite creature.

Therefore, no matter how long we may justifiably go on describing the world which faces us before making a decision, in the end all our thinking is directed towards that right action in which we choose the good and exclude the bad. The law of excluded middle applies at some stage in all processes of thought, and a two-valued logic is valid. Turning once more to my desk. Suppose that my friend and I are not going to devote our lives to describing it exactly. Suppose, instead, that he is working in Hamburg fitting up a refugee-ship with furniture and knows that I have a desk to spare which is more or less the same colour as the rest of the furnishings in one of the ship's saloons. He sends me a letter in which he says, "Please send me your brown desk imme-diately. It has just time to get here before the ship is due to sail". Do I respond by saying that my desk is not exactly brown and spend my time trying to work out a description of my desk which will be exact and at the same time allow me to bring it within the scope of a two-valued logic necessary for making a decision? Of course not. I apply the two-valued logic, send off my desk and accept the imperfection inevitable in any of my actions. Of course it does involve imperfection. And if I believed my action could be perfect I might spend the rest of my life working out a perfect description of my desk. But then I should be trying to achieve a perfection which is outside the scope of a finite creature; and it is less imperfect for a finite creature to accept his imperfection and act than to refuse to act until he is capable of a perfect action (which will be never in this life).

If, as we maintain, the two-valued logic is appropriate for thinking towards action, then such a logic can never be outdated, because men will always have to act. For this reason, also, Aristotelian logic commends itself to ordinary men in whose lives the need for action is ever present.

At the same time the Aristotelian mode of thinking has certain limitations which are not to be ignored, and which Semitic modes of thought do not suffer from. Like modern logic, Aristotelian logic is based upon the assumption that the purpose of thought is to formulate propositions about the world as it is; logic tests the validity of these thought-forms. Even to European students it sometimes occurs that human thought and speech are not directed entirely towards emitting propositions such as "It is raining". Sometimes we use it for giving orders—"Bring that lamp", "Stop bleating", etc. How can we formalize such statements? do we ask whether they are logically valid?

Our answer to orders such as these depends upon who is issuing them. If a person who has no authority over us issues them, then we may question their validity, turn them into propositions and judge them logically. On the other hand we sometimes receive orders from an authority whom we accept, in which case we *effect* what the words intend. This sort of word, this kind of language, are characteristic of the Semitic mind (both Hebrew and Arabic) which preaches to man on the authority of God's revelation. The Semitic languages (expressions of Semitic ways of thought) are the languages of divine authority. Words are used in these languages not simply to describe man and the world as they now are; they are intended to indicate man's destiny; they are the medium for prophecy and theology.

The most striking contrast between the mode of thought (or language) directed towards forming propositions and the mode of thought (or language) appropriate for searching man's destiny is found in the following comparison. Aristotle asks, "What is man?", and the Psalmist asks, "What is man?", but these questions, though formally equivalent, are asked in different modes. When Aristotle asks, "What is man?" he is trying to define man as he now is, to give man a biological classification. Consequently the answer to the Aristotelian question is in the form of a proposition—"Man is a rational animal", or "Man is a featherless biped". It is on the basis of such propositions that an Aristotelian formal logic can be developed.

The deepest contrast between the Aristotelian question-answer and that of the Semite lies in the absence of the time-factor in the first, and its supreme importance for the second. To state that "man is a rational animal" is to eliminate the time element—it states man's biological category, which is as valid at one time as at another. (This does not mean that it is eternal; eternal = not-temporal, *but*, not-temporal does *not* = eternal). Furthermore this classification does not say anything about what man is meant to be, because by eliminating the time element it excludes any possible reference to man's achieving in time what he is meant to be.

How different is the Psalmist's question, "What is man?" —"that thou art mindful of him". The Psalmist is addressing an authority; he is asking God to tell him his destiny. He already knows the proposition-answer, which he can work out for himself: man is a little lower than the angels. But that does not satisfy him, he wants to know his destiny; he is a creature and can receive an answer only from his Creator. "That thou art mindful of him"; in other words, what did you intend by creating me? And the answer comes back in the language of authority, in the language of prophecy. The

Psalmist *receives* the divine Word; he obeys it. The Word which the Psalmist receives is, in Hebrew, *Dabar*. But *Dabar* means a whole world more than the English "word"; it means also "history", it means "deed". And so whereas in English we use it as a word-photograph of reality, in Hebrew the Word is real—indeed it is in the Word that all things are made that are real.

When the Semite receives the Word he is not only instructed as to his destiny; he is shaped in his destiny by the Word. The Word is effective; it achieves what it intends (cf. pp. 140). When the Word, who is Jesus Christ, says to his disciples, "Fear not", they cease to fear; because the Word effects what it intends, producing peace by speaking peace. The disciples do not say, "How can we test the validity of this order, 'Fear not'?"; they cease to fear because they are obedient to the Word. The Word cannot be formalized; the Word is fulfilled.

This comparison between Aristotelian and Semitic modes of thought has been made in order to bring out two points. Firstly to show that words have other purposes beside their function as parts of propositions. Secondly to show that there are alternative modes of thinking, and, therefore, alternative logics appropriate to these various modes.

In regard to the first point it must not be assumed that it is only the Hebrews and Arabs who use a language of authority. In the West, also, we do so; and although it has become less frequent with the general rejection of authority in the West, nevertheless we do find, in our personal relationships, some reflection of the Word which effects what it intends. When someone whom we love, for instance, tells us not to worry, or tells us to be happy, they do not necessarily give us fresh reasons for being unworried or happy. But their very words produce in us what they intend, because of the relationship between them and us. Words are not only the means of reflecting reality in the form of propositions; they can also shape reality when they are effective words. Therefore, the positivist attempt to restrict words to propositions is a mistaken one, and rests upon a false philosophical assumption, viz. that

human beings have nothing to do except form propositions.
For no proposition in itself carries with it the motive for action.
If I were faced with one proposition about the world after
another I could reply to each of them, *ad infinitum*, "So
what?" Only when I received an *effective* word would I be
moved to action.

As to the second point, it might be objected that if there are
alternative formal logics then all thought is relative and we can
never arrive at the truth. Of course, this does not follow at all.
To begin with, people have arrived at truths very often without
ever having thought for a minute about how they arrived there
—just as men have built buildings to stand for hundreds of
years without knowing the first principles of stress and strain.
Again, the fact that one person arrives at Rome by one route
does not mean to say that no-one can arrive at Rome by any
other route. It all depends on their starting-point; if you start
off from Lyons the route will be different (formally different)
from the route of someone who starts from Naples. And the
same is true of the various philosophies and their appropriate
formal logics; the philosophies and their logics are determined,
in the first place, by their starting-points.

And it is here, in a consideration of their starting-points, that
we are most likely to get these various philosophies into perspective. For each of the starting-points has something to
commend it. Where they go wrong is in treating their own
particular starting-point as exclusive and disregarding the
others. The Aristotelian, for instance, who begins by taking
things as a basis for his philosophy is simply doing what most
ordinary men do; but if he ignores the possibilities opened up
by the positivist's concern with events he is going to cut himself
off from all the magnificent discoveries of modern science; if
both positivists and Aristotelians ignore the formation of society
they are isolating themselves from the world of modern govern-
ment and sociological enquiry; if positivists, Aristotelians and
Marxists despise the uniqueness of human experience stressed
by existentialists they are shutting their eyes to the secrets of
the human soul.

Once we refuse to be seduced into this one-sided approach

it is not difficult to bring these various philosophies into perspective. For example, the two philosophies which are at the moment most influential amongst intellectuals, logical positivism and existentialism, are generally regarded as poles apart, as contradictories. And yet, on our view, they are simply two halves of a sane philosophy, which could form a sane philosophy if they were brought together, but which lead to madness if they are not. Anyone who says that a half of one = one, would be rightly regarded as mad; the same is true of these philosophers who regard half the story as the whole story. If one puts together the two halves that are existentialism and logical positivism the resulting whole is not so very different from the traditional philosophy of St. Thomas.

To begin with, the existentialist is so conscious of the tremendous experience of existing that he can find no words to express it; all the definitions of existence which have been attempted are no more than straws in the wind. Language becomes vain in face of this tremendous experience, and anyone who imagines that he can define existence is only showing that he has failed to receive this experience. Beginning, then, with an awareness of this overwhelming experience the existentialist keeps pointing to the inadequacy of language. The reverse is true of the logical positivist; he begins by being oppressed by the inadequacy of language rather than the inexpressible experience, so that the most notable logical positivist, Wittgenstein, says: "My propositions are elucidatory in this way; he who understands them finally recognizes them as senseless when he has climbed out through them, on them, over them." And it is the same Wittgenstein who sums up what is, perhaps, the best motto for both existentialists and logical positivists, when he ends his discourse by saying, "Whereof one cannot speak, thereof must one remain silent". Though even Wittgenstein does not live up to the motto so well as did Cratylus, "whose folly reached at the last such a pitch, that he thought it was not meet to say anything, but, to express what he wished to say, merely moved his finger; because he believed that the truth he wished to enunciate about anything would pass away before his words were spoken".

Is this attitude so very much different from the position of St. Thomas Aquinas? who, at the end of a life of learning and close thinking, said, "I can write no more, for everything that I have written seems like straw, by comparison with the things that I have now seen, and which have been revealed to me." The similarity is obvious; the difference is more subtle and yet equally important. He is not saying that his writings are simply straws; he is saying that they seem like straw by comparison with the things which he now sees. When the whole light of God's countenance begins to reveal itself in his last days he sees that the fragments of that light which he had described in his writings were but fragments. But fragments *are* fragments; they are parts of a whole, and it is no good reason for saying that the part is nothing that it is not everything, is not the whole. To maintain that we cannot say anything simply because we cannot say everything is the mistake common to the despairing existentialists and the despairing logical positivists. True, we cannot define existence fully; but even to say that existence is indefinable is to give some fragmentary indication of existence; to say that one must remain silent about that whereof one cannot speak is a sign that we know something of the limits of speech and of what we are speaking about. These words that I am writing may not convey the whole of my meaning to the reader; they certainly do not convey the whole truth; but they do convey some meaning and do convey some truth. To expect the whole truth from a creature is to mistake the nature of creatures. St. Thomas' words show that he never did that.

Another illustration that logical positivism and existentialism are but two sides of the same coin, can be found in their attitudes towards human action. We have learnt how the existentialists scorn reason as a guide to action; it is the decision to act which itself reveals the appropriate action. We have also learned how the logical positivists refuse to allow that statements about ethics are characterized by truth; truth they accept as a canon of their formal, theoretical systems, but when it comes to action the canons are expediency, and fruitfulness (cf. p. 128–9). When Bertrand Russell, for instance, was asked whether he would condemn the actions of the criminals at Büchenwald he admitted that he would, but could not formulate any theoretical justification for his condemnation.

Obviously, however, we cannot go on permanently as blind existentialists in the field of action, nor, with the positivists, limit truth to questions of theory. The existentialist needs to see the *truth* in action, the positivist to see the truth *in action*. St. Thomas Aquinas did both these because, like the existentialist, he taught that human beings were on earth to act, to glorify their Creator in their actions, and not to return an inspector's report on the Creation; like the positivist, he saw that action cannot be wholly reduced to propositions characterized as true or false, for ethics is perfected not in a proposition but in an *act* of judgement. St. Thomas was able to do justice to both aspects of the case because he knew that on earth all our theorizing is directed towards truthful action, whilst teaching that the highest action of which we are capable is contemplation of the truth. Here theory and practice are perfectly joined in the contemplation of the truth.

But, it may be asked, this solution of the existentialist-positivist debate by St. Thomas would be accepted by both sides immediately if it were really so simple as that, would it not? It would, indeed, if man's condition in the modern world allowed him to exercise his will in accordance with his nature and his reason, but his condition makes it difficult for him to do so. The point of this explanation will be obvious if we recall our previous remarks about the effect of our attitudes before they ever reach the conscious, rational level (cf. p. 74). We noted how a person such as Chesterton, before he even begins reasoning about the world, already approaches it with reverence; how, on the other hand, H. G. Wells approached the world irreverently. These pre-rational attitudes are, broadly speaking, what St. Thomas means by *voluntas ut natura* (will as it expresses our total attitude towards existence), whereas the decisions taken at a later stage are expressions of *voluntas ut ratio* (will as it results from the process of discursive reasoning). If the pre-rational attitude is badly enough perverted no amount of reasoning will enable men to behave sanely; they will behave in accordance with their perverted nature.

We have already quoted sufficient witnesses to prove that the condition of modern man has been depressed into such perversion. We instanced such an existentialist as Heidegger. At what seems a remote philosophical level we could quote Bertrand Russell's perverse shying away from the obvious when he is discussing the essence of Socrates. He says, "The 'essence' of Socrates consists of those properties in the absence of which we should not use the name 'Socrates'. The question is purely linguistic: a word may have an 'essence' but a thing cannot".[1] Was there ever a more blatantly *negative* attitude towards the world? Socrates = not (the universe without Socrates)! How much one would give to have more men saying, with Chesterton, "I do not think there is anyone who takes quite such a fierce pleasure in things being themselves as I do." Chesterton could take pleasure in Socrates being Socrates but one can hardly expect anyone to take pleasure in Socrates when they believe, like Russell, that Socrates = not (the universe without Socrates). And yet neither Heidegger nor Russell nor Chesterton sums up the modern pre-rational attitude so well as did Jacques Rivière when he said, "I'm glad that I'm not satisfied any more, that I can find no answer in anything. That was the first thing that drew me away from Catholicism. I didn't want to be fed. I'd rather have my aching hunger, my anguish."[2] Emile Zola behaved in a like manner to Rivière after he had been to Lourdes and witnessed several striking miracles. In spite of this he wrote a very ungracious novel about Lourdes in which he failed to tell the truth. When he was in Paris Dr. Boissarie asked him why he had ended his novel with a conclusion contrary to the facts he had observed. Zola replied that he was master of his own books, adding, "What's more, I don't believe in miracles. And if all the sick in Lourdes were cured in one instant, I should still not believe."[3] Of course, no amount of rational argument can satisfy a person who has already adopted such a pre-rational attitude—he has already decided not to be satisfied. And that is how modern man so often reacts when confronted with the rational demonstrations of medieval thought; the five proofs for the existence of God are based upon the pre-rational axiom that it is good simply to be. Modern men do not believe that being and goodness mean the same thing; and therefore the five proofs are not *effective*. Confronted with them the perverse modern says, "So what?"—such perversion can only be overcome by God's grace, by his Word which *effects* what it intends.

Can we sum up in a few phrases the difference between the pre-rational attitude of St. Thomas and that of modern men? What is it that enables him to take the insanity of the existentialists, on the one hand, and the insanity of the logical positivists, on the other, and transform them into sanity? It is that St. Thomas accepts himself as a creature; and once he has humbly accepted his creatureliness everything that happens to him is a source of wonder and joy, the very fact of being rather than of not being he takes as a sign of his Creator's gracious loving kindness towards his creature. The man who refuses to accept his creatureliness believes that everything which happens to him could have turned out better, he even accepts his daily bread grudgingly; he thinks he knows better than God. He is guilty of the pride which caused the fall of man. He is possessed by a devil.

NOTES

[1] BERTRAND RUSSELL, *History of Western Philosophy*, p. 223.
[2] RÉGAMEY, *Poverty*, p. 46.
[3] cf. ANTON KOCH, *Homiletisches Handbuch*. Freiburg, Herder Verlag, 1937, vol. I, p. 156.

II

THE NATURAL SCIENCES

To HAVE headed this chapter "The Natural Sciences" does not in the least imply that we are going to attempt to discuss the evidence for and against any problems of natural science, or busy ourselves even with the so-called "philosophical implications" of the latest scientific theories. When two such noted scientists as Professor Dingle and Mr. Fred Hoyle become thoroughly bad-tempered with each other about these issues the layman is well-advised to keep out of the arena. But the natural sciences have come to affect our lives so intimately that each of us needs to clear his mind about their purpose and scope.

Generally speaking there are three levels at which natural science takes our interest; the popular level; the scientist's specific level; and that at which the scientist's assumptions and conclusions are examined by logic and methodology. Of the general public it is fair to say that their knowledge of the natural sciences corresponds to the view which scientists favoured some fifty years since. This situation is not difficult to explain; it is because the scientist at his own level is working with highly abstract ideas which only become intelligible to the general public when the scientist has spent some fifty years in giving them concrete representation. And even when he does make them concrete it is very doubtful whether they are the same ideas; because he thought it impossible to translate the scientist's complicated language into everyday speech (which is designed for a very different purpose) a well-known professor described Mr. Hoyle's lectures on "The Nature of the Universe" as, "the latest piece of mythology". And yet this does not mean that the general public has either to swallow the scientist's opinions wholly or else wholly spit them out, for the third level of which we spoke can be reached by the general reader. That is to say, he can examine the scientist's assumptions and his conclusions; here the scientist does not speak with the authority of an expert.

Fundamentally there are two questions on method that the general reader may put to the scientist, and to which he may expect answers in ordinary language. First, he may say, what are we trying to discover when we engage in the natural sciences? Secondly, what do the tools and methods available permit us to discover? Obviously the two questions are mutually dependent. For instance, it is no use asking ourselves whether Julius Caesar had a wart on the back of his neck unless we command the means of discovering whether he had. Our tools and methods determine the questions which we can attempt to answer.

And when we ask the natural scientist what he is trying to do, we must insist upon a precise answer. So often one receives a vague answer, such as, that he is trying to discover "the nature of the universe". Which is most unhelpful; it gives one the feeling of being on some great adventure, as though one is soon to be introduced to some great secret. One becomes sobered when one reflects that the natural scientist is, in fact, comparing the movements of various parts of the universe and trying to relate these movements to each other. It is the difference between allowing oneself to be caught into poetic meditation on "space" and "time", or, even, "space-time", and then realizing the following modest truths: when we speak about the velocity of something in the universe we mean the distance it moves divided by the time it takes to move; when we speak of the time it takes to move a certain distance we are relating this distance to the distance moved by some standard mover (e.g. a clock or a star); when we speak of the distance it moves we are multiplying its speed (i.e. $\dfrac{\text{distance}}{\text{time}}$) by certain standard units of the time (i.e.— $\dfrac{\text{distance}}{\text{speed}}$) which it takes to move.

Generally the natural sciences are always trying to state these relationships of speed, time and distance.

On the face of it this does not seem a very important task. It even seems superficial, and because it seems superficial (dealing with the appearances of things and their behaviour) the metaphysicians tend to scorn it. They triumphantly say, "But what *are* these things whose movements you are relating? You only deal with appearances whereas we wish to know things in themselves. To put it shortly, what is the *nature* of the things whose behaviour you are describing?"

What is the *nature* of an atom or a star? says the metaphysician. The natural scientist, if he is sensible, replies that he does not believe that concealed beneath the appearances of things they have a "nature" which only a metaphysician can unveil —a sort of secret sprite hiding within things and producing these odd external movements from inside them. As far as he is concerned, the "nature" of a thing is the sum of its behaviour, and not something over and above its behaviour. To which the metaphysician might legitimately respond, if the nature of a thing = the sum of its behaviour (cf. p. 150), we can never know the nature of anything. But if we do not know the nature of anything we cannot say why we pick out certain parts of the universe and assume that they are things; why, for instance, do we isolate a certain part of the universe and describe that part as "a frog"? and, even more, why do we speak of one part of the universe ("a frog") as being the *same* ("frog") as a spatially and temporary different part ("a frog after it has jumped a yard in three seconds")?

The answer to the natural science/metaphysics dispute seems to be this: whilst the natural scientist cannot tell us the "nature" (i.e. the whole sum of behaviour) of anything, nevertheless he can tell us in part (i.e. he can tell us of a good deal of its behaviour). And that the metaphysician can tell us very little more with certainty; the metaphysician will try to show us why we describe one part of the universe as "the *same* frog" as a different part of the universe ("a frog before it had jumped a yard in three seconds"); the metaphysician, in particular, will try to explain the motives of human actions which are beyond physical assessment (e.g. why we do not tell lies, etc.). But the metaphysician himself can no more tell us the "nature" (i.e. the whole sum of behaviour) of anything than the natural scientist; both of them are adding up partial calculations about

behaviour, but neither can ever give us the whole sum. Therefore, if we are going to continue to speak of the "nature" of
things, if we are to regard "nature" as equivalent to the whole
sum of a thing's behaviour, we have no choice but to ask
whether there is any source from which we can learn the
"nature" (i.e. the whole sum of behaviour) of anything.

Clearly there can only be one such source, i.e. the source of
"natures", the author of nature. And so if we are to use the
term "nature" strictly, in the natural scientist's sense, we can
only do so if the author of nature, i.e. God, has revealed the
ultimate destiny of the world and of creatures. Such a destiny,
since destiny includes and sums up the whole of a creature's
behaviour, is precisely what is signified by "nature". Therefore
"nature" is a theological term justified by revelation; when
the metaphysician uses it he is making a guess which only
theology can confirm or disprove.

Therefore, although the metaphysician can point out to the
natural scientist that the natural scientist leaves many questions
unsolved, the metaphysician himself can only raise the questions
—he cannot answer them convincingly. The metaphysician,
for instance, having heard the natural scientist's descriptions
of the movements of different beings, can ask, But why should
anything *be* at all? Is there any purpose in all these beings
which move around the universe? Are there non-physical
influences at work in the universe? etc. Yet the metaphysician
can only guess the answers to these questions; any convincing
answer depends upon revelation. The metaphysician raises
questions which would be insoluble unless we had received
divine revelation about them.

And so, although the natural scientist cannot give us any
final answer about the nature of things, his work is by no means
trivial. These humble descriptions of the behaviour of things
do give us a clue to their nature. And sometimes these humble
clues from the natural scientists prevent other specialists from
making rash judgements. For example, they can show us how
extreme heat or extreme cold influence a man's behaviour and
make certain actions difficult to perform; when the moralist is
aware of these influences he will be less ready to condemn

certain actions by a man enduring extreme heat or extreme cold.

But if one feels confident that the natural sciences can serve extremely useful purposes one is less confident these days about the methods and the tools which they have to employ for these purposes.

To cite a fundamental illustration. The basic method of physics is to measure things (length, speed, weight, etc.). This measuring presents few difficulties at the everyday level; in order to measure the length of my body I place my body alongside a measuring-stick and discover that my body is six feet six inches long. But difficulties arise as soon as we wish to measure more precisely, as soon as we are dealing in minute units of measurement. Suppose that we wish to measure the length of a rod minutely. What we have to do is to measure the distance between one atom at one end and another atom at the other end. Now each atom is a system of electrons; therefore the distance we are measuring is the distance between two electrons. We try to measure this by throwing light onto the electrons and observing the diffraction of the light. But since the light which we throw onto the electrons itself alters their velocity, we cannot calculate the position of the electron. And therefore we cannot measure the length of the rod!

Clearly this situation arises because the more precise our standard of measurement the less exactly we can apply that standard. It is the same ultimate puzzle as we were faced with when we found that the more precise we made our terms the less exactly we were able to apply Aristotelian logic (cf. p. 136).

This limitation inherent in our tools of discovery is brought out strikingly in astronomy. It has been discovered that light from the various nebulae produces changing effects on the spectrum, which "catches" the light, if the nebulae are moving away from us. If the nebulae are moving away from us the spectrum lines are displaced towards the red end of the spectrum, red registering low frequency. From this "red-shift" it is possible to calculate the speed at which the nebulae are moving away from us. The further away these nebulae are, the more quickly they seem to be moving away from us—or we from them—it does not matter how one states it. But if this is so, then the universe as a whole is expanding. It also means that if there are nebulae which are 1,750,000,000 light-years away from us they will be moving outside our field of observation, because, when the light from them reaches us, its frequency will be zero—it will have "moved off" the spectrum altogether. The nebulae, then, will be unobservable as far as we are concerned. Therefore, as far as we can know, there may be nebulae flying away from us, out of reach of detection by our finest instrument, which is light. We can only observe an area within a radius from us of 1,750,000,000 light-years. Anything outside that radius lies outside our ken.

These are illustrations of how the advances of modern science have shown even the simple process of measurement to be a complicated affair. As one may imagine, when we then go on to relate such measurements by scientific theories we face even more complications. In particular, it becomes difficult to decide which of two scientific "laws" is correct, because our theorizing, being the theorizing of finite creatures, does not exhaust the possible alternatives to any "law"—and, therefore, we have no means of asserting that one law excludes possible explanation of the facts by some other law. For instance, Newton drew up a formula for the Law of Gravitation which seemed to account for all the observed cases of gravitation. But a century ago it was observed that the orbit of Uranus did not correspond with the orbit which it should have according to Newton's Law. Therefore some physicists maintained that the Law needed to be replaced by a new Law. But other physicists said that the Law was fundamental. Amongst these other scientists was Leverrier, who said that since the Law was fundamental the deviation from the Law in the case of Uranus must be due to some unknown cause. By working out, on the basis of the Law, what kind of thing could account for the deviation, he came to the conclusion that there must be an unknown planet which disturbed the orbit of Uranus. Soon afterwards such a planet was observed, and given the name "Neptune". It seems, therefore, that Leverrier was justified.

But was he justified? For it was later observed that Mercury, amongst others, also showed deviations from Newton's Law of Gravitation. What course were scientists to adopt? Were they, like Leverrier, to assume that the Law was fundamental and to suppose that some unobserved object accounted for the deviation? Or were they to alter the Law and formulate the Law of Gravitation afresh? In this case most scientists decided against the Leverrier method. They adopted Einstein's alterations in his General Theory of Relativity. But some scientists did choose the Leverrier method—such as Seeliger, who accounted for Mercury's deviations from the Law by saying that the clouds of cosmic dust were responsible. It is difficult to test Seeliger's theory experimentally, but, in principle and from the point of view of method, we have no certain means of saying that Einstein is right and the minority who stick to Newton's Law are wrong—this is because the *possible* explanations are infinite: and finite creatures cannot exhaust infinite possibilities.

Having seen some of the difficulties in measuring, and having learnt how our formulae drive us towards the bounds of finite knowledge, it is possible for us to see how we could only know the *whole* truth about the very smallest part of the world if we knew the *whole* truth about the *whole* world. Consider, for instance, the interesting suggestion made by the mathematician, Hermann Weyl:[1] "Measured in the natural units, the gravitational attraction of two electrons amounts to E/r^2, where the pure number E has a value of about 10^{-41} . . ."; dividing the amount of matter in the universe (within the radius of our observation by light) "by the mass of the electron . . . one finds that the number N of particles present in the world amounts to about 10^{81}. Thus the mysterious numerical factor $E = 10^{-41}$ seems to be connected with this number N, which may well be accepted as accidental, by a relation like $E/1 = \sqrt{N}$. If this be taken seriously it would indicate that the gravitational attraction of two particles depends on the total mass of the universe."[2]

If the natural scientist, from his limited viewpoint, comes to the conclusion that we can only know the true formula for the gravitational attraction of two particles when we know the total mass of the universe, it is obvious that we can only know the *whole* truth about the very smallest part of the world if we know the *whole* truth about the whole world.

Clearly our considerations upon natural science have brought us to the stage where the philosopher has to be invoked to elucidate problems of method. Two such problems of recent years are worth glancing at in order to see how the philosopher can help to make the scientific position on some issue more precise. The first concerns the behaviour of radio-active substances (of which radium is the best known).

That is to say, all the radium in the world is gradually turning into lead, because all the time it is giving off something which is characteristic of radio-active substance but is not characteristic of lead. In each year a certain proportion of the radium is converted into lead, and the proportion is the same for each year. Which is all very satisfactory, from the scientist's point of view, since he can express this regular loss of radio-active substance by a *law* of physical science.

But the situation is less satisfactory when the scientist begins to examine more closely what is happening in the process. When he takes a screen, for example, which will record this break-up of radium through radio-activity he finds that the scintillations from the radium produced on the screen do not occur at regular intervals. In other words, he can find no formula which will enable him to predict the instants at which the screen will record scintillations. Assuming that the scintillations are due to particles being shot off from radium atoms, the scientist then says that the time that a particular atom will break up is unpredictable. But the worst is yet to come; for certain scientists maintain that this is due not simply to our being unable to detect the law governing the break-up, but to the fact that the break-up of each particular atom is not subject to any law whatsoever! From which it has been concluded that the ultimate particles of which the universe is composed are not subject to determinate laws; and therefore man (who is composed of these ultimate particles) is not subject to these laws—his behaviour is unpredictable, and therefore he has free-will.

Upon this process of reasoning we make the following comments.

(1) That *we* cannot predict when an atom will break up does not mean to say that the break-up does not occur in accordance with laws. Even if the latest theories are correct when they say that we shall never be able to predict the break-up, no matter how refined our instruments, it does not follow that there are no such laws. These theories are transferring our own inability to predict onto the objects of our attempted prediction.

This is not a question which the physical scientist can decide; it is a strictly philosophical issue. The fact that we cannot state the law for some particular case (e.g. radium atoms) does not mean that there is no such law. I cannot say, for instance, who or what threw a ball through this window; but that does not mean that no-one or no thing threw it through the window.

(2) The experts are agreed that radium does break up in accordance with laws (i.e. a constant proportion changes every year); but even so they say that *ultimately* nature is not subject to determinate laws because the ultimate particles of which it is composed behave unpredictably.

But why should these particles be regarded as in some sense more ultimate, more real, than the bodies they compose? Why should Eddington describe his desk as "a host of tiny electric charges darting hither and thither with inconceivable velocity—instead of being solid substance my desk is more like a swarm of gnats"?[3] This search for something more ultimate than the things amongst which we live is a most interesting psychological trait of many scientists. Why should atoms be regarded as in some sense more real than the cats, dogs, men and stars which they compose? In earlier times they would have occupied a lower place on the scale of being than plants, plants being lower than animals, and so on up the scale of being. It would have seemed absurd to have *reduced* the higher forms of being (such as animals) to the lower forms such as inanimate matter.

Furthermore these "ultimate particles" are not observable

F

in the same way that books or fish are observable; they are *assumed* to exist in order to explain certain unobservable happenings at a level where the microscope does not reach; they are entities invented by our minds in order to explain certain experiences, but they themselves are not directly experienced by us.   It seems foolish, therefore, to doubt whether there are laws governing the behaviour of physical objects simply because we cannot formulate laws for these hypothetical particles, when we *can* formulate laws for the non-hypothetical, directly experienced substances which are supposed to consist of these hypothetical particles.   To abandon the substances for the particles is to abandon the substance for the shadow.

Again, the simple truth that radium does behave in accordance with laws seems to show that the irregular behaviour of its hypothetical "particles" is governed by some overriding law—otherwise we should expect the irregularity of the "particles" to spread their irregularity to the substance, which does not happen.

(3) There is no reason whatsoever for connecting the problem of these particles with the question of human free-will. What has led scientists to do so, probably, is their habit of regarding their particles as more "ultimate" than human beings, and imagining that the supposed indeterminacy at one level involved indeterminacy at another.   However, it is obvious that human behaviour and the behaviour of "particles" invented by human beings cannot be reduced to the same level. To have attempted this is a gross error in method.

A similar failure in method has occurred in a field of work close to the field of radio-activity, which is the behaviour of light.   In recent years scientists have been asking whether light is a particle or whether light is a wave. On occasions they have to assume that it consists of particles and on other occasions they have to assume that it consists of waves. This divergence between wave and particle has led some scientists into the most alarming metaphysical speculations.   They might have done well to remember St. Thomas' simple methodological observation that just as there is no common

medium for a line and a point so there is no common medium
for the instant and duration. The scientists might have concluded from this that there is no common medium for the
particle and the wave; they would then have ceased trying to
combine the wave and the particle, realizing that they have
no common medium. But the fact of their having no common
medium in which to be measured raises no "ultimate"
difficulties; any more than ultimate difficulties are raised by
our being unable to flash onto a screen a view of Edinburgh
castle from the north side at the same time as we flash onto
the same screen a view of Edinburgh castle from the south side.
This absence of a common medium simply records the fact that
we are finite creatures and cannot see the world from different
viewpoints because we cannot both open and shut the same
window at the same time.

The wave view expresses one way of formulating our
experiments with light, the particle view a different one. The
fact that we cannot combine them simultaneously raises no
philosophical difficulties whatsoever; it simply urges us to seek
for tools which have a common medium such as "wave"
and "particle" do not have. But this is a problem for the
experimenter, not for the theorist.

From these illustrations of scientific method we hope to
have shown that the methods and assumptions of the physical
sciences are open to the judgement of all intelligent people.
But this judgement must only be made after a sober study of
what the physical scientists are, in fact, doing. The worst
possible approach is that of which certain religious people
seem particularly fond, whereby one either rejects scientific
theories out of hand or else expects them to answer questions
outside their scope (such as whether God exists, whether man
is free or determined, etc.). There is a story that a recent
Archbishop of Canterbury invited Einstein to a dinner so as
to discover from Einstein what bearing the theory of Relativity
had upon theological questions. When the question was put
to him Einstein replied, "None whatsoever".

And yet discussion between experts in the physical sciences
and experts in other disciplines can prove of immense profit to

both sides. The most illuminating instance of this occurred in the early years of the seventeenth century, when St. Robert Bellarmine and Galileo became involved in the controversy as to whether the sun goes round the earth (which is stationary), or whether the earth goes round the sun (which is stationary). The problem was not dealt with generally in a sober fashion, because the Galilean theory was supposed to contradict the teaching of Scripture.[4]

The interest of this episode is that in the course of showing that his theory did not contradict Holy Scripture Galileo enunciated principles for the interpretation of Scripture which have since become accepted by Catholic theologians. Galileo taught people how to read the Scriptures. At the same time St. Robert Bellarmine, in showing that Galileo's theory was a hypothesis and not an unchangeable truth, laid down principles of scientific method which have since become accepted by modern scientists. Bellarmine stated that the new theory (that the sun and not the earth is the stationary centre of the universe) was a hypothesis made to account for certain phenomena, and not an absolute metaphysical judgement, since it was liable to alteration. In fact the hypothesis has now been changed, and the theory of Relativity states that it is immaterial whether one takes the earth or the sun, or anywhere else, as the fixed point from which to measure relative movements in the universe.

The Bellarmine-Galileo dispute warns us against becoming excited over issues such as these, which can only be settled by sober investigation.

NOTES

[1] *Philosophy of Mathematics and Natural Science*, Princeton University Press, 1949, p. 289.
[2] cf. SIR EDMUND WHITTAKER, *Space and Spirit*, Nelson, 1946, pp. 110–111.
[3] *New Pathways in Science*, Cambridge University Press, 1935, p. 1
[4] cf. J. BRODRICK, S.J., *Cardinal Bellarmine*, Burns Oates, 1928, pp. 326–373.

THE QUESTION OF EVOLUTION

THE QUESTION of evolution, and the passions which it has aroused, well illustrate how a controversy should not be carried on. Instead of being discussed soberly with a deep concern for evidence and possible inferences from it, "evolution" has been turned into a religious issue. Amongst the biologists the "defender of evolutionary faith" was Thomas Henry Huxley. The scientific biologist, Darwin, was a much more reasonable person, ever aware that his hypotheses might need revision. Amongst ecclesiastics Bishop Wilberforce performed the rôle taken by Huxley amongst the biologists. Wilberforce belonged to an Evangelical school whose religion was determined largely by emotion. Consequently, when Wilberforce was faced with the evolutionary hypothesis, he simply projected onto Darwin and Huxley the deep doubts about Christianity which he had never consciously faced up to. He accused Darwin and Huxley of an infidelity which was rooted in himself and which could only have been uprooted by the use of his reason. Like so many Christians who attack "evolution", Wilberforce was fighting with his own shadow.

Darwin's modest attitude had its parallel amongst ecclesiastics in the attitude of Cardinal Newman. Faced with the evolutionary theory, Cardinal Newman said that it was nothing to get disturbed about; if the evolutionary hypothesis was true then it obviously could not contradict any truth of faith, because the truth cannot contradict the truth. And if at some point it seemed as though there was a contradiction, then either the evolutionary hypothesis needed modifying, or else we had misunderstood some truth of the Faith.

What strikes one, in comparing Wilberforce's reaction with Newman's, is not so much that Newman's knowledge of physical science was superior to Wilberforce's (though it was), but that Newman's theology was so much better than Wilberforce's. The "god" who seemed to be dethroned by evolution in the eyes of Wilberforce and his contemporaries was not the

Christian God but the god of the eighteenth-century Deists. According to these eighteenth-century Deists the supreme being (god) had so to speak kicked off the universe and then taken no more than a remote interest in it; occasionally the supreme being was called upon to intervene, to create the various species of animals and, in particular, to create man. But apart from these occasional interventions this remote god was not greatly regarded. Consequently, with Darwin's theory of evolution maintaining that the various species had gradually taken on their peculiarities by continuous development over the course of millions of years, it seemed unnecessary to invoke this distant god at all. Since they found this god to be unnecessary Huxley and many other scientists became agnostics; the general populace has more or less fallen in with their viewpoint during the past century.

And yet one may reasonably wonder whether the evolutionary theory would have brought about such a great crisis in men's religion in a truly orthodox age. It is difficult to imagine its causing any such crisis for St. Basil, when that great saint, simply on the basis of his own observation, wrote, " 'Let the waters', it is said, 'bring forth abundantly moving creatures that have life, and fowl that may fly over the earth in the open firmament of heaven'. Why do the waters give birth also to birds? Because there is, so to say, a family link between the creatures that fly and those that swim. In the same way that fish cut the waters, using their fins to carry them forward and their tails to direct their movements round and round and straightforward, so we see birds float in the air by the help of their wings. Both endowed with the property of swimming, their common derivation from the waters has made them of one family."[1] The orthodoxy of St. Basil would not have been scandalized by the theory that birds derive from reptiles.

Nor would St. Thomas Aquinas have felt it necessary to defend the god of the eighteenth-century Deists in the name of Christianity. With one dry sentence he provides the principle which enables us to see how the orthodox should regard the theory of evolution: "What can be done by created power need not be produced immediately by God."[2] If God created life-cells with the power of being formed into cows or pigs, then he does not need to intervene specially every time a new species is being formed. "But", the anti-evolutionists still retort, in their defence of the last Deistic ditch, "the life-cells themselves were created by a special divine intervention. Life can never be produced from lifeless matter." This phrase, "life can never be produced from lifeless matter", has almost been treated as an article of faith by certain Christian apologists— but it is not an opinion which would have commended itself to St. Thomas; he thought that the appearance of maggots in rotting matter seemed to argue for the spontaneous generation of life from lifeless matter.[3] Even though we may not accept this view of spontaneous generation it is obvious enough that St. Thomas would not have felt his faith shaken if physical scientists had one day produced living cells in their laboratory out of lifeless matter—the physical scientists would simply be revealing one way in which God's laws operate. By operating according to those laws the scientists would have produced effects in accordance with those laws, i.e. they would have produced "life" from "lifeless matter".

Fortunately, nowadays, it is the attitude of St. Basil, St. Thomas and Newman, rather than of Wilberforce, which is coming to be general amongst leading religious thinkers. Speaking as a Catholic theologian P. Dubarle, O.P., says, "The theory of evolution provides modern biology with a broad picture of the universe for which it has no other substitute. And the first law of religious thought on such an issue is precisely this: to accept frankly the scientific evidence. The Christian view of the world will not suffer, any more than it has suffered from accepting the sun as the centre of our universe . . . the similarity between the oldest man whose remains have come down to us and the higher apes is obvious".[4]

Unfortunately the reverse process seems to have operated amongst many biologists; they have become attached to certain theories about how the evolutionary process took place and defend their own particular theories as if they were defending an article of faith. Modern biologists who behave in this way are the spiritual children of Huxley in England and Haeckel in Germany. And they have done great harm to other disciplines by popularizing concepts taken from biology in these other disciplines, where they are no longer applicable. In particular it has become the common practice to speak of human events as "evolutionary processes"; historians speak of "the evolution of parliament", philosophers speak of the "evolution" of a man's thought, sociologists describe "the struggle for survival" of certain classes. The historian, the philosopher and the sociologist who use these terms are utterly falsifying their own studies, for whereas a biologist is speaking of a mechanical *process* applicable to *species*, the historian, philosopher, and sociologist are each in some way describing *free acts* performed by *unique human beings*. If they forget this they falsify their own disciplines, and in the end they come to regard unique human beings as merely instances of a species, to treat free human acts as parts of a mechanical process; they have bowed down to the evolutionary theory and regarded it as an object of religious faith. They are unscientific.

In order to escape from this overcharged atmosphere of religious strife let us state the position as soberly as possible, before describing certain problems in method which have arisen: "The question as to the ultimate motive-power of the evolutionary process eventually opens up the question of the source of all being. But the latter question cannot be solved by scientific methods, and so the problem of a contradiction between science and faith can obviously never arise; one supposition may be set against another supposition, one faith against another faith, but never science against faith". [5]

Once the atmosphere has been cleared by these preliminary observations we can glance at some problems in method which confront the biologists.

Frequently biologists are asked (and sometimes even ask themselves!) the question, "Well, what *is* life? You are studying *life* in its various manifestations, but you cannot even tell us what life *is*". This is a misguided question, as misguided as asking, what *is* matter? (cf. also p. 149). It is as if the questioner assumed that there is a universal, "life", of which all living beings are particular instances, just as materialists assume that there is a *thing*, "matter", in which all material beings have their share. If the biologist allows his questioner to make this illegitimate assumption, and ask his senseless question, he finds himself in the following predicament. There are certain viruses which sometimes behave like dead, "lifeless" matter but which on other occasions behave like beings endowed with "life". In the first case they have a structure typical of "lifeless" matter; they are crystals. But in the second case (when they are placed in certain cells) they act as parasites, showing the fundamental characteristics of "life", i.e. self-duplication and mutation. Can the biologist suggest why these viruses on some occasions receive this entity, "life", and on other occasions lose it? Of course he cannot, because there is no such entity!

The correct view seems to be that each living being consists of simple, chemical bodies organized according to a specific pattern—its form. Therefore the biologist's task is, *not* to find some universal form (named "life"), but to study particular forms, or organizations, compare them, and thus learn how each of these organizations is directed towards a particular mode of behaviour. He relates organizations (or form) to the behaviour he observes and so discovers how the being in question works. The biologist is investigating the behaviour of living beings; he is not discovering characteristics of a non-existent abstraction, known as "life".

If this view of what the biologist is doing is the correct one, then it solves certain pseudo-problems that have caused controversy. For instance, if one assumes that there is a mysterious thing, called "life", which some beings have and others do not have, it becomes difficult to offer any intelligible explanation of how "life" may have first been produced. Of course, to those who believe that there is a mysterious thing called "life" the obvious explanation is that it was a "miracle"; but physical scientists would never discover anything if they pronounced the word "miracle" over every difficulty which they encounter; moreover the science of theology would be in an equally primitive condition if theologians had adopted the same attitude. On the other hand, assuming that each living being is its chemical constituents organized according to a certain pattern, it seems reasonable enough to suppose that life first appeared on this earth when these chemical constituents came together into a certain pattern (in much the same way as water appears when its constituents, hydrogen and oxygen, come together in certain circumstances).

The biologist can work out, within limits, what the circumstances must have been under which living beings could be produced—which is something well worth knowing. Normally the biologist then goes on to say that the appearance of living beings was therefore due to "chance"; and it is this which annoys his religious brethren, and leads them to reject the biologist's claim that he knows what circumstances produced living beings. Each of the disputants is half-right. The biologist is right in trying to work out the conditions necessary for living beings. The biologist is wrong in describing these conditions, or circumstances, as "chance"; you can only describe the part (i.e. the circumstances) as "chance" if you believe the whole (of the universe) to be "chance". When someone describes the whole universe as "chance" he is not speaking as a biologist at all—he is expressing a philosophical opinion; moreover he is expressing an absurd philosophical opinion. But it would be foolish to reject his sound biology just because he favours an absurd philosophy.

At the same time one might have expected that biologists would nowadays have come to face up to this philosophical problem of the relationship between a part and its whole; for they cannot even continue to be sound biologists unless they take this philosophical problem into account (cf. also pp. 153-4). Let us illustrate this point from two difficulties which are facing biologists.

The first difficulty offers a parallel to the physicist's inability to state both the speed and the position of an atomic particle at the same time (p. 151).[6] In the same way, if we take a living organism and try to analyse it into its chemical constituents we either disturb its free organic functions, or else, in extreme cases, our chemical analysis kills it. Therefore, if we separate out its chemical constituents (its parts) we either kill it (in which case we are not studying a living organism at all), or else we disturb its free functioning—in which case we cannot study the living organism as a whole. Translated into philosophical terms: a part is a function of its whole; in order to analyse it we have to separate it from its whole; when we do this we are no longer studying the part (which is a function of its whole). This difficulty, as a matter of fact, was recognized on philosophical grounds long ago, long before modern experiments brought the biologists face to face with it. St. Thomas Aquinas pointed out that when you take a human heart out of a human body, it ceases to be a *human heart* once it is separated from the body to which it belongs. That this "modern" problem should have occurred to St. Thomas is not really so very surprising when we remember that the notions of "part" and "whole" are philosophical presuppositions which the biologist has to make in common with thinkers in every discipline.

The second difficulty, a beautifully fascinating one, arises from the recent discoveries in the branch of biology known as genetics. As a result of Mendel's experiments biologists have come to the conclusion that characteristics are inherited by means of "genes". No one has ever seen a "gene", of course; they are beyond the reach of the microscope, but biologists have to suppose that they are there in order to account for effects which they can observe. The position would be comparatively simple if each gene inherited by an organism produced a specific characteristic in that organism—if, that is to say, gene "a" always resulted in an unusual stomach formation, or gene "b" always resulted in blue eyes. But this does not happen. Genes do not act in isolation, they act in combination. Thus a characteristic of the organism, B, may be the result of the combined action of genes "a", "b", "c", "d"; and the characteristic resulting from the combination of genes "a", "b", "d", without "c", may be quite different. For genes have different actions according to what genes are their neighbours. Therefore, in order to know what effect a particular gene will produce we also need to know its relations with the other genes; it even seems likely that every characteristic of an organism is dependent on *all* the genes which it has inherited!

This situation is complicated enough, to begin with. But we also learn that different combinations of genes, at different times, may result in the *same* characteristic. And so characteristic B, may at one time be the result of a combination of genes "a", "b", "c", but at another time it may result from a combination of genes "x", "y", "z". When we remember that there are some 5,000 genes in even such a minute insect as the banana-fly (*Drosophila*) (and possibly four or five times as many in man) it can be seen what dizzy possibilities of combination and recombination we are faced with.

A further complication is that "most individual genes are, in all probability, themselves very complex, and attained their present state through a succession of small mutations".[7] Furthermore modern geneticists maintain that one cannot study the heredity of characteristics by studying one individual organism and its history; it is the whole breeding population of which the organism is one individual that has to be studied.[8] Strictly speaking, therefore, in order to describe any gene accurately, and predict its effect upon the characteristics of an organism, we not only need to know how it is combined with other genes in the organism; we even need to know the *history* of the gene in question, which involves its past combinations and relationships with other genes within the breeding population.

This complicated situation in genetics has several interesting consequences.

Firstly, from a practical viewpoint, it means that there is no possibility of breeding human beings according to plan so as to produce a "perfect" population. For in order to choose human beings who could procreate such a population we should not only have to choose specimens who are in fine condition now, we should have to know the whole genetic history of every specimen whom we chose—in order to be certain that flaws will not appear. In fact, we should need to know the *whole* genetic history of each human being (which, obviously, includes all his ancestors). This is clearly impossible![9]

Secondly, it means that whereas during the past century biological methods have dominated historians, now it is the historians who will have to show the biologists the need for *historical* method. Whereas historians had come to speak of human beings as though they were simply instances of a class or species it is now the turn of the biologists to acknowledge that even genes have their own unique history, and that the gene's history has to be studied by historical method and not only by laboratory experiment.[10]

Thirdly, we once again (as on pp. 151-2) find ourselves at the limit of human knowledge, a reflection of the fact that we are creatures with limited knowledge. Since we have again to recognize that we can only know the whole truth about the smallest part of the world if we know the whole truth about the whole world. The characteristics of any individual gene depend upon its relations with the rest of the universe and a complete knowledge of the gene would require a complete knowledge of the universe.

Another fundamentally philosophical difficulty, the neglect of which has led biologists into confusion, is that of classifying the organisms which they study. At one time this seemed simple enough; the structures of a man and an ape, or of a horse and a donkey, are obviously so similar that it seemed reasonable to assume that they have a common ancestor, and belong to the same family. By relating organisms in this way it was hoped to be able to classify them according to their family, their species, and so on. Even this system of classification encounters considerable difficulties; for instance, vertebrates (such as cows and crocodiles) have eyes, and molluscs (a sort of shell-fish) have eyes; but this similarity does not lead biologists to the highly unlikely opinion that these organisms with radically different structures belong to the same family.

Nowadays, however, biologists have other ways of relating organisms than by this *similarity in appearance, or structure*. Amongst other similarities they use the similarity in blood and chemical composition in order to classify organisms. These result in classifications which are often strikingly different from those obtained by the first method. Illustrations of how strikingly different they are would involve us in too much technical language. But a simple case is this: "The resemblance [between the woolly rhinoceros and the living white rhinoceros of Africa], especially in skull and teeth, is so close that it long seemed incontrovertible that they were extremely

closely related. This now appears not to be the case. The white
rhinoceros seems to be derived, with its relatively primitive
cousin, the more abundant black rhinoceros, from a different
Miocene-Pliocene ancestry, whereas the woolly rhinoceros is
descended from a long known line of dicerorhine rhinoceroses
related to the living Sumatran rhinoceros."[11] How great an
effect upon classification these newly-noticed similarities may
have is shown by the fact that we cannot even say with certainty
whether certain elementary organisms (e.g. the dinoflagellates)
are plants or animals. Certain characteristics seem to mark
them as plants but others suggest that they are animals.[12]

The question of *which* similarity to choose as fundamental
can only be decided either by blind faith in the biologist or
else by philosophical discussion. The blind-alley of the first
alternative is taken, for instance, by Julian Huxley when he
writes, "A quite reasonable definition of the term species is
that given some years ago by Dr. Tate Regan when Director
of the Natural History Museum at South Kensington—namely,
that 'a species is a community, or a number of related com-
munities, whose distinctive morphological characters are, in the
opinion of a competent systematist, sufficiently definite to
entitle it, or them, to a specific name'".[13] Which is a polite
way of saying that a "species" is what a competent systematist
says it is. Who is to decide on his competency, is not indicated.

A philosophical discussion, on the other hand, would reveal
that biologists, like the rest of us, often assume that when things
are similar in one respect they are similar in all other respects
—which is an entirely false assumption. For instance, they had
assumed that because the woolly rhinoceros and the living
white rhinoceros of Africa are similar in characteristics a (skull)
and b (teeth), therefore they had a similar ancestor, c (the
living Sumatran, as opposed to the Miocene-Pliocene ancestor).
This does not necessarily follow, any more than that because
A and B are both bald therefore they are both old—for A is
a baby, and B is an old-age pensioner.

The biologists are by no means the only people who commit
this elementary error. Many psychologists have assumed that
because the appearance of a mystic in ecstasy is similar to the

appearance of a neurotic in a trance, therefore the condition of each is due to the same cause (i.e. neurosis). Marxists assume that because one person hates Marxism through fear for his property therefore all who hate Marxism do so through fear for their property. The truth of the matter is that there must be *some* similarity between beings inhabiting the same medium, between fishes because they live in the sea, for instance, or between Eskimos who live in the frozen north; there must be *some* similarity between the vocal organs of all beings (whether frogs or débutantes) if these beings are going to produce noises in the same medium (i.e. the air around this earth of ours). But the differences between these beings are more important for certain purposes than their similarities. However, analysis of difference in similarity would involve us in a philosophical discussion of analogy; it would require a demonstration that it is more reasonable (*as it is*) to assume that the woolly rhinoceros and the living white rhinoceros have a common ancestor than to assume A and B to be old just because each is bald. These complicated issues, unfortunately, cannot be dwelt on here; they require space and time. It is enough if we have shown that biologists, in their classifications by *similarity*, of one kind or another, are making philosophical presuppositions which each one of us can examine for himself.

In the previous paragraphs we have been outlining the fundamental problems of method which must occur frequently to biologists themselves. In the following paragraphs let us attempt to bring out more of these problems by listening to some of the objections to the theory of evolution as far as the theory concerns other animals than man.

The most frequent objection to the theory of evolution states that "it is only a hypothesis, and is not yet proved". Whilst gladly admitting that this statement is correct one must point out that it is not an objection. To use it as an objection to the theory of evolution is to be guilty of irrelevance. Those who do so, saying "It is not yet proved", are applying an impossible standard of proof (cf. Ch. I.); they are demanding that evolution should be proved in the same way as one proves that hens hatch from eggs, or that magnets attract iron filings. Now these latter processes can be proved by reproducing them and watching them happen. But if we were to wait until biologists reproduce "missing links" (which we could watch evolving) before we accepted the theory of evolution, then we should wait for ever and a day; it will never happen. Neither, however, can historians reproduce King John and his barons; nor can Scripture scholars reproduce St. Paul and his sting in the flesh. But does that prevent us from believing that King John and his barons quarrelled, or that St. Paul had a sting in the flesh? Of course not; because we know that the proofs for these happenings are of a different kind from those by which we prove hens to hatch from eggs, yet they are none the less valid.

King John's quarrels and St. Paul's sting are past events, and like all past events can only be known on the basis of evidence presented to us from the past; on the basis of the evidence we form a hypothesis to account for it. Thus in the case of St. Paul our evidence includes a continuous tradition and literary documents; the same is true of King John. In the case of evolution we obviously cannot have either a continuous tradition or literary documents as evidence; we have to rely mainly on the evidence of the rocks. But we *have* that evidence, and can work out a theory to account for it which is neither more nor less of a hypothesis than any other account of past events. Therefore, to say of the evolutionary theory (an account of past events) that it is only a hypothesis (i.e. an account of past events) is like saying "one is one" or "men are men". It is not incorrect. It just has no bearing whatsoever on the question of whether the theory is true. In order to decide that question we must know the evidence which the evolutionary theory is trying to explain—otherwise we should be in the same position as a person who set out to judge whether a man was guilty of murder by refusing to hear any of the witnesses.

Applying these lessons to the debate on evolution: the person who is not a biologist cannot reasonably judge the hypothesis of evolution unless he is aware of some of the evidence which the biologist is trying to explain.[14] When the non-biologist tries to do so it is no wonder that the biologist becomes annoyed; because he himself sees evidence which the other person does not see, just as the mystic sees truths which are hidden from other men. And so the objection that evolution is "only a hypothesis" is no objection at all; the question is whether the hypothesis gives the most reasonable explanation of the evidence.

It is true that some of the evidence makes it difficult to imagine how the changes can have taken place which are asserted to have taken place according to the theory of evolution. How on earth the change took place, for instance, in reptiles so that they eventually became birds! Each change in the reptile's anatomy would disturb other parts of the reptile's anatomy so profoundly in the process of the bird's emergence that one cannot imagine how the reptile-bird ever managed to go on living at all—much less producing other reptile-birds. Any attempted explanation of these mechanisms of change on the hypothesis of continuous evolution is so utterly unconvincing that Schindewolf says, "The first bird hatched from a reptilian egg"! A similar blankness was registered by Berg when he remarked that "the probability that all useful variations will simultaneously occur is the probability of a miracle".[15]

The fact is that no biologist has been able to suggest a convincing account (based on the hypothesis of evolution) of the changes in structure that must have taken place in the transition from one family to another. But does this mean to say that the biologist should abandon the hypothesis of evolution? The answer is that, at the level of biology he cannot do so; at this level he is committed to explaining such changes in terms of agents which he can describe and investigate by biological methods. If he abandons this principle—and some of the difficulties might tempt him to do so—then he has to look for other *kinds* of agents, e.g. God. But the search for such agents could not be carried out by biological methods. Faced with this dilemma he has the choice of either recognizing the limitations of his science and continuing his search by other methods, or else he has to push the evolutionary hypothesis as far as it will go and accept even its highly improbable consequences.

Nor is the biologist behaving unreasonably when he chooses the latter alternative, for Leverrier made a similar choice when he remained faithful to Newton's hypothesis rather than

abandon it (cf. p. 152).   As we have seen, it led him to the
discovery of Neptune; and one imagines that it is the hope of
making similar discoveries by remaining faithful to evolution
which prevents the biologist from abandoning it. Whether or not
a human being should attach so much importance to making
discoveries about living beings is a question of a different order.
But the biologist can justifiably maintain that no-one abandons
a hypothesis which accounts for many things just because it does
not account for everything. For instance, religious people
maintain that God is at work in every event of their lives, but if
you ask them to give an account of how God is working at any
particular moment, how the hypothesis of God accounts for
some particular event, they are usually at a loss to do so. But
they do not abandon the hypothesis of God's providential workings in consequence. Yet, from the point of view of method,
their attitude is not so very much different from that of the
biologist who refuses to abandon his faith in the evolutionary
hypothesis.   It is true that for the believer there is all the difference in the world between his faith and the evolutionist's faith,
but the believer should have enough understanding to recognize
that they *look* the same to the outsider, the non-believer.

Yet whilst one is quite prepared to accept the biologists' good
faith, one's respect for their *science* would be increased if they
showed themselves more aware of the difficulties that they have
to face. For instance, one would expect to find them speaking
frankly of how odd it is that thousands of fossils have been
found in rocks that were on the earth's surface some 500 million
years ago but none in the rocks of earlier date. *On the face of it*
this suggests that these fossils are the remnants of organisms
which *suddenly* appeared, fully formed, some 500 million years
ago; according to the evolutionary hypothesis they must have
evolved from simpler organisms; but if so, it is very odd that
we have no remnants of these simpler organisms. There may
well be explanations for what seems a sudden appearance of
life on earth and the biologist must obviously seek some such
explanation; but on the evidence of the rocks it would seem
that living beings suddenly appeared fully formed.

Such oddities are frequent enough. For example, if we accept the evolutionary hypothesis we should expect to find traces of moss in the rocks before finding traces of ferns, because ferns are much more developed than moss and (according to evolution) are derived from moss. The evidence does not confirm this expectation. No traces of moss are found earlier than some 80 million years ago whereas full-grown ferns are found some 300 million years ago. Furthermore, at the time when the simplest form of plant, i.e. moss, does appear, there also appear the highest forms of plant, i.e. the flowering type. This makes it impossible to reconstruct the evolution of plants on the evidence of the rocks.[16]

Nor can the general reader fail to wonder whether there has been sufficient time after the first appearance of living cells for all the necessary changes to have occurred, if we assume that these changes have happened gradually.[17] It is dangerous, of course, to argue from the rate of change in one species to the rate of change in another, for these rates are different.[18] At the same time, the story of the horse has long been accepted as the classic illustration of an evolutionary process,[19] yet the changes recorded, though by no means very large anatomically,[20] have taken some 45 million years. When we see that it takes 45 million years for such small changes to take place we cannot help thinking that the evolutionists have not sufficient time at their disposal for their supposed changes to have occurred.

And it is the lack of time available for gradual evolution, as well as the lack of fossil evidence for intermediate types, that has led one biologist to say that evolution occurs in jumps. This biologist, Goldschmidt, believes that the hypothesis of gradual evolution (microevolution) requires supplementing by sudden large-scale changes (which he calls "macroevolution"): "Subspecies are actually, therefore, neither incipient species nor models for the origin of species. They are more or less diversified blind-alleys within the species. The decisive step in evolution, the first step towards macroevolution, the step from one species to another, requires another evolutionary method than that of sheer accumulation of mutations."[21] If the evidence forces Goldschmidt to believe in "another evolutionary method than that of sheer accumulation of mutations", then the hypothesis of evolution is so greatly modified that it can scarcely be described as the same original hypothesis. In fact, he is simply throwing the word "macroevolution" over the gap in our knowledge, and recording the fact that large-scale changes ("macroevolution") must take place, although the hypothesis of evolution assumes that all the changes are gradual and continuous. Therefore, from a biologist's standpoint there is nothing to choose between "macroevolution" and "God" as the explanation of "the decisive step", for both words record that the biologist has reached the limits of explanation according to the methods of his science.

But the moment at which the biologist must grow most conscious of his science's limitations is not so much when he is answering the kind of question of which we have been speaking, for all these questions are concerned with *how* the changes took place—what were the successive states of the various organisms. It is when he starts trying to say *why* these changes took place that the limitations become obvious, when he starts trying to discover the purpose of the changes. Indeed the question of purpose in nature is such a thorn in the flesh to someone such as Julian Huxley that he says that people only find purpose in nature because they project their own purposes onto nature. Which is really not a very intelligent comment, and one to which one might just as well reply that the reason why some people find nature to lack purpose is that they project the lack of purpose in their own lives onto nature. In any case, the biologist presumably has some purpose in studying living beings and it is not unreasonable to assume that if one living being, i.e. the biologist, has a purpose, so have other living beings.

In order to get this question about the "why" of living beings straight in our minds we have to see that it can be stated at different levels.

At the highest level, which is the most fundamental, we ask ourselves why anything should exist at all? This is not a question which only biologists ask; it is a question which each human being asks. Moreover the tools and methods of biology do not afford any advantage in answering the question. All of us are metaphysicians enough to ask this fundamental question; none of us knows enough to answer it unaided; we depend upon revelation for the answer.

At the second level, we say, "Granted that living beings do exist, why do they change at all?" That is to say, there was once a time when the earth was populated by very simple living cells; why did they change at all? They were going along reproducing in a very simple fashion and nourishing themselves in a very simple fashion; why did they start that process of change which has resulted in very complex beings, such as apes, which reproduce and nourish themselves in such a complex manner? Clearly the answer to this question is subordinate to the answer given to the first one; it is metaphysical, and the biologist commands no special means of answering better than anyone else. Yet it is precisely at this level that most confusion has been caused, for the biologists try to tell us why living beings change at all, yet restricting the *possible* causes of the change to causes which fall within the province of biology. But you cannot give a biological answer to a metaphysical question; if you try to do so you produce an absurdity. When we try to explain why a simple cell develops into a creature capable, for instance, of building a nest or spinning a web, we are faced with three alternatives: either it was unplanned and happened purely by "chance" (i.e. "natural selection") or else the cell thought it all out and planned it in advance, or else some being which controls the cell did the necessary planning.

Since no-one believes that the cell does the thinking it is only the first and the third alternatives that have to be considered. The objection to the first alternative is the same as we gave on p. 164: it expresses a philosophical opinion, and that opinion is absurd. The opinion cannot be contested on biological grounds, but only on philosophical grounds, as we pointed out on p. 164. How absurd it is philosophically is realized by some biologists such as R. A. Fisher who curtly comments, "Natural selection is a mechanism for generating a high degree of improbability".[22] In fact, it is interesting to notice that even those who maintain this absurdity do implicitly recognize it as absurd, because they try to endow their "chance" and "natural selection" with all the characteristics of the kind of being which is mentioned in the third alternative. Darwin, for example, said "We must suppose that there is a power, represented by natural selection or the survival of the fittest, always intently watching each slight alteration in the transparent layers."[23] This is truly a case of trying to have one's cake and eat it— to explain changes by "chance" and then attribute divine powers to this "chance"!

Obviously this question of *why* at the second level is a philosophical question, and not a biological one. If we try to say in biological terms why living beings change at all, we commit ourselves to an absurdity.

It is at the next level that the biologist comes into his own, when he says, granted that things do exist, and granted that living beings do change, what part in these changes is played by factors which a biologist can examine? All these factors ultimately are either hereditary factors or environmental factors, and it is these factors which the biologist can describe with all the skill of his special discipline. He can tell us, for instance, that certain changes in climate took place at a certain time, and that afterwards one found living beings with new characteristics; he can examine the way in which new characteristics appear after pressure of population has driven different species into areas of the earth which had previously been empty. And if he does so in the light of the principles which we have outlined, there need arise no quarrel between him and the philosophers or the Christians or any thinking person. The quarrels arise when the biologist introduces pseudo-philosophical notions; or when he isolates one factor in the changes and says it is the *only* factor.

An instance of a pseudo-philosophical notion is "natural selection". The very phrase is a contradiction in itself; if there is "selection", "choice", then it must be the work of some being capable of choosing, capable of making a rational judgement in favour of one course rather than another. But, in any case, "natural selection" offers no explanation whatsoever of why living beings *change*. Suppose, for instance, that there are two kinds of moths, black ones and white ones, which find themselves living in an area where the white ones show up against dark trees; it is only natural that the birds which eat

them should eat up the white ones which they can see. Therefore the black ones survive. This is an instance of what is
called "natural selection". But all that it tells us is how certain
representatives of the original moth-population *survived*; we are
not left with any *new* kind of moth at the end of it. Therefore to
put forward "natural selection" as an explanation of how *new*
kinds of beings are developed is pointless; it only tells us how
the old kinds survived. Though if "natural selection" were not
isolated as an explanatory factor it might serve some purpose.

But we have so often met this mistake of isolating one factor
and then saying it is the *only* factor that we are scarcely surprised to find the biologists disagreeing on account of it. The
way in which this isolation of factors leads to disagreement is
illustrated by the remark of a palaeontologist, "To them [the
geneticists] the idea that external conditions can so influence
an organism that in course of time their effect becomes heritable
is almost absurd; to me it is axiomatic".[24] And so, whilst
realizing that these questions can only be decided by experiment, is it presumptuous to suggest that all the factors indicated
have their part to play? One can conceive of evolution being
caused in the following manner. At a certain moment God, the
cause of all things, acts upon living beings by means of secondary causes, such as light-rays from the sun or the nebulae,
or eruptions on the earth's surface. This seems reasonable
enough, since God normally acts upon the world through
created things, secondary causes; also, since biologists have
recently been bombarding those little insects, *Drosophila*, with
X-rays in order to discover the effect upon their genes, and
subsequently their offspring, it may well be that God changes
living beings in a similar way, by throwing light rays upon
them. If this supposition is correct, then the part played by
genes is recognized, and the part played by external circumstances ("natural selection") is recognized, whilst the all-
pervading power of God makes the whole process intelligible
instead of being sheer "chance".

But, it may be objected, this account we have given of evolutionary theory, and our distinction between different levels, is
too clear-cut, since one would expect to find that the specifically

biological factors at least suggest sometimes that other factors are operating. That, in fact, is what we do find if we approach the evidence without a fixed notion that we are going to reduce it all to a certain few factors (cf. similar reductions in other sciences, p. 46, Marx, p. 203, Freud). If we have dogmatically decided, in advance, that there are only factors "a" and "b", then even when we find what looks like "c" or "d", we can always reduce them to "a(c)" or "b(d)" at a pinch.

For instance, certain features appear in animals which at the time of their appearance are more of a hindrance than a help, but which later prove extremely useful. Presumably the animal could not see the future use which these features were going to have, and so it seems reasonable to suppose that some other being (e.g. God) could see their future use (unless we assume that it was "chance"). It must have occurred to everyone that an elephant's tusks did not become useful until they had grown to quite a length. Other animals develop cones on their teeth which at first are of very doubtful functional use but later become of considerable functional importance. Unfortunately such instances are immediately "reduced" to a preconceived scheme, as we see from the following quotation: "Osborn, in discussing the gradual phyletic development of horns as 'rectigradations' in titanotheres, assumes that they have, in early stages, little or no selective value. Hence he concludes that their origin and growth is due to ill-defined 'germinal potentialities' and exemplifies his syncretic but (despite his denial) essentially mystical 'principle of tetra-kinetic evolution'. Recent genetic work, however, tends to show that even slight variants may be surprisingly effective as selective agents, and even a modest thickening of the bone in the potential horn region may have been, in the course of generations, influential in survival or (a field ripe for re-study) sexual selection."[25] The reader may judge for himself whether it is Osborn or the author of this paragraph who is most set upon "mystical" unknowns. At least it is obvious that the author is very concerned to reduce what appears to be a fresh factor to the preconceived factors, "survival or (a field ripe for re-study) sexual selection". Other glaring "reductions" are practised by biologists in the case of Weddell's seal and the emperor penguin.[26] We scarcely need to point out that these are instances of biologists trying to reduce to biological causes those processes which force them to look for higher explanatory causes.

Furthermore a wholly new world would be opened up to biologists if they ceased to regard all events in the natural world as reducible to a few factors. How easy it is to neglect the aspect of play in nature, of what seems like the spontaneous joy of being expressing itself in profusion. For instance, birds sing at their best when their singing has no functional value, when they seem to be singing for the sheer joy of singing.[27] Dogs join in the play of hunting when they are not seeking to satisfy their hunger.[28] Families of plants throw off far more forms of blossom, more leaves and forms of leaves than could ever be considered necessary or economical.[29] All this spontaneous growth and life and exuberance could, presumably, be reduced to "sexual selection" if we are prepared to attribute everything the biologist cannot account for to the all-embracing factor of "sexual selection". An unjaundiced eye might more readily see it as the play of God in creation, which plays to the glory of God.

Man's Evolution

Most of the arguments about man's evolution are confused by disputants having different notions of "man". One set of disputants believes that man's so-called mental and spiritual activities are nothing but functions of a body, and are expressions of that body's condition; if this is the case, then the whole of a man's life can be accounted for by bodily processes, and man is simply a kind of two-legged animal. The other set of disputants believes that man's mental and spiritual activities are a sign that he has a destiny beyond the time process, that his bodily actions are signs of his spiritual life and do not wholly determine it.

Clearly the evidence of fossils cannot decide the disputed issue for us, because a spiritual event is not recorded on the rocks in the same way that a fossil records the presence of some animal body. Bodily structures are recorded in the material world, and the records persist as long as the material persists in which they are laid. But spiritual events are not recorded in this way. If there was a man living in France 50,000 years ago we have a chance of learning what kind of a body he had because we may discover his skeleton. Yet if the man fell in love, saw beauty in the dawn sun, or worshipped God, none of these events will be recorded in the rocks (unless he drew pictures, etc., from which we can *guess* what was going on in his soul).

Therefore when it is asked, Did man evolve from one of the higher animals? the answer does not depend upon the evidence of the rocks but upon what we believe to be the subject of this evolution, i.e. what we believe man to be. If we believe that man is nothing but a body then clearly we will also believe that he derives wholly (in all his mental and spiritual faculties) from another body. We shall believe this whether we know the theory of evolution or not—the theory of evolution would not add any new belief but simply tell us *how* it all happened. On the other hand, if we believe that each man is unique and has a unique spiritual destiny, then we shall not believe that the story of where he derived his body from is the whole story— because it leaves out of account that which makes him what he is, his spiritual activity. The whole story would have to state the origin of his spiritual activities.

The disputants, then, are not talking about the same *thing* ; for a being which can be wholly explained in terms of bodily processes, and a being which is wholly explained by spiritual destiny, are different subjects. Since they are talking about different things these disputants obviously cannot arrive at the same conclusion. Perhaps some measure of agreement is possible, however, if we state the position as follows. It is an almost certain hypothesis that all living men derive their bodies, through their ancestors, from a common ancestor amongst the higher animals. It is quite certain that all living men are tremendously different from any of the animals. How did these differences come about? The religious man has one answer, the atheist another. But neither answer can be confirmed by the evidence of fossils, for "all attempts to determine where the gap lies between 'still an animal' and 'already a man' are just as vain as trying to say at what exact moment a child becomes an adult. Both processes took place slowly. But just as our appreciation of this continuity does not prevent us from recognizing countless differences between the child and the adult, no more should our appreciation of the gradual transition in the remote past from animal to man prevent us from seeing that, no matter how it happened, man to-day is a fundamentally different being from all animals." [30]

Are we not faced, in fact, with a similar situation to that which confronted us when trying to describe a desk as either "brown" or "not-brown"? (p. 136). We know perfectly well what we mean by "brown", just as we know perfectly well what we mean by "man", but this very precision of our terms makes it impossible for us to say exactly at what point in space we come to "not-brown", or at what point in the past we come to "not-man". Therefore, although we can usually state whether a fossil belonged to "man" or "not-man", we cannot state this definitely of every fossil, and we never shall be able to do so.

In the past this confusion about "man" or "not-man" has been increased by the biologists' over-confidence in drawing conclusions about the being which was the source of a fossil from the fossil itself. Leaving aside such fantastics as the man who announced the discovery of "dawn-man" on the basis of a tooth which later turned out to be a pig's, we find respected investigators equally confident. Broom has discovered *Plesianthropus*, who walked erect, on his two feet; what he found, in fact, was an upper arm-bone. In 1907 Heidelberg man was announced; Boule thought that if the jaw had been found without the teeth it would have been attributed to an ape, whereas if the teeth had been discovered apart from the jaw they would have passed for those of "modern" man. In 1941 three teeth were found and became *Gigantopithecus blacki*. Just before his death, in 1940, Dubois announced his opinion that his famous find of 1891, Java man, was a gibbon. These are a few instances, amongst many, of the slender evidence that is found, and of the care with which inferences from it have to be made.

But if we have to be hesitant in reconstructing bodily structures on the basis of a tooth or an arm-bone, how much more hesitant we must be to speak of the mental life of the source of some fossil, as the following illustrations show.

Calculating brain-capacity from skulls one discovers that Anatole France and Gambetta, for instance, had half the brain-volume of the primitive Pekin man. Similarly most modern men have a much smaller brain-capacity than the primitive Neanderthal man. Consequently, when Broom discovered a skull in 1948 with a brain-capacity of 850 c.cm. he was not necessarily correct in believing that the owner belonged to a high intellectual level—since brain-capacity alone is no guarantee of intellectual capacity. The accepted way of measuring intellectual capacity is to relate the body-weight to the brain-weight and place those on the highest level whose brains are proportionately the heaviest. In order to apply this test to Broom's discovery (*Paranthropus Crassidens*) we should have to know the weight of *Paranthropus Crassidens* ; if it happens to be a giant form, with a large body-weight, then its brain-weight is actually low in proportion.[31] But we cannot know this until we know more about *Paranthropus Crassidens*—which is exactly what we are trying to find out. And even the proportion between brain-weight and body-weight does not provide an absolute standard for measuring intellectual capacity, since certain small apes of South America have a far larger proportion of brain than do modern men.[32] But no-one would conclude from this that these small apes have a greater intellectual capacity than modern men. In fact, arguments about intellectual capacity cannot be convincingly based upon either the size or the shape of skulls. [33]

But if we have to scrutinize arguments from fossils to bodily structure very carefully, and increase our caution when discussing intellectual capacity, how vain are our efforts to decide upon spiritual destiny from such evidence. The problem does not arise, of course, for those who do not believe in the spirit, but those who do believe might realize the flimsiness of such arguments from the following consideration. According to Christian teaching the soul is infused into the body at the moment that conception takes place in the mother's womb. From that moment onwards the foetus in the mother's womb has a spiritual destiny. Would anyone, confronted with such foetus in the early stages, believe that it has a spiritual destiny? Almost certainly not. And yet it has. So little can we infer with certainty about spiritual capacity from physical appearance.

Once we have these guiding principles in mind it should be possible for us to introduce order into our thinking on man's evolution and its relationship to theological declarations about man. We are assured by a Catholic biologist that the development of man's body from a pre-human form "is the only hypothesis which a competent biologist can accept in the light of contemporary research".[34] And, indeed, it is difficult to imagine what evidence would convince opponents of this hypothesis, if they do not accept it on the basis of the fossils that have already been found. If an anti-evolutionist had been asked some eighty years ago what kind of fossils would have to be found before he would accept evolution he would have named just those kinds of fossils which have been brought to light during the past eighty years. The cheap gibe that "the only certain thing about the missing link is that it is missing" has completely lost its point, if it ever had any.

At the same time, the detailed efforts to construct a family tree indicating man's descent can scarcely be described as successful. The difficulty arises through our having to argue from similarity in one respect to similarity in other respects when we are trying to reconstruct man's descent. We have already pointed out some of the obstacles to this procedure (p. 167). A fine instance of the falsities spread by those who do not appreciate the obstacles was the famous "recapitulation theory" of Ernst Haeckel. Haeckel maintained that the human child in embryo recapitulates the evolutionary process during its months in the womb, repeating in the womb all the developments of the evolutionary process. As proof of his theory he pointed to what he called "gill-slits" in the human embryo —which he said showed that the embryo passes through a "fish stage", just as man developed from a fish. This over-hasty conclusion based upon superficial similarity had two evil effects: it prejudiced a genuinely scientific attempt to reconstruct man's family tree; and it delayed the recognition of the precise and

valuable function of the so-called "gill-slits" in the growth
of the embryo—for they are not "gills", and they serve a quite
different purpose from a fish's gills. A salutary warning of the
need for precise philosophical thought to work out the difference
as well as the similarity of different beings.

Another illustration of the failure to establish the human
family-tree upon a basis of some specific similarity comes from
the attempt to do so by blood-tests. For many years it has
popularly been assumed that chemical similarity in the blood of
two living creatures was a proof of their having the same family
tree. We have already learned to suspect such arguments,
and our suspicions are justified when we learn that this blood-
relationship test, if strictly applied, would lead us to the following
conclusions. Some whales are in a closer family relationship
to man than some monkeys are; some men are more close to
monkeys than they are to their fellow-men; eels are more nearly
related to new-born rabbits than to adult rabbits.[35] These
absurd conclusions show that the blood-relationship test (for
the present, anyway) cannot afford us any sure method of reconstructing man's family tree. Perhaps the experimental technique
in classifying blood will one day be perfected and give us the
necessary information, but for the moment it does not help.

One can sympathize with the biologist who, after surveying
present-day evidence, declares exasperatedly that apes are more
likely to have descended from man than man from apes! [36]
For the discovery of so many fossils has increased the number
of possible lines of man's descent and made it correspondingly
more difficult to select the most probable one; and though it
is sometimes said that fresh discoveries will help to clear up
the obscurity, in the past fresh discoveries have actually
deepened this obscurity.

Put quite simply the position is this. Once the theory of
evolution had been put forward, and it was assumed that man
was descended from the family of the great apes, all that was
needed to confirm this particular theory of descent was an
ape-like man or a man-like ape. The discovery of Neanderthal
man, near Düsseldorf, of Java man (*Pithecanthropus*), and of
Heidelberg man, seemed to provide the necessary confirmation,

and the descent of modern man (*Homo sapiens*) from Neanderthal man seemed to give us modern man's family tree. But during recent years other discoveries have shown that beings which have to be classed as "modern man" (*Homo sapiens*) were living long before the type known as Neanderthal man. Therefore modern man cannot be descended from Neanderthal man.

The discoveries of "modern man" at a very early date include several whose great age has been doubted because they did not fit in conveniently with the theory of descent through Neanderthal man—though it is revealing to notice that they might have been accepted apart from this preconceived notion of certain biologists. [37]   Such finds were the Galley Hill, Castenodolo and Calaveras man. Yet no one doubts the great age of the "modern" Swanscombe man, Piltdown man, and Fontéchevrade man; and it is agreed that Reck's discoveries at Oldaway in East Africa and Leakey's discoveries at Kanjera in East Africa reveal the presence of "modern" man as long ago as some 500, 000 years. These finds raise a pretty problem; for if "modern" man was on earth so long ago, what are we to say of the Neanderthal types. Are they really men? and, secondly, the further back "modern" man goes, the more difficult it becomes to find a single ancestor for him (since there have been men tremendously different from the apes, almost as long as there have been apes) and we are once more tempted to exclaim with Professor Wood Jones that the apes are more likely to have descended from man than man from the apes!

Some biologists try to solve the second problem by maintaining that the present races of mankind are derived from different pre-human stocks by processes of parallel evolution. There are many weaknesses in this theory, and it cannot be accepted by Christians, because it is incompatible with the unity of the human race, which fell in Adam and is redeemed in Christ. The theory has been explicitly condemned by Pope Pius XII in the encyclical *Humani Generis*. [38]

But the first question, about Neanderthal man, is not so puzzling as once appeared. It was only puzzling if the so-called "primitive" features of Neanderthal man (e.g. massive brow-ridges, long arms, etc.) represented a stage in between the apes and "modern" man, and if Neanderthal man was an example of this stage. For in this case one cannot explain why "modern" man is found before the more "primitive" Neanderthal man.

However it is now generally agreed by biologists that so-called "primitive" features in either a man or an ape do not necessarily show that such a man or an ape represents an early stage of the species' development. It seems that these "primitive" features very often indicate decadence, a falling-away from a level that had already been attained. [39] And so the "primitive" features in Neanderthal man (and in many other types) may well be explained by the theory that Neanderthal man went down a branch-line, becoming gradually more primitive, and eventually becoming extinct. The supposition that Neanderthal man went down a branch-line is strengthened by the discovery of Mount Carmel man in Palestine. Mount Carmel man dates back beyond Neanderthal man yet is closer to "modern" man in bodily structure and has a quite advanced culture. Therefore the most likely story is that the men from the Mount Carmel area, as they spread westwards throughout Europe, became more "primitive" both in their bodily structure and in their culture, eventually dying out when they had reached the condition of Neanderthal man. [40]

And therefore it seems quite definite that Neanderthal men were men in the theologian's sense of the word; they have a spiritual destiny. One might anyway have concluded so from their own burial customs, since they themselves seem to have believed that they had a spiritual destiny; and one cannot believe that a being who could conceive such a spiritual end had no spiritual capacity.

Whilst recognizing that it is important for biologists to try to reconstruct man's family tree one must regret that these attempts have generally led biologists to propagate an entirely inadequate view of what man is—even from a biological standpoint. In their eagerness to show the continuity between man and the higher animals they have stressed the similarities between them and thus blinded themselves to the enormous differences. This blindness is one instance of a mistake which we have frequently noticed; it is the mistake of thinking that we can study

a flower simply by examining its roots and never bothering ourselves with the flower itself; it is the mistake of thinking that
"electrons" are more "fundamental" than the things composed
of them. It is the mistake of trying to understand man by asking what kind of ape he was, studying a hypothetical ancestor
whom we cannot see instead of studying man, whom we can see.

Several biologists in recent years have realized what a profound mistake this has been, and have begun to remedy the
situation, with interesting results (which, unfortunately, can
only be glanced at here.) [41] Their main thesis is that from the
very moment of his conception in the womb, man's physical
characteristics are ordered towards specifically *human* activity.
In other words, you cannot study the human being in embryo
by relating his physical proportions to the physical proportions
of the ape embryo: if you do so you give a false picture of the
human embryo, every detail in whose development is directed
towards specifically human activity. It is a mistake to think of
man as if he were three layers ape and one layer human; man
is thoroughly human at every level. For instance, the children
of other mammals are able to look after themselves from a very
early age, but human children are helpless for long enough
and only develop control of their bodies over the course of
years. But this helplessness is not to be interpreted negatively;
what would be a weakness of man if he were merely an animal
is actually his glory as a human being. For it means that man
is essentially social, dependent upon other human beings for
his education and upbringing; his very helplessness brings him
into intimate communion with other human beings from the first.
Furthermore the human being only arrives at physical maturity
after fifteen or twenty years whereas some apes do so, for instance,
after two years. Therefore this need for education and the instil-
ling of right habits, the handing on of traditional ways of doing
things, is embedded in the very *physical* constitution of human
beings. Physically he is formed for specifically human activities.

Superficial similarities between apes and men should never
lead us to neglect what is thoroughly human. For instance,
the comparatively short legs of the human child at birth are
not a reminiscence of the short legs of its hypothetical ancestors.

G

It is much more likely due to the fact that the human child's brain is so large (in proportion to the adult human brain much larger than the young ape's brain is to the adult ape's); consequently the rapid development of the child's body (legs included) seems to be retarded until this large and complex brain-structure has accommodated itself to the rest of the body. And so the legs begin to grow longer more quickly when the child itself is making its first efforts to stand. They had remained proportionately short for specifically human purposes.

These biologists, who have taken the view that man is not most profitably studied by asking whether he is a decadent ape, have proposed similar positive, human accounts of the rest of man's body. The human eye, for instance, does not have anything like the keenness of a vulture's; Helmholtz declared that he would give an extremely low mark to any optician who constructed such an imprecise instrument as the human eye. And, indeed, for the specialized tasks of hunting or spotting an enemy the human eye is very imperfect. But surely the most reasonable explanation is that our eyes are not intended primarily for that purpose. For purposes of seeing the world as a whole, catching the interrelations of things, for appreciating beauty, and affording a contemplative mirror of the world, our eyes are admirably adapted. And since our eyes are admirably adapted for this purpose it may well be because we are not vultures, nor predatory animals, but beings who are meant to gaze in wonder at the beauty of the world, to reflect that beauty in ourselves, and to see that it is good.[42]

A similar positive interpretation of our having so little hair on our bodies has been proposed. The explanation is not that we are decadent apes who have lost our hair. On the contrary, the fact that our skin is bare of the ape's thick hair means that it is many times more sensitive; it leaves room for a far greater number of nerve endings, which itself demands a very high level of central nerve-structure such as only human beings possess. And so the hair-distribution peculiar to man tremendously increases our range of feeling; it enables us to be more sensitive to the world, to catch its intensity and fine shadings very much as our eyes catch its beauty.

Other parts of the human body have been studied along the same lines, and it has been shown that laughing and weeping and talking are essentially different from animal activities (which, at a superficial glance, seem so similar), for laughing, weeping and talking are specifically *human* activities.[43] The net result of all these studies is to show that, from a biological point of view, man is a comparatively unspecialized creature, because his various bodily organs are not specially shaped for any biological purpose in the same way that, say, the vulture is specially fitted for preying upon other creatures. For instance, whereas all the apes have hands specially shaped for some particular task, such as climbing,[44] the human hand is not shaped for any of these particular purposes. This lack of specialization may seem an imperfection, in that men cannot climb as well as apes nor pick out objects so well as vultures, but it is, in fact, the essential condition of that freedom which sets man above these creatures, for man has a hand which he can turn to any purpose. Man's whole constitution (his eyes, his sensitive skin, his unspecialized hand, etc.) means to say that his range of vision, feeling and activity opens up an immensely wide horizon; as a non-specialist creature he is not confined to the grooves into which their specialized organs force other creatures. This creature, man, is a free creature, as even his bodily constitution suggests.

Furthermore, there are certain aspects of human behaviour which, as the biologist must surely see, have to be examined in their human context and cannot be paralleled in any animal context. For instance, human societies in every age have attached a special human dignity and value to those of their members who refuse to satisfy their fundamental biological urges. These people (ascetics, such as priests, monks, nuns, etc.) freely deny themselves their desire for nourishment and for sexual intercourse, and by doing so place themselves outside biological categories; their lives are, on any judgement, as real as the life of an ape, but the values which they embody cannot come within the scope of biological judgement. And an even more clinching illustration of how totally inadequate biological categories are for judging man, is provided by the case of the man who lays down his life for his friends, whether in war or in peace. From a biological standpoint such a man is committing suicide; in his death he reaches the very lowest biological level; from a human standpoint such a death is the noblest of human acts, and by it man reaches the very highest level of all. Man is a sacrificing animal who lays down this mortal life in the hope of eternal bliss.

And so the study of man by biological methods leads us to suppose that there is a principle of activity in man which cannot be derived from his bodily needs. This principle we call spirit. According to Christian teaching this spirit was breathed into the first man by God; and in the light of what we have been saying so far, this Christian account of man's origin fits in with the hypothesis of sound biology.

If a biologist could transport himself back to observe the formation of the first man he would have to look for a protected place, rich in natural food and drink; for only in such a place could the biologically helpless creature, man, hope to survive with his offspring.[45] This place is known in the Christian tradition as the garden of Paradise. In comparing this man with his immediate ancestor our modern biologist would observe that there were radical *physical* differences, and he would say that this was an "instance of a large mutation" or "macro-evolution" (cf. Goldschmidt p. 173, Schindewolf p. 171). Of course, the biologist would not be able to observe the infusion of spirit into this man, but he would be able to observe some of the startling physical differences from the man's immediate ancestors, which this infusion of spirit caused. The eyes would be different, and the hands, and he would be less hairy. Above all he would be struck by the man's ability to speak, for when the spirit was breathed into him the man began to say "Thou", saying "Thou" to other creatures and to the Spirit from which he had received the spirit. The biologist would realize that the man had *received* this word, this ability to speak, from the Spirit, because "it is impossible to imagine a being whose mental condition is mature enough to discover words and does not already possess words."[46] He would also realize that these changes he observed must have taken place simultaneously, for even one of them, if it had occurred in isolation, would have unbalanced the creature's anatomy and nervous system. This simultaneous change of the whole system (due to the infusion of the tremendous spirit) would escape him in part. But the fact that this man said "Thou" might lead him to examine the new vocal system. He would discover that whereas the sympathetic system of other animals was essentially coupled with their sexual regions, in man the essential link is between the sympathetic system and the vocal system. So that the energy which at one time was directed towards sexual satisfaction can now receive expression in the genuine spiritual communion of a being who says "Thou".[47]

"In the beginning was the Word". Remembering this phrase the biologist might seek for some explanation of these events in the Bible. Being a good scientist he would not be content with the second-hand account of the Biblical story given by many Christians. For many Christians would revolt in horror at his remark that they derive their bodies from other creatures—though, the biologist would note with a smile, they seem to have no objection to their being derived from the slime of the earth! And he would scarcely be happy with those who claim that this all happened only 4,000 years ago; he knows better than that, just as he knows that man has an equal number of ribs on either side, and so did not give up one rib for the formation of woman. He would, perhaps, reflect that the biologists can at least teach people how *not* to read the Bible, feeling glad that he in his humble way had taught people something about God's ways. He would remember the years in which theologians had rejected this knowledge about God's ways just because it did not fit in with their preconceived notions, and just as they had refused to learn from Galileo. He and Galileo had taught Christians how to read the Bible better, anyway. Not content with this negative attitude he begins to read the Bible for himself, but soon realizes that the English translation may translate words but cannot translate primitive Hebrew modes of thought and speech. For instance, "the dust of the earth"—what did that signify for the person who wrote under the guidance of the Spirit? Nearly all words for physical things in Hebrew carry a moral connotation along with them, and the writer probably had in mind that God had raised up

man from the lowest, from nothingness.[48]   Again, some Semites
speak of their best friend as their "rib"; was there not some
such meaning in the statement about Eve's formation from
Adam's "rib"?[49]   Again, our biologist might wonder, is there
not some special significance in the fact that Adam, the first
man, was "cast into a deep sleep" during the formation of Eve?
Does that not suggest that recent theories of deep psychology
might throw some light on this passage?[50]   Pondering upon
these events he would conclude that the interpretation of the
Bible needs a good deal more thought than it has often received,
and that God sees that it is good for us to use our knowledge
of all the sciences of biology, psychology, history and all
others, in order to appreciate God's play in creation.

NOTES

[1] Quoted by E. C. Messenger in *Evolution and Theology*, p. 22.   For a
fine illustration of how bad theology complicated the situation, compare
the attitude of Philip Gosse, one of the Plymouth Brethren.   He maintained that God created the world about 4,000 years B.C., complete
with fossils, so that it looked as though evolution had taken place!

[2] *S.Th.* I. Q. 21, art. 2.

[3] c.f. *Q. disputatae de Potentia*, Q. 3, art. 11 and 12.   For a brilliant
discussion of the Thomist viewpoint cf. Père Salman O.P. in *Revue des
Sciences Philosophiques et Théologiques*, 1949, pp. 390–421.

[4] *Herder-Korrespondenz* 1948, p. 247.   Catholic theologians who have
expressed themselves similarly include P. Teilhard de Chardin, S.J.,
Mgr. de Solages, Abbé H. Breuil, F. Rüschkamp, S.J.   F. Rüschkamp says
quite definitely, "E. Haeckel postulated that there was a *Pithecanthropus*,
i.e. an early man with ape-like characteristics; E. Dubois looked for him
and found him, and the excavations in the cave-dwellings of early man
at Peking have confirmed this.   The classical form of the evolutionary
theory is no longer a hypothesis." (quoted by Gerhard Benl, *Philosophia
Naturalis*, Meisenheim/Glau., Westkulturverlag Anton Hain, 1950, p. 123.)

[5] GERHARD BENL, *Philosophia Naturalis*, p. 131.

[6] cf. MAX BORN, *Science News*, No. 17, p. 26.

[7] cf. H. J. MULLER in *Genetics, Palaeontology and Evolution*, ed. G. L. Jepser,
E. Mayr, and G. G. Simpson, Princeton University Press, 1949, pp. 421–425.

[8] cf. for example, the question of "drift", *Genetics, Palaeontology and
Evolution*.

[9] It is interesting to notice that Professor J. B. S. Haldane recognizes
this, whilst the Anglican Bishop of Birmingham does not.   Even from a
scientific point of view there are disadvantages in always trying to be
one step ahead of the scientists.

[10] W. R. Thompson. (*Science and Common Sense*, Longmans Green & Co., 1937, p. 218) quotes the remark of Alfred Giard, "We shall never make protoplasm, because protoplasm has a *history*". Thompson himself then says, "If, therefore, the transformations of the organic world are due in all cases to individual successions of fortuitous events, it is clear that any theory of Evolution that would enable us to give an exact scientific statement as to the causes and course of any stage in this transformation is impossible, and that we are dealing not with Science but with History—in the absence of documents or testimony on which, alone, history can be built".

[11] H. E. WOOD, *Genetics, Palaeontology and Evolution*, p. 187.

[12] cf. LECOMTE DU NOUY, *Human Destiny*, Longmans Green & Co., 1947, p. 59.

[13] JULIAN HUXLEY, *Evolution, The Modern Synthesis*, Allen & Unwin, 1942, p. 157.

[14] There are other factors to be considered, of course, such as hypotheses, which seem well-founded but are not in accordance with it.

[15] cf. the similar remark of Schroedinger (*What is Life?* Cambridge University Press, 1945, p. 46) where he points out that from the point of view of statistical physics the "regular and lawful activity" of the gene "borders on the miraculous". More and more this notion of the miraculous is being invoked the further statistical methods are used in the physical sciences.

[16] cf. OTTO SPÜLBECK, *Der Christ und das Weltbild der modernen Naturwissenschaft*, Berlin, Morus-Verlag, pp. 106–107.

[17] cf. G. G. SIMPSON, *Tempo and Mode in Evolution*, Columbia University Press, 1944.

[18] "Phyletic taxonomic rates of evolution vary inversely with the inclusiveness of the taxonomic category involved. Subspecies evolve more rapidly than species in the same group, species more rapidly than genera, and so on. This appears obvious, but it has an important bearing on evolutionary theory, because it does not seem (to me) to be consistent with the view that species, genera or higher categories normally arise by 'systematic mutations'." G. G. SIMPSON, *Genetics, Palaeontology and Evolution*, p. 216.

[19] Though cf. Simpson's *Tempo and Mode in Evolution*.

[20] cf. D. M. S. Watson, "All or at least the great majority of characters in horses whose evolutionary change is known are (or may be) due to the effect of increasing size and the necessary food and mechanical requirements that go with it". *Genetics, Palaeontology and Evolution*, p. 52.

[21] GOLDSCHMIDT, *The Material Basis of Evolution*, New Haven, Yale University Press, 1940, p. 183.

[22] Quoted by Julian Huxley, *Evolution, The Modern Synthesis*, p. 474.

[23] *Origin of Species*, p. 146.

[24] Hopwood, quoted in *Genetics, Palaeontology and Evolution*, p. 222.

[25] A. S. ROMER, *Genetics, Palaeontology and Evolution*, pp. 105–6.

[26] Ibid., p. 83. The "reductions" in these cases are more difficult to believe than even the farthest-fetched instances of telepathy.

194   RECENT THOUGHT IN FOCUS

²⁷ cf. Bally's excellent book, *Vom Ursprung und von den Grenzen der Freiheit*, p. 25. Basel, Benno Schwabe & Co., 1945.

²⁸ Ibid., p. 26.

²⁹ cf. HANS ANDRÉ, "*Überwindung des Biologismus durch die Biologie*" *Katholische Gedanke* 1946, and MAISIE WARD, *Splendour of the Rosary*, p. 128, where she tells of T. H. Huxley saying that the very existence of flowers, with their gratuitous beauty, was the most convincing argument for a Creator.

³⁰ B. Bavink. Quoted by Gerhard Benl, *Philosophia Naturalis*, 1950, p. 127.

³¹ J. KLÄIN, *Hochland*, April 1950.

³² W. KOPPERS, *Primitive Man and his World Picture*, (English ed.) Sheed and Ward, 1952, p. 68.

³³ cf. Koppers, pp. 67–69.

³⁴ KÄLIN, *Hochland*, April, 1950.

³⁵ cf. VERA BARCLAY, *Darwin is Not for Children*, Jenkins, 1950. p. 60.

³⁶ WOOD JONES, *Hallmarks of Mankind*, Bailliere, 1948, pp. 79–86.

³⁷ cf. Sir Arthur Keith's *The Antiquity of Man*.

³⁸ *Humani Generis*, English translation, Catholic Truth Society, p. 21.

³⁹ cf. L. S. B. LEAKEY, "The Early History of Man", *Science News* 17.

⁴⁰ e.g. the Ehringsdorf skull, the earliest known Neanderthal skull, is one of the least "primitive", whilst the La-Chapelle-aux-Saints skeleton is very "primitive", and yet it comes from a later time, when Neanderthal man was approaching extinction.

⁴¹ cf. ADOLF PORTMANN, *Biologische Fragmente zu einer Lehre vom Menschen* Basel, Benno Schwabe & Co., Verlag, 1944: GUSLAV BALLY, *Vom Ursprung und von den Grenzen der Freiheit*: A. GEHLEN, *Der Mensch*. It is interesting to notice that these "modern" observations had been observed in principle by St. Thomas, *S.Th.* I. Q. 76, art. 5.

⁴² cf. HANS ANDRÉ, op. cit.   He refers to Goethe's acute observations on the human eye.

⁴³ cf. H. PLESSNER, *Lachen und Weinen*, Arnhem, 1941: G. RÉVÉSZ, *Ursprung und Vorgeschichte der Sprache*, Bern, Francke AG Verlag, 1946.

⁴⁴ cf. the division of these specialized hands in Kälin, *Hochland*, April 1950.

⁴⁵ cf. PORTMANN, *Biologische Fragmente*, p. 134.

⁴⁶ The phrase is from G. RÉVÉSZ, *Ursprung und Vorgeschichte der Sprache*.

⁴⁷ HANS ANDRÉ. Op. cit.; and KÜLENKAMPFF. "Über den Einbau des Sympathicus-Systems in das cerebrospinale System", *Hippokrates*, No. 17, Stuttgart, 1950.

⁴⁸ cf. CHAINE, *Le livre de Genèse*, Paris, Editions du Cerf, 1948.

⁴⁹ cf. *Downside Review*, 1951, p. 29.

⁵⁰ The application of deep-psychology to Scripture is still very tentative, but an excellent example of the insights it affords is to be found in Dr. Schärf's "Die Gestalt des Satans im Alten Testament" (in Jung's *Symbolik des Geistes*, Zürich, Rascher Verlag, 1948).

III

PSYCHOLOGY

At first sight one may find it curious to have a chapter on psychology following chapters on biology rather than those on philosophy, because the study of the soul would seem to be more nearly related to philosophy than to the natural sciences. But this order is in accordance with the principles of St. Thomas, who says that psychology is to be classed firstly amongst the natural, or physical sciences[1]—because the soul is the form of the body, and physical functions are most intimately related to mental functions.

Nevertheless St. Thomas was well aware that the methods of the natural sciences do not provide an exhaustive account of the human soul, and referred to other aspects of psychology, which require a philosophical and even theological explanation. Indeed, since every science is the result of operations by a human soul which can investigate any aspect of the universe, the study of this human soul itself is related to every science. Since psychology is related to every science, no matter how remotely, it means that psychology itself has almost as many branches as there are sciences, each using very different methods. For instance, one group of psychologists, the experimental psychologists, more or less conform to the quantitative measuring methods of the physicists; another group, the graphologists, try to discover persons' temperaments through reading their handwriting; while yet others, the psychical researchers, try to sift the evidence for communication taking place between different persons without the use of sense perception. And each of these methods has recorded successes. As a result of experimental psychology, for example, it has been possible to cut away parts of certain melancholy people's brains, after which they have become cheerful. Or we encounter the case of a graphologist who not only correctly predicted that a certain person would kill himself, but even predicted the method he would use, i.e. by hanging himself. Furthermore, the psychical researchers have gathered evidence for extra-sensory perception which must be taken into account by anyone who in future attempts a comprehensive treatment of psychology. Such comprehensive treatment, clearly, is out of the question here, where we have only a few pages at our disposal, and which we therefore intend to devote to surveying the implications behind the researches of Freud and Jung. This is a very restricted subject (but not, therefore, a simple one!), and is of particular importance, because many Freudian and Jungian concepts have gained popular acceptance without always being critically tested. For those of us who are primarily concerned with method, this critical examination of concepts and their practical consequences for our lives are of first importance.

When considering Freudian theories about human behaviour we have to remember the principle stated on an earlier page: that you cannot satisfactorily judge a theory or hypothesis until you have seen a good deal of the evidence which it is meant to account for. Applying this to Freud's studies, it means that you need to examine some of the cases of mental disorder which Freud was trying to cure before you can judge the theories by which he attempts to account for these disorders. In other words, Freudian theory follows from Freudian practice; and therefore many of the objections to the theory can scarcely help seeming academic and unreal to the Freudian. His reply is often reminiscent of the blind man in the Gospels who answered the casuistry of the Pharisees by saying, "All I know is that once I was blind, and now I can see". Similarly the Freudian can reply that his methods may be "unscientific" in the sense of not producing "laws" comparable to those of the physicist, but that he does at least *cure* people on the basis of them. And since his psycho-analysis is a practical science the test of whether it is scientific is whether it does, in fact, cure people. Of course, the story of the blind man in the Gospels does not afford an exact parallel, because it is very easy to determine whether a person is cured of blindness but not so easy to determine whether he has been cured of mental troubles. But there are occasions when the parallel needs to be borne in mind, because the surest way to see what Freud is getting at consists in reading through the case-histories which he describes.

Freud however was not only a doctor; he was a first-class doctor, who observed a good deal more than his patients' symptoms. Freud noticed that a great many symptoms of physical disorder were to be traced to conflicts in his patients' minds. He saw that mental conflicts can result in illnesses of the body. And therefore, in spite of a wide-spread opinion to the contrary, Freud unwittingly showed the inadequacy of an ex-clusively physical account of man, ranging himself on this point with St. Thomas Aquinas. For St. Thomas states that mental disturbances, such as fear and anger, may harm the body, that sadness does so most frequently ("and sometimes leads to melancholy and madness").[2]

Freud, however, went further than St. Thomas. Whereas St. Thomas mainly concerned himself with conscious mental conflicts Freud located the source of neurosis in *unconscious* con-flicts. It may happen, for instance, that a person goes blind, really does not see things, although there is nothing physically wrong with that person's eyes. A possible explanation is that the person unconsciously wants to shut out the world from sight and therefore (for motives which he has driven into the uncon-scious) goes blind. The way to cure such a person of blindness is to bring the unconscious motives to consciousness, and get him to face up to the real reason why he wishes to shut out the world, thus resolving the conflict and curing the blindness.

In his "discovery" of the unconscious and its workings Freud has proved himself a pioneer of the first order;[3] he has shown that a human being is rather like an iceberg, four-fifths of which is below the surface, just as four-fifths of a human being is below consciousness. And yet it is precisely this magnificent discovery of Freud's which has been disputed on most trivial grounds. The objectors have said, for instance, that if you can become con-scious of the unconscious then it is no longer the unconscious, therefore there can be no science of the unconscious.

This trivial objection implies a complete failure to understand scientific method. For the "unconscious" is something we postulate in order to account for certain aspects of conscious behaviour which would be incomprehensible apart from the assumption of an "unconscious". This method is exactly parallel to that by which we speak of "genes" in biology or "electrons" in physics; the "unconscious" is an explanatory concept referring to non-conscious activity and to which we can attribute certain characteristics in order to account for conscious activity—just as we attribute certain qualities to "genes" (which we cannot directly observe) in order to explain characteristics which we can observe directly. And the fact that there is a parallel between postulating an "unconscious" and postulating "genes" or "electrons" helps us to see that investigation of the unconscious may proceed scientifically. We have already learnt not to deny that a method is scientific—so long as it gives us knowledge—although it is not the method of the current dominant science. Undoubtedly Freudian analysis has brought us knowledge about the unconscious; therefore we do not ask ourselves whether this knowledge is scientific but *in what way* it is scientific.

Now the scientific method of psycho-analysis is not altogether the same as that of Aristotelian science, which proceeds from the particular to the general. For instance, the analyst does not assume that a particular image in a dream— say, a lamp-standard—allows him to generalize about lamp-standards in dreams generally, since different people may dream about lamp-standards for quite different reasons, depending upon the circumstances of their lives and their past experiences. Nor is the scientific method of psycho-analysis the same as that of Newtonian physics, which infers universally applicable laws from events. For example, an analyst may be confronted with a dream in which a policeman is thrown into a pond and changes into a mermaid; he does not try to work out whether there is a relationship of cause and effect between the event of a policeman being thrown into a pond and the event of a mermaid's appearance. Instead, he has to relate the images of the policeman, the pond and the mermaid, not to each other but to the dreamer and his whole past—for any event in the dreamer's past *may* be related to the occurrence of these images. Since according to Freud the appearance of these images is a result of the dreamer's past history the method employed to explain their appearance is more nearly the method of *history* than of the physical sciences. And therefore the scientific status of psycho-analysis is bound up with the scientific status of history (cf. p. 193 for the historical basis of evolution, and p. 167, for genetics).

Leaving aside any detailed examination of Freudian method (a subject which has been brilliantly dealt with by Roland Dalbeiz[4]), what are the most striking happenings for which we seek an explanation in the unconscious and which allow us to see how the unconscious works? One such type of happening is the *Fehlleistung*, when we do something or say something which gives away what is going on in our unconscious. Everyone is aware of having committed a *Fehlleistung* at one time or another. For example, the manager of a business firm has been ill for a long time and his deputy has been to see him many times during his illness. One day as the deputy is leaving the manager's house after such a visit, the two of them are talking about future plans and the deputy, instead of saying, "When are you going to come back?", says, to his horror, "When are you going to retire?" His *Fehlleistung* has betrayed what was going on in his unconscious.

An even more frequent manifestation of the unconscious is given in our dreams, for, according to Freud, our dreams represent to us, in a disguised form, the desires which we have consciously repressed. Therefore the study and interpretation of dreams is the key to the unconscious. On the basis of his dream-interpretation Freud constructed a picture of the human person—or rather, he constructed several pictures, that of his later writings being rather different from the earlier one. In the earlier one the components of the person were the conscious and the unconscious, with a "censor" as it were regulating the traffic between the two. Any unconscious drive which would not have seemed respectable to the conscious was held up by the censor, and disguised in obscure images; it was the psycho-analyst's task to penetrate these disguises and reveal the unconscious desires. In his later theory Freud presents rather different components, the ego, the id and the super-ego, the last-named of which may be either conscious or unconscious. The fact that his earlier and later components are rather different does not mean to say that Freud was inconsistent. It merely indicates a refinement of his theories, since the ego, the id and super-ego were intended to fulfil very much the same functions as the conscious, the unconscious and the censor. But, in any case, all these concepts are hypothetical, and so obviously subject to revision that their value can only be adequately assessed in terms of case-material. However, so long as we are constantly aware of their being hypothetical we shall no more fall into the habit of thinking of them as real *things* than of imagining that "genes" are real *things*.

It is because Freud did not always remember how subject to revision his concepts were that he committed errors in method. Once these errors are pointed out and Freud's teachings put through the screen of criticism, there is no reason for not accepting a chastened Freudianism into our integrated vision of the world.

Freud's primary mistake[5] lay in a tendency to turn his empirical psycho-analytical concepts into a philosophy of man, using operational notions such as "Oedipus complex" as if they were metaphysical judgements upon the nature of man. This transference of concepts sometimes produces fantastic results, as when one of Freud's most earnest disciples assures us that "it is not far short of the mark to say that the human race can be divided up into hysterical, obsessional, depressive, alcoholic, hypochondriacal, paranoid, schizoid and psychopathic *types*, meaning thereby that they exploit in their individual and social relations unconscious mechanisms which if more exaggerated would give rise to classical neurotic, psychotic or psychopathic symptoms."[6] (!)

This transference of notions was particularly dangerous in the case of Freud because he was unaware that it was taking place, as he admits: "even when I have moved away from observation I have carefully avoided any contact with philosophy proper. This avoidance has been greatly facilitated by constitutional incapacity."[7] But here Freud was deceiving himself, for he was influenced by the pessimist philosopher Schopenhauer; furthermore, he unquestioningly accepted the *philosophical* assumptions embedded in the biology which was current in his youth. Consequently he had an unconscious philosophy in terms of which he interpreted the cases he examined. It was not only that he *constructed* a philosophy on the basis of his psycho-analytical work, it was that he viewed his patients in the light of his own unconscious philosophical presuppositions.[8]

As illustration of his biologically determined philosophy, combined with Schopenhauer's pessimism, consider his teaching that there is in each human being a "death instinct". Biologists in those days used to employ the word "instinct" whenever they wanted to explain some aspect of human behaviour, and Freud simply took over this pseudo-philosophical concept. But the concept of "instinct" is so vague as to be almost meaning-less; one can invent an instinct (or a complex) corresponding to any situation in human life, and different investigators have named hundreds of "instincts". In view of the number of people with a craving for cigarettes, why not say, for instance, that modern man has a "smoking-instinct"? Furthermore, in view of the wide-spread belief amongst human beings that they survive death, would it not be more reasonable to attribute to man an "immortality instinct" rather than a "death instinct"? Freud's choice of the latter alternative, we may suppose, was a result of his pessimistic philosophy rather than of scientific considerations. And his "death instinct" seems an even less convincing hypothesis nowadays, when biologists themselves have begun to see how inadequate is the concept of "instinct".[9] The whole story of the "death instinct" is a warning against scientists' accepting pseudo-philosophical presuppositions from another science—for these presuppositions change very rapidly, leaving those who have rested upon them high and dry, as Freud was left high and dry by developments in biology.

How fatal his uncritical acceptance of a particular philosophy proved is obvious from his declaration that the language of psychology must necessarily remain metaphorical and un-satisfactory, "until we shall be able to substitute the proper physiological and chemical terms for it. Though the latter are also metaphorical, they are at least more familiar and perhaps also simpler".[10] Here Freud is blatantly declaring his prejudice in favour of a materialist philosophy which aims at reducing all psychological events to bodily processes. This philosophical programme involved him in difficulties even with his psychology since it led him to teach that each instinct must have a bodily organ corresponding to it;[11] but in that case what is the bodily organ corresponding to the death "instinct"?[12] Of course, Freud could find no such bodily organ and so he was compelled to reduce all manifestations of life to variations of the sexual instinct—because at least you can point to sexual organs.

And therefore Freud's method left him faced with the formidable task of explaining the whole of human activity as so many variations upon the sexual instinct. How did he carry out this task? Having narrowed down human activity to sexual activity, how did he account for the varied and many-sided aspects of human behaviour? Quite simply by broadening the meaning of "sexual" until it included all these varied aspects; so that in the end we find him saying, "thus the Libido of our sexual instincts would coincide with the Eros of poets and philosophers, which holds together all things living."[13] But if "sexual" means all that, if it means everything that poets and philosophers mean by "Eros" then the term has become so inclusive as to provide no means of distinguishing between the various principles upon which human beings act. We are left with the possibility that a regular Don Juan may, in fact, be a perverted mystic whose desire for God has been turned into sexual channels; or the other possibility, that the mystic may be a sexual pervert whose sexual desires have been turned towards an imaginary God.

It is worth while stating the method by which Freud arrived at this indecisive position,[14] because it illustrates several points made earlier in this book.

The main point is that Freud's method is positivist (cf. p. 37); he is so concerned to discover a few factors which cause the mental states of human beings that he pays scant attention to the mental states and their complexities.[15] Being in such a hurry to discover *causes* he does not give an adequate description of the *states* he is explaining (he does not appreciate the need for a phenomenological method—he is so absorbed in the roots that he does not see the flower).

. Having begun by simplifying the situation, and isolating a few explanatory factors, he then paints a picture of human beings in terms of these few factors. When he looks at his picture, he sees, like all positivists, that the human beings whom he lives with are not recognizable as the ones he has painted. His original explanatory factors, therefore, are not sufficient causes for the activity he is trying to explain; in order to make them sufficient he broadens their meaning until they are almost beyond recognition. Consequently Freud comes to speak of libido, which was at first narrowly sexual, as "holding together all living things". The process by which this change of meaning occurred is a warning to us to make an adequate phenomenological description at the beginning of our enquiries, otherwise we have to make drastic revisions of our theories at the end (cf. the way in which Darwin isolated the factor of "natural selection" and then had to broaden the scope of the term until it became "a power, always intently watching each slight alteration").

These observations upon Freud's philosophy have inevitably been negative because his philosophy was itself so inadequate. They are not in the least meant to cast doubt upon Freud's greatness as a psychologist, for his discoveries about the unconscious will certainly prove to be of incalculable importance in the future development of human beings. Nor is it necessary for us to deny that sexual excitement plays a great part in all our lives; it is only necessary to point out that this factor is not the only one to be considered. As a matter of fact Freud's protest against sexual repression can be taken as a symptomatic protest of the European mind against that disrespect for sexual activity with which Europeans had become obsessed for centuries. This horror of sexual activity is ultimately an insult to the Creator who created us with sexual organs, and is clean contrary to orthodox Christian teaching—although the insult has often been voiced by Christians.

One cannot help wondering sometimes what the reaction of

a prudish Christian lady would have been if she had received the message of the Annunciation. Not, one imagines, the clear, pure answer of the Mother of God, who said to the angel, "How can that be, since I have no knowledge of man?" Here is neither repression nor obsession; the Mother of God simply and humbly accepts the fact that she is a creature; she naturally expects to give birth to her Child in the same way as all other creatures; but if her Creator decides otherwise, then she welcomes this new manifestation of his will just as humbly.

Again one wonders what such Christians make of the liturgy for the blessing of fonts on Holy Saturday, when the Church makes unhesitating use of sexual symbols. In the prayers the priest mentions "the immaculate womb of this divine font" (the womb of our Mother, the Church); he then plunges the Paschal Candle into the water three times, singing each time in a higher tone, "May the virtue of the Holy Ghost descend into all the water of this font . . . and make the whole substance of this water fruitful and capable of regenerating."

Finally, once we accept the fact of sexual excitement in our lives we can integrate it into a sane view of the world, and it ceases to be an obsession. Those Christians, for instance, who feel sexual excitement at the height of their devotional life will not be worried by it. For since we are whole persons, since we commit our whole persons, body and soul, to God, the tension of this self-giving produces tremors, no matter how slight, at every level of our organism, stirring of our wills, of our intellects and of our senses, including those associated with sexual activity. To accept these stirrings as part of our human condition is a sign of a healthy psychology, for which we are considerably indebted to Freud.

The second great name in modern psychology is that of Alfred Adler, who, like Freud, came from Vienna. The depressed level of society from which he came led Adler to attach primary importance to social maladjustment, rather than to sex, as a cause of neurosis. For in place of the sexual instinct Adler sets the drive for power: human beings are constantly working out an adjustment between their drive for power and the claims of society. For instance, a mother, whose daughter is about to marry, unconsciously wishes to maintain her power over her daughter, but will not consciously admit this to herself; consequently a complex arises. She develops a neurotic illness which makes it necessary for her daughter to wait upon her hand and foot; the daughter and her husband cannot establish a separate home of their own as a result. In this way the mother has managed to realize her unconscious drive for power.

This example could be paralleled by similar ones from each of our lives, which fact alone is enough to show how widely Adler's principles may be applied. [16] Nevertheless his psychology is open to the same fundamental objection as Freud's: he takes one factor in our behaviour, and treats it as if it were the only factor. He makes the desire for power into an absolute, just as Freud makes the sexual instinct into an absolute. From the point of view of *method* they are both open to the same objection.

It is because he avoids these common errors in method that Jung (the third great name) must be considered here at rather more length.

Even in his very approach to a patient the Jungian analyst's attitude differs strikingly from Freud's or Adler's, and eliminates one-sided interpretations. A Freudian, like all positivists hurrying towards causes, approaches the patient convinced that he is going to find a sexual cause for the conflict—and, of course, he does; for once a person is convinced that he is going to find such a cause he will say that he does so—despite appearances to the contrary. If, that is to say, the patient's unconscious does not display images and symbols obviously associated with sexual activity then the Freudian explanation is not that the conflict is non-sexual, but that the sexual instincts have been so deeply repressed, pushed so far down, that the sexual contents have been almost completely disguised. He then goes on to strip off these disguises and reveals naked sexual causes. In other words, he is playing "heads I win, tails you lose"; since the Freudian will not accept any other explanation than a sexual one he will go on analysing his patient until he comes to something which he declares to be sexual. [17]

The Jungian's approach, on the contrary, is typically phenomenological; he is in no hurry to reduce the complexity of the patient's symbolic activity to any single, isolated factor, for this activity is an expression of the patient's whole personality. And so the source of the conflict only becomes apparent as the patient's personality unfolds itself during the course of analysis. Of course, it may turn out to be mainly sexual, or it may turn out to be mainly a question of social adjustment; but in any case the Jungian does not decide in advance what it is going to be.

A further distinctive feature of Jung's approach is that it is positive rather than negative (by an odd twist of language negative attitudes are characteristic of "positivists"!). Whereas Freud sees neurosis as a sign of disease, [18] for the causes of which one has to look backwards into the past, Jung sees neurosis as a symptom of the diseased person's desire for health, pointing to the future; the neurotic symptoms represent a protest on the part of the organism against being diseased. They are, therefore, not only backward-looking but also forward-looking, looking forward to wholeness and health. Consequently to reduce the symbolic activity of a neurotic to a sexual cause would be, quite literally, to miss the point, [19] to miss the pointer towards health which nature is holding out in the form of neurosis. All neurosis, according to Jung, is an attempt to find a substitute for *legitimate* suffering; when God asks us for one thing we give him another. Jung's task, as he sees it, is to get his patient to face up to his legitimate suffering, thus eliminating the illegitimate substitute (i.e. the neurosis). [20] But the clue to the legitimate suffering will be found in the content of the neurosis itself, which points forwards to the solution as well as backwards to the origin of the conflict.

Even in his very approach towards mental disorder, then, Jung displays a fundamentally hopeful and positive view of life. He knows perfectly well that a flower has roots in the dark earth but this does not convince him that the flower is "nothing but roots"; on the contrary he sees the blossoming of the flower as the purpose which the roots are meant to serve. Similarly he does not regard art, religion, heroism and other qualities of culture as nothing but perversions of the sexual instinct. On the contrary, he believes that libido is there precisely to be

formed into beautiful art, devout religion and heroic virtue, as well as promoting sexual intercourse. The fact of transformation is just as well established as the fact of sexual intercourse, and from a strictly psychological standpoint there is no need to make either of them primary—but neither of them can be denied. That will be the time to accept Freudian pessimism when apples refuse to grow on apple-trees and roses refuse to bud.

This fact of the *transformation* of psychic energy may be regarded as the central one for understanding Jung's thought. It enables him to do justice to all the *forms* which that energy takes, the sexual forms, [21] the religious forms and the artistic forms; none of the *actual* manifestations of psychic energy is treated as illusory just because it cannot be immediately reduced to some *hypothetical* sexual cause. Furthermore it enables Jung to paint a picture of the human person which is not unlike the persons we encounter in our everyday life. But before singling out the elements of the Jungian picture one must repeat that the picture itself is only a by-product of Jung's work; it is, in fact, a sketch to which Jung occasionally turns to add some fresh line when he pauses from his main task, the healing of human beings.

Beginning on the circumference of human beings we encounter what Jung calls the "persona". This "persona" is very far from being the same as our word "person" (which signifies that in nature which has the greatest perfection). "Persona" is a Latin word for the mask which actors used to wear, and therefore, in Jung's scheme, a human being's persona is the mask, as it were, in which he faces the world; it is the function which he believes himself (sometimes rightly) to perform in society. A human being who identifies his persona and his self, who allows himself to be completely absorbed into his office or function, remains an empty shell—he lacks profundity. Examples of those who do this are professors who act the part of professors all the time and are small-minded outside the lecture-room, or civil servants who kill their real selves in their office. Other instances of it are those men who present virtuous and immaculate faces to the world but who, once we penetrate

behind their masks and see their behaviour at home, are seen
to be quarrelsome and vindictive.

Immediately behind the persona we find, not the real *self*,
but the ego, the conscious part of man. It is the ego, the
conscious, which directs the movements of the persona. Once
more, just as some people identify themselves with their persona,
likewise others identify themselves with their conscious part,
their ego; and the results are just as disastrous. By treating
their conscious part as if it were the whole of themselves they
court disaster, for they cut off consciousness from its roots in
the unconscious. To isolate a part of oneself is the sure way,
in Jung's view, to produce a complex, for the harmonious
relationship of whole and part is destroyed. The type of person
who does this is easily recognized. Very often he is a self-made
man (the very phrase betokens the pride that comes before a
fall—or a breakdown); very often he is a director or leader of
men, a captain of industry or a captain of empire; he boasts
about never letting the light of consciousness set upon the
empire of his ego. If the disease becomes severe enough he may,
in fact, start dreaming that he *is* the sun (the Sun-God)
circling round and round the earth, who has to keep on circling
round, because he, the sun, is needed to maintain life on earth.
If he were to go to sleep, if he were to accept his unconscious
side, then he would be admitting that he is not the master of
his fate nor the captain of his soul. And so it becomes more and
more difficult for the captain of empire or of industry to go to
sleep—until nature shows to him that he is not the centre of the
universe; he breaks down—but the earth continues on its course.

After the persona and the ego it would seem that we come
to the real *self*. But that is not accurate, for the *self* is the whole
of a human being, conscious and unconscious, finally integrated;
and just as we have seen that we can never know the whole of
any thing or any one until we come to heaven (cf. p. 150),
similarly Jung teaches that the self, the ultimate integration, is
unattainable in this life; the self symbolizes our final *destiny*
rather than expresses our present *condition*. And so, in spite of
(or even because of) the supreme importance which he attaches
to the self, Jung has little definite to say about it, since our self

is not what we are at this moment but the whole that we are continually trying to achieve. [22]

The symbol of the self takes us to that side of our nature with which analytical psychologists are specially concerned, the unconscious. But whereas Freud spoke of the unconscious as though it were something entirely personal, [23] Jung distinguishes between a personal and collective unconscious. For Freud the unconscious is made up of what has been pushed down into it by the conscious: it is full of repressions. And his task, in analysis, is to get rid of those repressions, to prevent them from doing harm. But while Jung also obviously recognizes that each of us has a personal unconscious into which we have cast our repressions, his work has convinced him that there is also a collective unconscious which each of us inherits—and therefore he is bound to regard Freudian analysis (which never reaches beyond the personal to the collective) as superficial.

The occasion which first set Jung on the track of the collective unconscious is worth relating. In 1906 he was treating a patient who believed that he could see a tube coming out of the sun and that it is through this tube that the wind comes to us; four years later scholars discovered the Greek text of a Mithraic liturgy which accounts for the origin of the wind in the same way as Jung's patient. [24] From that moment onwards Jung began to be alive to the number of times that he found symbols and images in his patients almost identical with the symbols, images and myths from the ancient peoples and the literature and folk-lore of many countries. On the basis of these similarities Jung postulated that there is a collective unconscious which each of us inherits from the past of our race. The contents of this collective unconscious may be symbolized in our dreams just as they have been symbolized in the myths of our ancestors, and this information allows us to argue from the meaning of the myths to the meaning of our dreams. Thus we are in a position, so to speak, to interpret what is going on in the unconscious. The practical importance of this was illustrated by the way in which Jung found the myths of Wotan, Thor and other Teutonic gods occurring in the dreams of his German patients during the years preceding Hitler's coming-to-power;

these myths were a foreboding of the worship of the old
Teutonic gods which broke out under the Nazi regime.

Clearly there are many objections to Jung's belief in a collective unconscious,[25] and it could scarcely ever be a well-defined
notion; but it is still true that the figures which Jung attributes
to the collective unconscious do account for obscure aspects of
human behaviour. In other words, it is a valuable hypothesis.

It is from the unconscious that each of us derives his or
her "shadow"; the "shadow" is the dark side of our personality, the side that our conscious is unwilling to recognize.
But each of us has a "shadow",[26] and we have to accept our
"shadow" and bring it into the light, if we are to attain our
true selves. We have to assimilate our shadows, a process
which will only be completed when we know ourselves without
any shadow in heaven; there will be no shadows there because
they will have been assimilated into our selves. But meanwhile
we are usually unwilling to accept our dark side as part of
ourselves; since we do not attribute this dark side to ourselves
we attribute it to other people, we *project* it onto them. In
this way we observe an imaginary mote in our brother's eye
which is really a projection onto him of the beam which is in
our own eye. Thus those Christians, for instance, who harbour
an unconscious hatred for Christ may project this shadow, this
hatred, onto other people, especially onto the Jews, to whom
they attribute a hatred for Christ which is really in themselves.

By studying the content of projections and of dreams, Jung
was able to detect some constant symbols which are part of the
constitution of the unconscious. These he named *archetypes*.
He chose this name because they seem to operate like switches
directing psychic energy into typical patterns of behaviour; and
because each human being throughout the ages has been involved in certain typical situations (relationship to mother,
father, God, society, etc.) the unconscious mechanism for
dealing with these typical situations is described as an archetype. Consequently Jung lists archetypes of Father, of Mother,
of God, of Self and so on, which he has discovered in the
unconscious of his patients. Amongst the archetypal functions
are two in particular which seem to occur with remarkable

frequency. In order to understand these two functions we have to remember that each one of us has a feminine and a masculine side;[27] our feminine side is known as the *anima*, our masculine side as the *animus*. Males, obviously, spend most of their lives stressing their masculine side, they give free play to their *animus*, whilst females usually give free play to their feminine side, their *anima*. But no man or woman is exclusively masculine or exclusively feminine, and both need to give free play to their other sides if they are to achieve wholeness, if they are to be themselves.

What happens if they do not do so? Jung maintains that for centuries European men have, in fact, been failing to give play to their feminine side; they have concentrated so much on their analytical, reasoning faculties, that they have neglected their intuitive, emotional side, which is no less part of them. As a result, European men find themselves in the condition so accurately described by Charles Darwin: "My mind seems to have become a kind of machine for grinding general laws out of large collections of facts, but why this should have caused the atrophy of that part of the brain alone, on which the higher tastes depend, I cannot conceive. . . . The loss of these tastes is a loss of happiness, and may possibly be injurious to the intellect, and more probably to the moral character, by enfeebling the emotional part of our nature".[28] If such a condition were the only result of men concentrating exclusively upon their masculine side it would be regrettable enough, but in fact much worse happens normally. For the *anima* cannot be permanently suppressed, and if it is not given normal expression then it is projected on to someone else. As an illustration of the regularity with which such projection takes place we might consider how frequently intellectual types marry very earthy types of women, ageing professors fall in love with their female students and respectable business men succumb to their secretaries. What is often happening in such cases is that these men, having neglected their feminine side, their *anima*, find their *anima* in the earthy type, the student or the secretary. Their marriages, or their liaisons, are an unconscious substitute for accepting, and reconciling themselves to, their own feminine side. Having married a projection of their own unconscious they then find themselves living with a person who has a real, independent life of her own, sometimes with unhappy results.

Examples of this process occur so often that they provide strong confirmation for Jung's postulate of archetypes. A young man, for instance, devotes himself wholly to his scientific studies and starves his intuitive, emotional desires. Then one day he unconsciously begins projecting his intuitive, feminine, side on-to a girl; the girl becomes for him a redeeming woman, she is everything beautiful, wonderful and good; she is to him as Beatrice was to Dante, or even as Mary, Mother of God, is the redeeming woman to Christians. But it must be remembered that the archetype occasioning the young man's visions is like a switch, which can turn on a negative as well as a positive current. When he is seeing the girl as if she were Beatrice the young man is under the influence of the positive current, from the archetype. Since few girls, however, are really like Dante's Beatrice, the girl in question will at some time act in a way which proves beyond doubt that she is *not* Beatrice! When this happens the young man does not condone her failings as human frailty—because he is not, in fact, looking at a real human being but at an image from his *anima*. He believes that the girl is *completely* different from what he thought she was. Immediately the positive current is changed to a negative current; and the feminine side which he now projects onto her is represented not as Beatrice, but as a witch; she is no longer the redeeming woman but the seductive woman, she is Eve leading man to lose his integrity. (It is no accident that witch-hunting became the sport of European man at the very time that he began to abandon the receptive, feminine, contempla-tive life and started idealizing instead the masterful, he-man captains of empire and trade. In attacking witches he was unconsciously attacking a part of himself which he despised—his neglected feminine side.) This sudden switch-over from a positive to a negative image is an almost certain sign that projection has been taking place.[29]

How to resolve the difficulties arising from a false relation to the unconscious is a problem which occupies many analysts every

day, and does not concern us in our present enquiry. But there
are two aspects of the unconscious, as described by Jung, which
are relevant to our theme. The first, that Jung has been led
to assume in a man a basic psychological need for religion; the
second, that his description of the function of *symbols* is very
reminiscent of what we said earlier about the effective word.

Putting it quite bluntly, Jung said, "During the past thirty
years people from all the civilized countries of the earth have
consulted me. Among all my patients in the second half of
life—that is to say, over thirty-five—there has not been one
whose problem in the last resort was not that of finding a
religious outlook on life. It is safe to say that every one of them
fell ill because he had lost that which the living religions of
every age have given to their followers; and none of them has
been really healed who did not regain this religious outlook".[30]
In psychological terms, each of us has to accept the archetype
of God in our unconscious; the archetype must work in us
whether we like it or not. If we do accept the archetype its
energy becomes integrated into our self; but if we try not to
do so, we block the healthy expression of this energy which then
discovers an outlet in an unconscious religion, a perverse religion full of our own projections. Therefore our religious needs
are just as real as our need for food and drink, and we have to
satisfy them in one way or another.

If this thesis of Jung's is correct it explains certain features
of contemporary philosophy to which we called attention previously. It explains, for instance, why Marxism is an unconscious, perverted form of religion; why the existentialists are
constantly stating problems in terms which they imagine to
be philosophical but are actually religious. It would also
explain why the logical positivists discuss minor matters of
language with theological passion; the passion is a symptom
that they are blocking the energy from their God-archetype.
Perhaps more interesting still, Jung's assumption that each of
us has religious needs would account for the ardour with which
many psycho-analysts, although professing no religion, are in
the habit of "excommunicating" each other. They describe
each other as "heretics", or "schismatics",[31] and treat those

who diverge from their point of view as if they had lapsed from the faith. When one observes men who pride themselves on being emancipated acting in this sectarian manner it seems as though they are satisfying their religious instincts in a perverted form. The Freudians seem to have strong religious instincts.

The second aspect of Jung's discoveries relevant to our enquiries lies in the function of *symbols*. The word "symbol" is normally used in a very loose fashion, and Freud certainly was guilty of confusing its meaning [32]—a departure from scientific rigour which his followers who accuse Jung of being "unscientific" would do well to remember—for Jung uses the word "symbol" rigorously. The contrast between a "sign" and a "symbol" brings out the symbol's function most clearly. A sign is that which points to something else which we already know; for instance, a wooden sign at a cross-roads with the name "Malvern" on it is only helpful to us if we already know that it is the custom in England to use pieces of wood as signs, and if we can already read English letters, and know that "Malvern" is a proper name—(that it does not mean, say, "This is the *Principality* of Malvern"). A symbol, on the other hand, expresses some experience that we cannot consciously formulate or define—if we could define the experience it would have to be in terms which we already understood, and therefore a sign would do quite adequately. Thus Freud is using words incorrectly when he says that a stick is a "symbol" for the sex organ; in fact, a stick may be a *sign* for the sex organ, but it is not a symbol, any more than is the word "penis" or— "male sex organ". But a symbol is used precisely in order to convey some experience which is inexpressible in consciously-chosen terms; therefore, in the very nature of the case, any experience which is being conveyed from the unconscious to the conscious must take the shape of a symbol. If we already knew the message from the unconscious we should not be saying that it came from the unconscious—for the simple reason that we were already *conscious* of it—and a sign would express it adequately. Since the experience is conveyed from the unconscious, however, it has to take a unique form. These forms are what Jung calls "symbols", because they represent the

inexpressible in an unsurpassable way.[33] Among the countless
symbols which he meets with in his patients are the Cross,
the Serpent, and the Tree of Life, to name but three. And
these symbols occur in the dreams especially of unbelieving
people, who have thrust religion out of their conscious life,
and whose unconscious is presenting them with these symbols
in order to convey the religious experience of which they have
starved themselves.

What *function* do these symbols serve for those who receive
them? On the basis of his case-work it seems to Jung that the
symbol actually *does* something to the persons who face it; it
initiates them into an experience, enables them to share in an
experience which the symbol conveys to them. The symbol is
the psychological mechanism for transforming psychic energy,
for making the untapped power of the unconscious into energy
available for serving the self. The symbol opens up a world of
experience which the patient has been shutting out, a new
world in which he will find wholeness and health. The experience is not pointed to, as a sign points: it is conveyed, as a
symbol conveys. Bridging the gap between the realm of reality
and the realm of signs lies the symbol, as it bridges the gap
between conscious formulation and experience from the unconscious. The symbol is not a dead letter or sign, for it is
charged with life-giving energy.

It can be seen that the function of symbols corresponds very
closely to the function of the *effective word*[24] which we discussed
in the section of logical positivism (p. 140). And granting this
function of the symbol, it raises the whole question of whether
twentieth-century men have not banished the symbol from their
lives as they have banished the effective word, and are therefore
dried up, hollow and ineffective? For in earlier centuries
human beings inherited traditions containing symbols; they
received abundant life and energy through the liturgical symbols
of the Church, or else, if they were pagans, they inherited myths
whose symbols initiated them into the deep mysteries of birth
and rebirth, death and marriage. Even such a simple myth, for
instance, as that of St. George and the dragon has tremendous
power to transform our energies and mould our characters.

In St. George we are dealing with a man who has his desires fixed, as a child has, upon his mother, in the manner of Oedipus. By his decision to serve Christ he succeeds in destroying those evil forces which are trying to blot out from his gaze the charms of femininity (these forces are the sea-monster devouring the young women—the danger that his fixation upon his mother will abrogate his right to love young women). Then he puts himself at the service of the young woman, and can, without fear or danger, undo the belt by which she is fixed to the dragon. He returns to the city with her, leading the dragon along behind him. Now the hero goes off to carry out more valiant deeds, after having baptised everyone in the city. His instincts having been put to the service of woman, everything he now does for society is done at a sublimated level; the whole of society has made the same choice as himself and lives through its trials in the service of Christ, who is the life and the resurrection. The whole of this legend is a symbolic expression of the psychological trial which male human beings go through: at maturity their sexual, emotional and mental life is integrated into the order of society and acquires a sacrificial character. By sacrificing themselves for their deeds, for their offspring and for society, they acquire, at this critical stage of their development, that natural capacity for sacrifice which may lead on to a capacity for supernatural sacrifice.[35]

At one time such myths, packed with a wealth of symbols, were handed on from one generation to another, as families were gathered round the hearth, or as grandparents sat in the sun with the children. In this way men's minds received life-giving symbols from their traditions, and they were equipped with energy available for handling the critical situations of life. But nowadays traditions are being destroyed; mothers no longer hand on the rich symbolism of their country's legends,[36] and children are growing into manhood with starved souls, their only nourishment the insubstantial "shadows" which other starved souls have projected onto the screen of the cinema. But there is a law of compensation at work, and it may well be that Jung's investigations will help us to recapture our life-giving symbols—if not, there is every indication that

Marxism will successfully capture the dominant archetypes, and man will surrender himself to one of his shadows, the shadow of the hammer and sickle.

After this Jungian description of our psychological structure we are naturally prompted to ask how far it squares with the traditional Christian view. There is no denying, at any rate, that it often helps us to cope with situations in which religious decisions are involved. The following case is one example. There was an unmarried woman, aged 38, whose life seemed very dry and meaningless. And then one day she met a man who wakened in her loving desires; she was in love with him and she was lifted up from the meaningless boredom of her everyday life. But the laws of the Church made marriage impossible. She seemed to be doomed to a fruitless and despairing existence, until she dreamed a dream by which she was led into the way of salvation:

"I was standing with my sister in the north room of our house, when I looked through the door into the south room, where my mother was distributing something sacred. I noticed her let something fall on to the ground, which looked like a portion of a Sacred Host. She did not notice it. So I went to the spot where I thought the Host must be, got down on my knees to look for it and found a piece of red-coloured egg-shell with a tiny piece of egg next to it. I recognized it as the Sacred Host yet did not dare to take it into my hands; but it could not be left there, and so I picked it up lovingly and reverently. Then I noticed that a little flame was flickering in the palms of my hands. And a little ball of light began to move in it like a tiny sun. Immediately the light began to grow brighter, streaming up from my hands in golden-yellow flames; overcome by a holy awe I knelt upright and raised my hands to the heavens as if offering a burning sacrifice. The room became radiant with light and I suddenly saw a Crucifix on the wall above me— its head, like the burning flame in my hand, was being more and more transfigured by the light until it revealed the indescribable glorified face of Christ. In ecstasy and dread at this vision my whole being was raised in surrender. No words can describe it. For the palms of my hands with their burning sacrifice—they were the images of my ardent prayers. Gradually the light faded from the glorified head of Christ, and the flames in my hands went out. I stood up and went into the north room, back to my sister—and woke up." [37]

This dream came from the depths of her being; from her unconscious she was learning her true condition and how it was to be transformed. This transformation is effected through symbols. The mother and the egg symbolizes her natural sexuality, her desire to be a mother and a wife. She was not pretending that she didn't have these desires, but picked up the egg; out of it sprang flames, searing, painful, transforming fire; fire, the symbol of transformation. In her dream she surrendered herself utterly to this transformation, which brought her face to face with Christ on the Cross; God working her transformation through the burning suffering of the Cross. She had understood this and was now formed for her task; she went back to her sister—*to the Sisters*. For she found her health, her holiness and her love in a community of religious Sisters.

Such an incident brings out for us the religious function of the unconscious, which has been so much neglected in recent Christian tradition. For there is every reason to believe that God speaks to us through the unconscious [38], just as he speaks to us through events in the external world, which are equally outside our conscious control. God's Word comes into our consciousness both from the external world and from the interior world of our unconscious. St. Paul, for example, seems to have received the Word of God through his unconscious when he had a vision of a man called Ananias coming in and laying hands on him, to cure him of blindness. Though we have no evidence, it seems unlikely that St. Paul's eyes had been physically harmed to the point of blindness. Possibly he went blind because his unconscious (i.e. God through his unconscious) directed him to go blind. Nor does this interpretation mean that it was "purely psychological", since, if our minds are open to the

unconscious on one side as our eyes are open to the external
world on the other, God may work just as effectively through
"psychological events" as through external events. [39]

And yet one cannot immediately assume that Jung's psychology may be taken over completely without further discrimina-
tion. There is a sense, indeed, in which Jung's postulates may
mislead Christians more than Freud's or Adler's do, precisely
because they *look* so very religious and Christian; and when the
similarity is so close it requires the gift for the discernment
of spirits to divide the good from the evil. [40] Since dividing the
good from the evil is so very difficult let us content ourselves
with indicating the chief weakness in Jung's approach; it is
from this weakness that all his subsequent shortcomings will be
found to derive.

The weakness is that Jung's postulates may prove misleading
if they are not controlled by sound metaphysics; without a
sound metaphysics one is always in danger of slipping off into an
imaginary world instead of keeping one's feet in the real world.

We have already described Jung's method of working as the
phenomenological one. In the section of phenomenology it
was pointed out that this method does not afford us any criterion by which to test the truth of an assertion (cf. p. 73),
and that the phenomenological method, unless anchored to a
metaphysics, leads to intellectual chaos. The lack of an adequate criterion of truth certainly does strike one when trying
to grasp the implications of Jung's psychology. For example,
although Jung did detect the upsurge from the unconscious
which eventually swept Germans into the Nazi movement, his
lack of metaphysics prevented him from being able to make a
judgement upon it. He could not say whether the energy was
going into the right or the wrong channels. He knew that
something tremendous was going to come out of it but could
not himself adopt a firm stand which might have helped to
make it terrifically *good* instead of terrifically *bad*. Again, at a
more personal level, how are we to tell when we are *projecting* our
unconscious onto the external world, and when we are making
a *judgement* about things as they are? Are Jung's own statements

H

projections, or are they judgements? He, presumably, believes that they are judgements, but he does not provide us with any means of judging whether they are or not. Only after we have judged things as they are can we make allowances for the way in which our view of them is distorted by our projections.

The quarrel between the Jungians and the Freudians illustrates this need for a criterion most strikingly. For when a Freudian cures a patient, a Jungian is inclined to say that he has unwittingly touched on some archetype; when a Jungian cures a patient, the Freudian says that he has unwittingly released some repression rooted in infantile sexuality. Which of them is right? Without some judgement upon the nature of man it is impossible to decide; such a judgement involves a metaphysics.

Jung has never worried too much about the possible metaphysical implications of his work, however, from the very understandable fear that his work, which is empirical, might be perverted if he came to it with preconceived metaphysical notions;[41] metaphysics might pervert his psychology. In fact Jung sometimes almost seems to have a complex on the subject of metaphysics; there is a certain passion in his statement that "metaphysical assertions are made by the psyche, therefore they are psychological. This self-evident truth strikes the western mind . . . as an unacceptable negation of metaphysical 'truth'."[42] But to say that metaphysical statements are psychological because they are made by the psyche, whilst true, only constitutes a half-truth. For metaphysical statements, though made *by* the psyche, are not usually *about* the psyche; they are about things which have their own existence, such as cats and mice and men and trees. To neglect the object of a metaphysical assertion would be to render it non-metaphysical —for the simple reason that it would no longer be *about anything!* In fairness to Jung it must be pointed out that he does not say that metaphysical assertions are "only psychological";[43] at the same time he does not seem to recognize that, if metaphysical statements have a psychological aspect, likewise psychological statements have their metaphysical aspects. For instance, I am quite interested to hear that Jung thinks I have a God-archetype in my unconscious which is going to help to

integrate me; but I am much more interested in *knowing* whether
or not there *is* a God who created heaven and earth. Nor is
it any use Jung assuring me that it is good for my integration
to believe that there is a God—I want to *know* whether God *is*.
Similarly Jung assures me that the symbol of the Cross has a
salutary effect upon my psyche; but that still leaves me wanting
to *know* whether Jesus Christ actually suffered death upon the
Cross at a certain date under Pontius Pilate. In other words,
I want to *know* things as they are; I am, like all other men, a
"metaphysical animal". Nor is it any use saying that men
should stop seeking the answers to these different metaphysical
problems but should simply accept what is good for their
psyches; the desire to know is, in fact, a far more obvious part
of man's psyche than are symbols, archetypes and shadows
(which are all hypothetical). And since the desire to know is
an essential part of man, ought not Jung's well-grounded fear
of metaphysics' perverting psychology be accompanied by an
even stronger fear that *lack* of metaphysics might warp the
psyche? The answers to metaphysical questions have a profound effect upon the psyche and their neglect can only do it
harm. Jung spoke better than he knew when he said that
"metaphysical assertions are psychological"; they are indeed;
their truth or falsity has profound effects upon the psyche,
and the analytical psychologist who is indifferent to their truth
or falsity may harm his patients.

Arising directly from this indifference to metaphysics, [44] to
that which has existence independent of the psyche, is Jung's
unconvincing description of what it means to achieve integration. Into what are we integrated? Into our own isolated
selves, devoid of real relationships and communion with other
things and other persons? This must be the case unless we
have real relationships with others who have their own existence which we know to be their own, to be *other* than our own
existence. Take the man, for instance, who is in love with a
woman; is it a matter of indifference to him whether she
actually exists and does love him, or whether she is no more
than a projection of his feminine side? Is he loving her, or is
he simply loving his own image? He cannot believe that his

relationship with her is a real one unless he trusts his ability
to make judgements about people and things as they are. These
judgements are metaphysical and it is they which open up to him
the possibility of communion with other things and other persons.
It is in this communion that true integration is achieved.

There is a genuine danger, in Jung's psychology, of encourag-
ing people to regard integration as an esoteric process which
leaves them in the happy possession of their own tidy little
well-balanced psyches, indifferent to the love and the suffering
of other people.[45] But true integration does not leave a man
in isolated splendour; it comes when he gives himself in the
ecstasy of communion with others, really sharing in their love
and their suffering. Though never fully achieved in this life,
integration means sharing in the utter self-giving of three
Persons, the Father, the Son and the Holy Spirit.

NOTES

[1] *De Anima*, Lib. I Lectio 2.

[2] *S. Th.* I–II, Q. 37, art. 4 ad 3. Perhaps the mental causation of illness
has been most aptly described by Franz Kafka, the novelist, who said of
his own tuberculosis, "My head has made an appointment with my
lungs behind my back".

[3] Though it is worth noting that the Romantics had grasped the
importance of the unconscious. But whereas they expressed their awareness in poetry and romance Freud stated his discovery scientifically.

[4] ROLAND DALBIEZ, *The Psycho-Analytic Method and Doctrine of Freud*,
Longmans, 1941.

[5] A whole list of these mistakes is out of the question. Some people
have pointed out that Freud himself was never properly analysed, and
suggest that in his Oedipus theory Freud was rationalizing his own
protest against his "fathers" in psycho-analysis, Charcot and Bernheim.
This would explain why he cut out the use of "suggestion", to which
they attached so much importance. (BAUDOUIN, *De l'Instinct a l'Esprit*,
Études Carmélitaines, Bruges, Desclée de Brouwer, 1950, p. 151.)
Others have pointed out that the Oedipus legend, which Freud treated
as if it were a universal one expressing a universal situation, is in fact
confined to a very small part of Asia Minor; and therefore provides no
grounds for generalizing about human nature. (RUDOLF ALLERS, *The
Successful Error*, Sheed and Ward, 1941, pp. 120, 185–6.) Because he
did not alter his statements about the Oedipus situation doubts have
been cast on Freud's scientific method; moreover, it is disturbing to find
him saying that he suppressed certain evidence for telepathic phenomena
which he had encountered on the ground that to reveal it would shake our
present scientific world-outlook. (Quoted from Ehrenwald by L. J. Bendit,

Paranormal Cognition, p. 26.) In general there is much to be learnt about Freud from studying the peculiar atmosphere of the Vienna in which he operated (cf. STEFAN ZWEIG, *The World of Yesterday*, Cassell, 1943).

[6] E. GLOVER, *Freud or Jung*, George Allen & Unwin, 1950, p. 95.

[7] *An Autobiographical Study*, Hogarth Press, 1935, p. 109.

[8] His later talk of *meta-psychology* (cf. *The Psychopathology of Everyday Life*) is tantamount to admitting this. (We have now collected from modern learning, a metapsychology, a metamathematics, a metalogic, a meta-language—but the word "metaphysics" is avoided like the plague.)

[9] cf. GUSTAV BALLY, *Vom Ursprung und von den Grenzen der Freiheit*.

[10] I cannot find the work from which I took this note.

[11] cf. the discussion in BAUDOUIN, *De l'instinct a l'esprit*, pp. 247–249.

[12] He does not seem to have faced the difficulty of finding an organ for the death instinct.

[13] *Beyond the Pleasure Principle*, International Psycho-Analytical Press, 1922, p. 64.

[14] Similar indecisiveness in many matters shows how unfair it is to neglect the development of Freud's teaching. In his earlier days he regarded masochism as a derivative of sadism, but later thought it was the other way round. Most important; at first Freud believed that it was sexual repression which produced conditions of anxiety, but came to the view that anxiety precedes repression—it is a fear of losing love. One appreciates how Freud's thought becomes more *human*.

[15] RUDOLF ALLERS in *Conflict and Light*, Sheed and Ward 1952, p. 55.

[16] "Theologically considered, Adler's diagnosis of the condition of fallen man goes deeper than Freud's. Freud stops at the *malum poenae* ("the evil we undergo") which is the immediate outcome of the Fall and which Western theology since St. Augustine calls *concupiscentia inordinata*, the *inordinatio* which is at the root of all human ills. Adler takes us further to that *malum culpae* (the "evil we do") which, by sundering the grace-relationship with God, is the cause of this *concupiscentia* itself and of the conflicts and disintegration which follow upon it. This latter the theologians call *superbia*—the self-assertion of the individual ego over against the Absolute, and, as a consequence, over against the community and the exigencies of integral human nature itself. But for that very reason the tendencies of Adler's "Individual Psychology" would seem to be even more hostile to Christianity than Freud's "Psychoanalysis". Adler in effect conceives the basic drive in human nature to be precisely that which constitutes its *fallen* condition; for him the ultimate and irreducible psychological factor is that which the Christian believes to be most in need of integration and redemption." VICTOR WHITE O.P. *The Frontiers of Theology and Psychology*, p. 24 (The Guild of Pastoral Psychology, Lecture No. 19).

[17] cf. GLOVER, *Freud or Jung*, p. 90 "a frustrated anal type is either excessively untidy or ritualistic to the point of absurdity". You are caught either way.

[18] The extent of this disease in the modern world is noteworthy. . . . "The official estimate of the British Medical Association is that at least

$33\frac{1}{3}$ per cent of all patients going to doctors are not suffering from any
primarily organic disease, but from functional nervous illness. . . .
Many experienced doctors put the figures for neurosis at 50 per cent".
(GUNTRIP, *Psychology for Ministers and Social Workers*, Independent Press
Ltd., 1949, pp. 87–88). According to Jung, neurosis affects Protestants
more than Catholics. Furthermore, he asked educated Protestants and
Catholics whether they would rather go to the doctor or to the priest
when they were in spiritual trouble; 57 per cent of the Protestants and
24 per cent of the Catholics preferred the doctor to the priest. cf. JUNG,
Die Beziehungen der Psychotherapie zur Seelsorge, Zürich, Rascher Verlag, 1942.

[19] Of course, in practice, Freudians and Jungians are not so much at
cross-purposes as they are in their theories. How do both parties explain
the successful cures of the other party? Jungians would say that
Freudians unknowingly deal with archetypes, e.g. that the phallus is not
simply sexual but symbolizes the power of the father archetype, or that
the womb symbolizes the *Magna Mater*. Similarly Freudians would say
that these archetypes are rooted in infantile sexuality—which accounts
for Jungian practice being better than Jungian theory.

[20] "According to the teaching of St. John of the Cross and St. Francis
de Sales, it is not sin which necessarily prevents the soul's ascent towards
God, so long as the sin is sincerely regretted each time with the firm
purpose of never committing it again in future; much more harmful is
an habitual and conscious will to hang on to something, no matter how
small, when God asks for it". P. PHILIPPE DE LA TRINITÉ, *Conflict and Light*,
Sheed & Ward 1952, p. 44.

[21] In view of the ease with which this theory might be used to
transcend rather than *transform* our instinctive desires, it is worth
insisting that "all instinctive desires must be satisfied either in the flesh
or in the spirit". (J. LAYARD, "The Incest Taboo and the Virgin-
Archetype", *Eranos Jahrbuch* xii, p. 265). If a person sacrifices wealth it
is for the sake of spiritual riches; if a person sacrifices fleshly marriage it
is for the sake of spiritual marriage; if a person sacrifices power it is to
stand in judgement on the very angels.

[22] Many Christian writers have used spiritual terms to express this
wholeness attaching to the "self". Some speak of "the apex of the soul",
others of "the fine point" of the soul (Lady Julian "saw God in a Point").
In Pascal's "The heart has its reasons which the reason does not know",
we have an echo of it. A most lovely statement that the self, the heart,
is more than the ego, the conscious, is found in the words, *Ego dormio,
sed vigilat cor meum*—"my ego sleeps, but my *heart* keeps watch".

[23] Baudouin, p. 219, maintains that Freud was moving towards the
notion of a collective unconscious. However, Glover interprets Freud
otherwise, *Freud or Jung*, pp. 38–39.

[24] *Contributions to Analytical Psychology*, pp. 108–9.

[25] Some of a biologist's doubts are given in "Die Urbilder in
biologischer Sicht" by Adolf Portmann, *Eranos Jahrbuch* xviii.

[26] "Sin is with us; if we deny that, we are cheating ourselves; it means
that the truth does not dwell in us" (1 John I. 8). For a study of the

"shadow" in the life of St. Thérèse of Lisieux c.f. Hans Urs von Balthasar's *Therese von Lisieux* p. 314 et seq. A Christian mystic's teaching on the "shadow" is discussed in *Walter Hilton: an English Spiritual Guide*, by Victor White O.P. (Guild of Pastoral Psychology, Lecture No. 31).

"God is light, and no darkness can find any place in him" (1 John I. 5).

[27] It is not insignificant that when God created human beings he created them male-and-female. The taking of Eve from Adam's side is an indication, perhaps, that males are not wholly masculine, but also have their feminine side; whilst Eve's origin out of Adam may indicate that females have their masculine side.

[28] Quoted by Kenneth Walker, *Meaning and Purpose*, Pelican Books, 1950, p. 198, who also quotes a passage from J. S. Mill which might well have been written by a Jungian, "The spirit of analysis has a tendency to wear away the feelings . . . when no other mental habit is cultivated, and the analysing spirit remains without its natural complements and correctives".

[29] The notion of projection still needs much clarification; here let us at least indicate the exciting lines of research upon which it has recently set Jung working.

Projections normally occur when the mind is faced with an unknown, a blank screen, as it were, onto which the mind unconsciously projects characteristics from the archetypes. Thus simple men projected unconscious contents onto the unknown heavens; they described the planets as "gods", attributing to these gods the characteristics of the unconscious archetypes. (Virgo, Leo, Saturn, Mercury, etc. all have these characteristics in ancient astronomy, or astrology).

Besides the outer heavens, another blank unknown facing man is "matter"; i.e. matter appears to be formless. And yet we find certain people, the alchemists, attributing wonderful characteristics to matter, one form of which, the philosopher's stone, they believed to be the elixir of life. Assuming that the alchemists were projecting their unconscious contents onto "matter" it seems that the alchemists were projecting outside themselves a process which was going on inside themselves. Their search for a process which would transform base matter into the precious metal reflects their search for a process of integration which would transform their own psyches ("the dust of the earth") into glorious, eternal life (integration). The connection between the two processes is given by a 13th century writer when he says, "Make a round circle of man and woman, extract therefrom a quadrangle and from it a triangle. Make the circle round and thou shalt have the Philosopher's Stone" (quoted by Jung, *Psychology and Religion*, Oxford University Press, 1938).

Having decided that the astrologers and alchemists were projecting the contents of their unconscious on to the heavens and the earth it would seem that they have little more to offer us. But we should hesitate to translate the phrase "were projecting" as though it meant "were *only* projecting". May there not, in fact, be some connection between events in the heavens and on earth and the events in the psyche? At least those who believed in such a connection were at home in the

universe; they were in a living communication with it, as opposed to
modern men, who are split off from the universe into an isolation which
not infrequently leads to madness.   Paracelsus was describing this
supposed connection when he said, "He that knoweth the origin of
thunder, winds and storms, knoweth where colic and torsions come from
. . . he that knoweth what planets' rust is and what their fire, salt and
mercury, also knoweth how ulcers grow and where they come from as
well as scabies, leprosy and serei".   (Quoted by Owsei Temkin, in
Science and Civilization, ed. R. C. STAUFFER, Madison, University of
Wisconsin Press, 1949, p. 187.)

Men such as Paracelsus believed that the outer world and the inner
world were related as father to son; God creates the inner world
(including man's) according to his image.   Man's inner world is an
image of the outer world; for there exists in the inner world "the kind
of the dragons, the kind of the snakes, the generation of vipers and
adders, also the nature of wolves, sheep, etc., also of all elements, likewise
health and disease".   Allowing for the confused way in which Paracelsus
thinks, one can at least appreciate how his obscurely apprehended
father-son relationship no longer exists in modern minds, and that its
severance corresponds to the split in modern man, for whom the silent
heavens and the brute beasts are utterly alien.

Of course, the fact that it makes men feel more at home in the
universe would not be a good enough reason for believing that there is a
connection between events in the outer spaces and events in the unconscious.   But recent observations of "parapsychology" (cf. the whole
discussion in Jung's "Der Geist der Psychologie", *Eranos Jahrbuch* 1946),
suggest that there is, in fact, some connection between the outer and
inner events (as was believed by St. Thomas Aquinas *S.Th* I. Q. 115,
art. 4.   Also the Bible: "And there shall be signs in the sun, and in the
moon, and in the stars; and upon the earth distress of nations, by reason
of the confusion of the roaring of the sea and of the waves. . . . But
when these things begin to come to pass, look up, and lift up your heads,
because your redemption is at hand".   Luke 21, v 25 and v 28.)   Jung
does not believe that there is a direct and necessary *causal* relationship
between the two spheres which would make man, for instance, a plaything of the stars in their courses.   The relationship between the two
sorts of events is rather a relationship of complementarity, so that they
are synchronized.   There is a rhythm in the events which is shared both
by the outer and the inner worlds, that sort of rhythm which accounts
for the belief that there is music in the spheres, a heavenly music which
can be heard by those whose psyches are attuned to it.

It seems as though modern psychology, as well as modern physics (cf.
Prof. Pauli, quoted by Jung, "Geist der Psychologie" p. 482) is moving
away from the notion that the "laws" of nature are the kind of laws
which a dictator imposes upon his subjects, a craftsman imposes upon
the material he moulds or a draftsman on his blueprint.   Instead they
are seeing the "laws" of nature as the kind of "law" which describes the
playful relationship of a father with his children, in which there is a free

rhythmic response, a harmonious relationship of give and take ("complementarity"); the kind of play that befits a creator rather than a tyrant.

So far these are only suggestions, straws in the wind. But they do coincide with the way in which A. J. Toynbee rejects the notion of historical "laws" (in the dictator-subject sense) and suggests *rhythmic responses* as the true terms for interpreting history.

Moreover, if there is this close correlation of heavenly and earthly events it would strengthen our suggestion that the evolution of species owes something to influences from astral bodies (p. 177).

[30] *Modern Man in Search of a Soul*, Kegan Paul, 1933, p. 264.

[31] cf. especially Glover's descriptions of Jung in *Freud or Jung*, and the description of the Adler/Freud warfare in Phyllis Bottome's *Alfred Adler* (Faber & Faber 1939 ch. vi.). Glover, p. 164, also quotes Freud's statement, "One would like to count oneself amongst the believers so as to admonish the philosophers who try to preserve the God of religion by substituting for him an impersonal, shadowy, abstract principle, and say, 'thou shalt not take the name of the Lord, thy God, in vain'". There speaks the man whose ancestors had heard God's message, "I am, who am."

[32] Dalbiez, op. cit., Vol. II, p. 99ff., esp. 105, quoting Jung, "Those conscious contents which give us a clue, as it were, to the unconscious backgrounds are by Freud incorrectly termed symbols. These are not true symbols, however, since, according to his teaching, they have merely the role of signs or symptoms of the background processes. The true symbol differs essentially from this, and should be understood as the expression of an intuitive perception which can as yet neither be apprehended better nor expressed differently".

[33] It is no accident that the Christian creeds are described as *symbols* —they represent the inexpressible (i.e. the Faith) in an unsurpassable way. The Greek word "*symballein*" means "to hold together"; Freud's "sexuality" is "that which holds all living things together"; it is, in fact, a *symbol*.

[34] An example of how a person may wander for a long time in the realm of signs without his life being effectively changed comes from St. Augustine's *Confessions*. Still unconverted, he one day flung himself below a *fig-tree* in the garden at Milan; and there he heard a child's voice singing, "*Tolle, lege. Tolle, lege*". Immediately he was *moved;* he took up the Scriptures and was converted. Why this sudden conversion? unless that God had moved him by the effective word, the life-giving symbol.

We speak of symbols *moving* us, as music or art etc., moves us. After being *moved* by symbols, by music and art, we are in a relaxed condition; we are in a contemplative disposition, no longer filled with bad humour. David knew this when he played to Saul to relieve him.

The relationship between the function of the symbol and the Christian sacraments is touched on by Fr. Victor White in "Psychology and Symbol" (*Life of the Spirit*, June 1949, p. 558).

[35] FRANÇOISE DOLTO, *Satan*, Études Carmélitaines, Bruges, Desclée de Brouwer, p. 439–40. Dr. Dolto adds in a footnote, "This psychoanalytical interpretation of the St. George legend in no way removes the aesthetic and spiritual value of this legend. On the contrary, this analysis helps one to understand the symbolic importance of the legend and the rôle it may play in forming children's moral characters".

[36] A most attractive account of such symbols has been written by Dorothy Donnelly, *The Golden Well*, Sheed & Ward, 1950.

[37] JOSEF GOLDBRUNNER, *Heiligkeit und Gesundheit*, Freiburg, Herder Verlag, 1948, pp. 56–59.

[38] A study of how God uses dreams for his messages in the Scriptures would be very valuable cf. Nabuchodnosor's dream in Daniel iv, which shows the truth of Jung's view that the dream corrects our conscious attitudes.

[39] It is worth noting that man's highest capacity, according to St. Thomas Aquinas, is his *potentia obedientialis*, his power to obey. Man, a creature, receives everything from his Creator—he is *capax Dei*, a vessel for receiving the waters of Divine Life, which come down from the heavens, but also come up from the hidden wells below the earth (i.e. the unconscious).

[40] An illuminating, though brief, discussion of the Gnostic tendencies in Jung's thought has been written by Fr. Victor White, *Dominican Studies*, October 1949, pp. 398–400.

[41] We have every sympathy for Jung when he protests that in his study of the psychology of the Trinitarian doctrine he had no intention of treating the religious validity of the doctrine (*Symbolik des Geistes*, Zürich, Rascher Verlag 1948, pp. 323–326). Some theologians reacted to his study as though they were positively frightened that the doctrine of the Trinity might mean something, and be relevant to our lives.

[42] *Tibetanischen Totenbuch*, Zürich, Rascher Verlag 1935, p. 18.

[43] Ibid. Other psychologists have been less wise. Some have even reduced *logic* to psychology; they maintain that the law of excluded middle and its two-valued logic is an expression of the sexual desire to exclude the father, also expressed in the Oedipus myth!

[44] Indifference to metaphysics (which is the work of the conscious faculties of the intellect and the will) itself arises from minimizing *conscious* functions. It would be a pity if the discovery of the unconscious were to lead to a loss of consciousness—which is *psychologically* disastrous. No one has protested more vigorously against such disastrous tendencies than Jung himself.

Jungians also need to remember Pascal's remark (*Pensées* 669), "The Jews loved symbolic things so much and attended to them so closely that they failed to recognize Reality when it appeared in the time and manner foretold".

[45] Nor, obviously, can one analyse away either the guilt or the effects of original sin. Remembering that the root of all sin is pride, one fears for the analyst who is daily facing the temptation to be as a god towards his patient, a temptation which cannot be analysed away.

IV

CONCLUSION

AT THE end of this attempt to use modern learning as a focus for viewing the world into which we are born and in which our destiny is so hard to discern, it seems fitting to end by estimating whether we are now in any better position for discerning our destiny.

In the beginning we learnt the value of an old distinction which modern scholars too often ignore, the distinction between the kind of knowledge which is easy to come by and the kind of knowledge which we really desire from the depths of our hearts. Expressed in the terse statement of St. Thomas Aquinas, "the slenderest knowledge that may be obtained of the highest things is more desirable than the most certain knowledge obtained of lower things".[1] Therefore it would be misguided for us to cram our minds with any and every piece of information which happens to come our way; we should try, instead, to direct our attention towards the highest things, towards the knowledge we desire in our heart of hearts.

If we approach the story of mankind in this spirit, surveying the history of nations, the fluctuation of political power and the humble joys and sorrows of those who went before us, we come face to face with one person who, even on the most materialist assumptions, has profoundly affected the past and continues to affect the world into which we were born. Every historian, no matter what his beliefs, has to face up to Jesus Christ and make some decision about him. It is no use the historian's saying that he will suspend judgement about this person; he cannot do so. For Jesus Christ said, "Whoever is not for me is against me"; and therefore the historian cannot suspend judgement, but has to make a decision for or against Christ. "What think ye of Christ? Whose son is he?" The answer to this question is crucial. Whereas a historian can study the career of Napoleon, for instance, with a detachment which leaves his own personal life undisturbed, his decision about Jesus Christ is not only a decision about history but a decision about himself, and the whole of his personal life is thrown into a different light according to his decision.

And so there is at least one piece of knowledge which needs to be known above all others, i.e., knowledge of Jesus Christ, who claims to be God.

If the study of history brings us face to face with Jesus Christ, does philosophy help us to make a decision about him? Actually we need to link together our lessons from history and our lessons from philosophy. Remembering that history, if it is to be worthy of the name, brings us knowledge of *persons* ; remembering also how the poverty of propositional expressions makes it inevitable for us to speak the language of an "I" to a "Thou", we can at least realize that reverence for the person, the "Thou", whom we are approaching is absolutely essential if we are to come to the truth on this all-important issue. Reverence, at a level of our personalities deeper even than our reasoning faculties, must characterize our approach. And the other truth which our philosophy taught us: before making such a decision we should use the phenomenological method, searching the Scriptures and discovering the many-sided life of the Christian Church, its liturgy and learning, its saints and sinners, pilgrimages and miraculous shrines. Unlike the positivists who would "reduce" all these manifestations of spiritual life to a few "natural" causes, we must make quite sure that, to begin with, we do not neglect any of the manifold riches in the Christian tradition.

And yet we have to make a decision; although our study of scientific research has taught us how difficult it is to acquire certainty about anything. The tools which are at our disposal limit the range of knowledge which we can exact from the world. And these limitations seem particularly oppressive in dealing with the Christian Church, for we obviously cannot transport ourselves back to ancient Palestine to question Jesus Christ. As a matter of fact, we are not so unfortunate in this respect as is commonly assumed. There is little ground for the widespread opinion that it was easier for people in those days to believe that Jesus Christ is God than it is for us. Many people who had seen him in the flesh did not believe, whilst others did. It is not the fact of seeing, therefore, which can act as our tool to give us knowledge on this issue.

What instrument for this "experiment" do we then possess? Often it is maintained that we have no such instrument, that we have no means of verifying the statement, "Jesus Christ is God"; it is maintained that people may believe this, but have no process whereby to verify it. Yet there *is* an instrument for the "experiment", and there *is* a process of verification. Our very selves are for each one of us the instrument; and the whole of our life is the process of verification. If any man desires knowledge of Jesus Christ he has to surrender his self, to lay down his life for love of his friends. The verification is found in the fruits of such lives; "by their fruits ye shall know them". Ultimately there is no other process of verification except the growth of these fruits, just as there is no other instrument for the experiment except our very selves. Both the instrument and the process are unique; there is no substitute for either; without them we cannot acquire knowledge of this crucial issue. This is a hard saying—but, then, we have learnt that life is hard, a battle to be fought against the powers of darkness, and we are not so foolish as to imagine that victory comes easily.

No one can make this decision for us. It is absolutely personal, unique, the secret of our innermost conscience. So intimate is this decision that no amount of reasoning can *force* us to choose one way or the other; its sacred quality even led St. Thomas Aquinas to say that if a man's reason told him not to believe in Christ, then that man would be doing evil by believing.[2] And so all the reasoning which we have used so far leaves us face to face with a decision which each one of us must make for himself.

May we be permitted, nevertheless, to conclude with a description of how a person whose reason brings him to believe, thereby enters into a life of wholeness and health—such whole-

ness and health as the sanest modern psychology teaches us to
expect when we acknowledge the truth about ourselves and
our world.

This life begins with the time of Advent, a time of expectancy,
a time of waiting. A creature, owing his very existence to his
Creator, man waits breathlessly and in silence for the word
from his Creator. All human creatures since the fall of man
have known this time of expectancy, waiting upon the word
from the Creator, preparing to receive this annunciation with
joy and gladness and shouts of thanksgiving. But the preparation is made in silence. "All the number of those who wait for
thee, O Lord, shall not have hoped in vain". The Church
waits quietly, as a bride for the bridegroom. "Behold the Lord
is coming and all his saints; and in that day there shall be a
great light".

It becomes man to hold himself ready to receive the message
of his destiny, straining for the light in the obscurity of Advent.
And then, after this period—from the fall of Adam until now—
out of the silence, God in his graciousness sends us his Word.
The Word is made flesh. It is the season of Christmas and
Christians raise songs of joy over the Child who takes upon
himself our creaturely nature, showing us from the manger how
to acknowledge our helplessness, our complete dependence
upon our Creator. This Child we take into our hearts, and
ourselves become as little children, gaily playing before the face
of God with the gifts he has given us—the endless beautiful
things of this our blessed world.

From the time that the Child is with us he grows in natural
knowledge, as we also grow, through our studies of the various
branches of learning. When he grows to his full stature we
walk with him through the world, speaking to him intimately
as a man to his friends. He teaches us the goodness of things,
the beauty of flowers and the companionship of sharing our
bread with our neighbours. And it seems to us as though
nothing could ever disturb the tranquillity of these days lighted
by the joy of human friendship. Yet, slowly, fearfully, we begin
to discover a shadow falling across our joy. He is without
shadow, completely guiltless; the shadow that we see is our own

which we are casting on to him. We realize that he has taken upon himself the weight of our sins.

This is the season of Lent. It is a time when we turn inwards upon ourselves, seeing more clearly each day the darkness of our very natures. And as the days pass by, the powers of darkness seem to become ever stronger, to threaten our light and our joy with destruction. Until at last we come to the day when there is darkness over the face of the whole earth; there seems no light in any place, and our joy is brought to destruction. On Good Friday we see that our sins have crucified him who is guiltless. And in our grief over our sins we break into a dance of mourning around the Cross, trying to comfort ourselves as we cry in rhythm, *Agios O Theos; Agios ischyros; Agios athanatos, eleison imas*; and again we cry *Agios O Theos, Agios ischyros, Agios athanatos, eleison imas*.[3] But there is no reply from the Cross; only the Cross, stark against the sky; and as night draws in we go down with our love into the darkness of the tomb.

Everything is finished. Death has brought to nothing the beauty of flowers, the joyous gifts of human friendship, the bread that we took in common. It is all turned to ashes, in a silence which is no longer expectancy but despair over our loss, our nothingness. We are naked in the silence and darkness and loneliness.

Then suddenly, in a flash, our light and our joy breaks forth from the tomb. He is victorious over the powers of darkness. Christ is risen. *Resurrexit sicut dixit*. Once more he is with us in the flesh—with a body that is glorified, shining with the glory of the victor, a glory in which we also are called to share. That for which we dared scarcely hope is realized; we see fulfilled the prophecy from out the ages, "I know that my Redeemer liveth; and in my flesh I shall see God". Nothing that we had feared to lose is lost; it is treasured for us with our glorified Lord, safe with him for ever. We see the new heaven and the new earth, where God shall wipe away all tears from our eyes; and death shall be no more, nor mourning, nor crying, nor sorrow shall be any more, for the former things are passed away. "He that shall overcome shall possess these things, and I will be his God; and he shall be my son".

In the strength of this victory the Christian goes forward without fear to the conquest of the world, armed with the Spirit which at Pentecost is poured forth upon all flesh. For the rest of his days, now, he fights his fight against the powers of darkness, wrestling with them in his own nature and in the rulers of this world. It is a fight to which there will be no end in this life, and it leaves the Christian warrior exhausted at the hour when his beloved Master calls to him. But at evening, as the heat of battle recedes from him and its noise dies away from his hearing, the Christian's beloved Master appears to him under a different figure. Entering into the garden of peace there is no longer any place for strife, "for winter is now past, the rain is over and gone. The flowers have appeared in our land, the time of pruning is come; the voice of the turtle is heard in our land: the fig-tree hath put forth her green figs: the vines in flower yield their sweet smell". And the Christian hears the words of his joy, "arise, my love, my beautiful one, and come . . . and the spirit and the bride say: Come". Come, Lord Jesus, come.

NOTES

[1] *S. Th.* I. Q. 1, art. 5, ad 1.
[2] *S. Th.* I–II. Q. 19, art. 5.
[3] O holy God; O holy strong One; O holy immortal One, have mercy upon us. (From the liturgy of Good Friday).

Appendix I

PLAY

THERE IS an interesting little paragraph in St. Thomas Aquinas' works[1] which refers to play. He has been describing how every action is performed towards some end, with some *aim* in view. Then he breaks off, and says that there are some actions which do not seem to be for any end, such as contemplating, playing —and stroking one's beard! Leaving aside the beard-stroking (which St. Thomas accounts for as would a modern analyst), he sees close similarities between contemplation and play. That is to say, contemplation does not have any end outside itself, because it is its own end; likewise with play, for although we sometimes play so as to study better afterwards, we also play for the sheer delight which is in the game itself. Therefore there is obviously a close similarity between the playful and the contemplative attitudes: they have no end outside themselves.

Given the space one would like to develop the Thomist account of play. For instance, St. Thomas begins an exposition of Boethius[2] by quoting from the book of Ecclesiasticus (xxxii, 15) where man is told on rising to run first to his home, and there recollect himself and play. St. Thomas uses the quotation in order to explain that he is undertaking this exposition because the contemplation of wisdom (the recollection) is itself a delightful game which requires no exterior aim for its justification. Furthermore, he points out, the Scriptures themselves compare the divine wisdom to the delight of play, for in Proverbs viii, 30, we hear how "I was with him forming all things; and was delighted every day, playing before him at all times". In view of which one is not surprised to discover St. Thomas saying that a man may commit sin by not playing sufficiently.[3]

But delightful as a Thomist theology of play might prove, it must give place here to a very simple "phenomenology of play" based upon the ordinary observations of our everyday life.

If we take as an example of play the games of cricket which many families play on the beaches during summer time, what features of the game are particularly striking?

Adopting a hint from St. Thomas we notice that such play involves a suspension of time, so that each second of the game is treasured for its own delight, and not as a means towards the next second. In this respect the game on the beach is like contemplation, for in contemplating also there is a suspension of time—time is left out of consideration and the mind relaxes from the anxiety of time into the peace of eternity. Is it not possible, then, that in a game where the players are enjoying every second for its own sake, they are, in fact, having some slight foretaste of the joys of eternity? By accepting each second in itself, and not in its relation to other seconds of time, the players may well be seeing it in the light of eternity. Play, perhaps, is the working man's mode of contemplation.

A related feature of this game of cricket on the beach is the relaxation which it affords. Instead of suffering from the tension of time, the anxiety of waiting for what will happen next, the players have thrown off care. In this mood of relaxation they are able to see everything as a whole, taking in the sights and sounds of the beach without straining to plan what use these sights and sounds may serve. In their workaday lives their minds are continually tensed to discover *what use* things may serve; all the time, whether consciously or unconsciously, they are asking *what use* is this, or that, or the other? But now, in their play, they are simply *enjoying* things, enjoying them for their own sakes. And in this they are not, perhaps, unlike the blessed in Heaven, who never ask themselves what use anything is but simply enjoy it.

The third feature of our game on the beach is that the result does not matter. Whereas in most of our working lives it is the result which decides whether our activities have been successful or not, it is not the result of a game which determines its success or failure. The result is irrelevant to the essence of the game. Even those who lose the game are the richer for it, since the loss cannot remove the enjoyment which they have had. "Who loses, wins"—truly this can be said of those who know how to play. And he would be a blind man who could not see in this "Who loses, wins" of the players some reflection of the Christian notion that "everything worketh for good to them that love God". For the Christian, also, believes that we have to lose our life in order to gain it, and the Christian who watches his life in this world brought to nought can laughingly cry, "Who loses, wins".

These features of cricket on the beach are more sharply realized if we contrast them with the features of cricket when it ceases to be play, becomes a professional occupation, and is treated as work.

When cricket becomes an occupation there is not the suspension of time which characterizes play. With one eye on the clock and another on the state of the game the professional cricketer cannot afford to enjoy each second for its own sake; each second is seen in its relationship to other seconds. It is all brought beneath the tyranny of time; and, indeed, the tyrant time may even be used in order to sway the result of the game by a timely declaration or the use of the new ball. Here it is eternity, and not time, which is shut out.

Again, there is no relaxation for the professional cricketer, who must be oblivious to the sights and sounds of the spectators around him, or the whistle of the passing train. Or, at worst, he may even try to *use* these sights and sounds in order to disturb his opponent's concentration and secure an advantage over him. What *use* is it? must be his constant question, preventing his clean, fresh enjoyment of the play.

Finally, in professional sport, "Who loses, loses". The result determines success or failure. And this baleful concentration on the end (a contradiction of play) becomes increasingly harmful to play in proportion to the importance attached to the end. If, for instance, a spectator gambles 2*d.* on the result of a game the interference with his enjoyment of it may be slight; but if he gambles £2 on the result he will become so concerned and tense about the result as to lose all enjoyment. His concentration upon the result will have destroyed the ele-

ments of play in the game. To set an end to play is to destroy
its essence.

In case these reflections on the beach seem out of place in
a serious book ("Play and seriousness are sisters" says Plato)
may we point out that many modern thinkers have been led
astray through asking always what the *use* of everything is, and
losing their capacity for *enjoyment*, for *fruition*, which is inciden-
tally developed by play. It has been noticed how Freud, for
instance, could see roots (which have some *use*) but could not
even *see* the blossom, the fruits, which are to be enjoyed (p.
203). Similarly the biologists who cannot enter into the "play"
of nature actually lose their ability to see nature as it is (p. 179),
because play is a real aspect of the world, and they are ignoring
it. A list of the harmful effects upon learning produced by
destroying play would prove most enlightening; here it is sufficient to call attention to Bally's stimulating book on the subject:
Vom Ursprung und von den Grenzen der Freiheit. Bally points out
(p. 132) that Archimedes set about working on the problem of
how to weigh the King of Syracuse's gold, but was unable to
solve it during all the time that his mind was concentrated and
tense, narrowed to that immediate problem. The solution
came to him when he was relaxed, in his bath, in a "playing"
disposition. Perhaps if Archimedes' successors amongst modern
scientists would learn to relax, as he did, they would acquire
deeper insights than they at present enjoy.

Furthermore, the game on the beach could prove a very
enlightening introduction to a neglected aspect of Christian
theology.[4] For the Christian revelation is unique amongst
religions in that it teaches us an astounding truth about God's
creation of the world: God created the world *out of nothing.*
Our astonishment at this truth is nowadays not so fresh in our
minds as it should be, because we have been brought up within
a tradition which accepts it. But God's creation of the world
from nothing is a truth which should never be just calmly
accepted; it should surprise us into daily renewed reflection
upon its mystery. God is his own happiness; he does not *need*
anything outside himself, and yet he creates the world. His
creation of the world, therefore, was not necessary to him, but

supremely free. Obviously, then, this free act of God's had no
end outside itself. In having no end outside itself the act of
Creation has its analogy in contemplation and play, neither of
which, according to St. Thomas, has an end outside itself.
The activity of play is the best analogy by which most of us
can reach towards some conception of God's creative act. By
thinking of God as the sovereignly free player who creates the
world in his bounteous, gracious playfulness, we dimly perceive
the eternal play of God's will at each moment of time. Each
moment of time has its eternal treasure, which God eternally
sees, and see that it is good.

In order to illustrate this element of play within the Christian
tradition we have gathered below a few texts, which we present
without comment in the hope that the preceding paragraphs
have made a commentary unnecessary:

"When he compassed the sea with its bounds, and set a law
to the waters that they should not pass their limits: when he
balanced the foundations of the earth: I was with him forming
all things: and was delighted every day, playing before him at
all times, playing in the world: and my delights were to be
with the children of men." (Prov. viii. 28-31.)

"But David and all Israel played before the Lord on all
manner of instruments made of wood: on harps and lutes and
timbrels and cornets and cymbals." (II Kings vi. 5.)

"And David said to Michol: Before the Lord, who chose me
rather than thy father, and than all his house, and commanded
me to be ruler over the people of the Lord in Isreal, I will
both play and make myself meaner than I have done, and I will
be little in my own eyes: and with the handmaids of whom thou
speakest, I shall appear more glorious." (II Kings vi. 21-22.)

"Thus saith the Lord of hosts: There shall yet old men and
old women dwell in the streets of Jerusalem, and every man
with his staff in his hand through multitude of days. And the
streets of the city shall be full of boys and girls, playing in
the streets thereof." (Zach. viii. 4-5.)

"And we came near to a place, of which place the walls
were such, they seemed built of light; and before the door of

that place stood four angels who clothed us when we went in with white raiment. And we went in, and we heard as it were one voice crying *Sanctus, Sanctus, Sanctus* without any end. And we saw sitting in that same place as it were a man, white-headed, having hair like snow, youthful of countenance; whose face we saw not. And on his right hand and on his left, four elders; and behind them stood many other elders. And we went in with wonder and stood before the throne; and the four angels raised us up; and we kissed him, and with his hand he passed over our faces. And the other elders said to us: *Go ye and play*. And I said to Perpetua: Thou hast that which thou desirest. And she said to me: Yea, God be thanked; so that I that was glad in the flesh am now more glad". (*Passion of SS. Perpetua and Felicity*, 12.)

" . . . in this work [the work of santification] . . . strain not thy heart in thy breast over-rudely nor out of measure; but work more with a list than with any idle strength. For the more listily thou workest, the more meek and ghostly is thy work. . . . This is childishly and playfully spoken, thou thinkest peradventure. But I trow that whoso had grace to do and feel as I say, he should feel good gamesome play with him, as the father doth with the child, kissing and clasping, that well were him so!" (*Cloud of Unknowing*, Chap. 46.)

"For some time past I had offered myself to the Child Jesus, to be His little plaything; I told Him not to treat me like one of those precious toys which children only look at and dare not touch, but rather as a little ball of no value that could be thrown on the ground, tossed about, *pierced*, left in a corner, or pressed to His heart, just as it might please Him. In a word, all I desired was to amuse the Holy Child, to let Him play with me just as He felt inclined" (and more in the same vein, St. Thérèse of Lisieux, *Histoire d'une âme*, trans. Taylor, Burns Oates, p. 115.)

"MY BELOVED LITTLE SPOUSE,—I am well pleased with thee! All the year round thou hast amused Me by playing at *ninepins*. I was so overjoyed, that the whole court of Angels was surprised and charmed. Several little cherubs have asked Me why I did not make them children. Others wanted to

know if the melody of their instruments were not more pleasing
to Me than thy joyous laugh when a ninepin fell at the stroke
of thy love-ball. My answer to them was, that they must not
regret they are not children, since one day they would play
with thee in the meadows of Heaven. I told them also that
their smiles were certainly more sweet to Me than their
harmonies, because these smiles were purchased by suffering
and forgetfulness of self. . . . Thy little Brother,

Jesus.

(St. Thérèse of Lisieux, op. cit. pp. 319–20).

Finally an Orthodox monk, describing the ascetic life, says,
"You deny yourself sleep by night and sacrifice the hours of
day, never sparing yourself, and when you realize that this is
all play—then you are in earnest." (Quoted by Rahner,
Eranos Jahrbuch xvi.)

These witnesses to the play of God in man throughout many
centuries seem to strike an alien note in our own society. We
of the twentieth century have abandoned the creaturely receptive attitude of contemplation or play and replaced it by the
ideal of the captain of commerce who wrests time and nature
to his purpose. When he says that "time is money" the
modern captain of commerce is quoting a formula for the
destruction of himself and our culture. Under cover of this
formula he destroys the growth of trees and of crops by forcing
them to grow at *his* rate, forgetting that growing things require
their own time and, if forced, are forced to destruction. In the
name of the same formula he insists that he and his workmen
should each produce a certain amount of work in a certain
time—for "time is money"—forgetting that each one of us has
his own time and rhythm, and that our nature gives us a nervous
breakdown when that rhythm and time is not respected.
"Time is money", he says, and thus throws everyone else into
nervous anxiety, because they fear lest they should lose some
time. With his ally, the tyrant Time, he destroys his own
nature, the nature of his workmen, and of all growing things.
Having for centuries asked what *use* everything is, he has

eventually turned his eyes towards our play. When we tell him that we do not need to state a *use* for our play—because it is delightful in itself—he is incapable of understanding us. He has so thoroughly perverted his own nature that he is incapable of *enjoying* anything, including our delightful play. And so, in his jaundiced perversity, he has even turned what was our play into an article of commerce, by inventing professional sport, and making it an occasion for gambling. Having lost the capacity for play, he has poisoned the play of others.

But this captain of commerce will not have the last word. For if you wander into the cities which his bombs and shells have reduced to rubble, you will still find "the city full of boys and girls, playing in the streets thereof". They laugh as they play over the captain of commerce's destruction; in which they prove themselves true men (following St. Thomas's definition of man: "a rational animal capable of laughter"). And in the last day they shall laugh, these children of the rubble, when they walk the streets of the New Jerusalem, playing before the face of God.

NOTES

[1] *Summa Contra Gentiles*, Book III, Chapter 2.
[2] *Expositio super Boëtium de hebdomadibus.* Prologue.
[3] *S.Th.* II–II. Q. 168, art. 4.
[4] For what follows cf. Hugo Rahner's "Der spielende Mensch", *Eranos Jahrbuch* XVI.

Appendix II

FREEDOM

DURING THE twenties of this century certain leaders of thought were behaving in a very curious fashion. In regard to man as an individual they were denying that he is free, saying that his actions are determined by his circumstances, his social position, etc. At the same time they were demanding boundless freedom for man in society, saying that man's freedom should not be restricted by divorce-laws, drink-laws, moral laws, etc. These leaders of thought do not seem to have realized how absurd it is to demand that a man be allowed to exercise his freedom whilst at the same time asserting that man is not free by nature.

Why did they defend these absurd statements? Since they are absurd there can be no rational, philosophical explanation for them, and the answer is to be found in their personal psychology. Not to put too fine a point on it, they wished to sleep with any woman whom they could seduce, and indulge their sensual appetites (therefore they said their freedom should not be restricted by social laws); but at the same time they did not wish to be held responsible for their actions (therefore they maintained that man is not free because his actions are determined by circumstances, etc.). They wished to have their cake and eat it.

This example should be enough to show how the word "freedom" is abused, and it has been quoted to express my belief that the question of whether man is free, is not to be taken seriously. How futile such a question proves may be illustrated from the way in which it is normally treated.

If a Catholic man, for instance, loves a lady who is herself already married, he faces an alternative. Either he runs away with her and puts himself outside the communion of the Church, or else he remains within the communion of the Church and does not run away with her. If he chooses the first course, and runs away with her, then the determinist says his action was not free, but was determined by his passion for the lady. Likewise if he chooses the second course, and does not run away with her, the determinist says that his action was not free, but was determined by his fear of the Church.

The defender of freedom who is confronted in this way with a determinist skilled at playing "Heads I win, tails you lose", realizes that he is being tricked, but cannot discover how. In desperation he will say, "Let us take another case". Whereupon the determinist takes another spin of the coin, calls "Heads I win, tails you lose", and, to his opponent's dismay, wins again. What is the secret? Surely it is that the determinist's call is making any other answer but his own impossible. In other words, if you begin to discuss whether man is free by analysing certain of his actions in terms of the possible desired objects which influenced him, you cannot avoid coming to the conclusion that it is the desired objects which determine his actions, and not the man himself. The conclusion that man is the slave of these objects is absolutely inevitable, granted the terms of analysis.

For we have always to remember that an analysis can never give us any information of a different type from the type contained in its terms. Suppose for instance that I place a number of rugby balls and a number of soccer balls into a crate, some of the rugby balls and some of the soccer balls being painted black whilst others of the rugby balls and of the soccer balls are painted white. I then go along to a friend and ask him to analyse the contents of the crate into black and white by throwing the white balls into one room and the black ones into another room, counting them as he does so. Eventually he announces that he has finished. I ask him for the results of his analysis, and he replies that there were 65 black balls and 35 white balls in the crate. If I then say, "If there are 65 black balls and 35 white balls, that shows there were no rugby balls or soccer balls, doesn't it?"—obviously he explodes, and says that he was analysing them into "black" and "white" not into "rugby" or "soccer". In his frustration he is comparable to the defender of freedom confronted with a determinist. My friend has used terms for his analysis ("black", "white") which do not allow of an answer to my question ("rugby" or "soccer"). Similarly the defender of freedom is being asked to use terms for his analysis ("desired objects", "fear", "passion", etc.) which do not allow of an action's being described as free.

Unless our analysis of an action, therefore, includes terms for the *subject* as well as for the *objects* of desire, fear, etc., our analysis can give us no information whatsoever about the *subject*, which in this case is man. Consequently we cannot say, from such analysis, whether man is free or not. In fact, since the term "man" would need to have a precise meaning before it could be used for such an analysis, we cannot profitably begin the analysis until we already have a clear conception of the nature of man.

It is no part of our task to outline our conception of man; we are only concerned to point out that certain customary methods for discussing man's freedom are worthless: the aim of the discussion is cancelled out by the means adopted. We hope, at least, to have shown that certain questions should not be asked, because they cannot be answered. We also hope to have shown that statements about man's free acts only become intelligible when they refer to those acts or expressions of a particular nature, i.e. man's, with all that nature's powers and limitations. When someone says, for instance, that I am "free" to jump across the English Channel my reply is that my nature is a "not-able-to-jump-across-the-English-Channel nature"; the word "free", in this context, is totally unrelated to my nature, and therefore meaningless. Likewise when someone says, the law should give us "freedom" to have several wives, my reply is that man's nature is a "not-able-to-have-several-wives nature", and that such "freedom", being contrary to nature, is quite meaningless.

Appendix III

WHOLE AND PART

THE RELATIONSHIP of a part to its whole can be described at three levels, the material, the organic and the spiritual. If we take a slab of butter and cut away a portion we say that we have taken a part away from the whole; the relationship between the part and the whole in this case is at the material level. If we next take a cat and remove its kidney we also say that we have taken a part away from the whole, but in this case the relationship between part and whole is at the organic level. And it is worthwhile noticing immediately that the material notion or "part", which is quite adequate at the level of butter, is inadequate when applied to a kidney—because the kidney's relationship to the whole cat is more intimate than the relationship between the part and whole of butter; therefore the kidney is more properly described as a "member" of the cat. When we reach the third level, that of a spiritual whole, we are even more struck by the inadequacy of language, because this language is directed towards describing material things; and though this language may cover material relationships, and—less adequately—organic relationships, it cannot reach to the intimacy of spiritual relationships. So intimate is the relationship between a spiritual "member" ("part") and its spiritual "body" ("whole") that we cannot illustrate it by saying, as we did at the other two levels, "If we remove a 'part', or 'member' . . .", because the act of removing a "member" from a spiritual "body" can only be carried out by the "member" himself—it is a *free* act. So far is it from being external (so intimate is it) that only the "member" himself can carry out this act of separating himself from the whole, and he does it freely, e.g. a man leaving the Christian Church.

Many difficult problems about the spiritual life would be cleared up if it were generally realized that the logic which we use in discussing such matters is a logic based on a language which was itself invented to account for material relationships, and therefore falsifies the issue if it is applied to questions for which it was not intended, i.e. spiritual relationships.

For instance, a characteristic of material things is that they can be distributed but cannot be shared, whereas it is the essence of spiritual goods to be shared. Suppose I have a bar of chocolate (a *material* thing); this bar of chocolate is capable of being distributed between myself and, say, two friends, for each of us may take a third part of the chocolate. But no-one else in the world can eat the part which I eat, or the particular part which each of my friends eats; because a material thing may be distributed, but it cannot be shared; the more one person takes of it the less there is for anyone else. If I indulge my enjoyment by eating every particular *part* of it I put the *whole* of it beyond anyone else's enjoyment.

Suppose, on the other hand, I have a friend (or I write a poem, or discover some truth—that is, enjoy some *spiritual* good). This friend of mine cannot be split up and distributed in parts, like a bar of chocolate; but his friendship can be *shared*. Indeed, if my friendship for him is true friendship and not possession such as one exercises over material things, then it is not only possible, it is absolutely certain that I shall share my friend with other people. Furthermore, whereas in distributing a part of a bar of chocolate the amount of chocolate left for myself diminishes, in sharing my friend with others I do not have any less of his friendship—I actually find myself enjoying more of it. Therefore, it is not mysticism but common sense to recognize that whereas material goods are diminished by being distributed, spiritual goods actually increase by being shared and communicated. "Goodness is self-diffusive", as the medieval philosophers used to say; so true is this that if we ever find ourselves enjoying something which we do not wish to share, then it is a sure sign that what we are enjoying is not a spiritual good.

In relation to spiritual goods, therefore, the logic of whole and part, which is appropriate for material things, no longer applies; for whereas we *distribute parts* of a material thing, we actually *share the whole* of a spiritual good with all who share in it—all who share in a friend, or in a poem or a truth, share the *whole* of these spiritual goods. In so far as there is any limitation in each sharer's enjoyment that limitation is found, not in any limitation of the whole into parts, but in each sharer's restricted capacity for enjoying the whole.

Let us illustrate this wonderful, essential feature of spiritual goods by calling on a few witnesses from the Christian tradition:

"Spiritual wealth acts like the sun, both dividing itself to all who see and being present as a whole to each."[1]

"This is the great and wonderful happiness that awaits us in heaven. God has created between himself and his creatures, between the manifold orders and degrees of angelic spirits, between the innumerable types of Saints, an all-embracing friendship, so that each one loves the other as himself. The result is that as each individual rejoices in his own happiness so he finds joy in the happiness of his neighbours; and the beatitude of each individual is the beatitude of all, and the *sum total* of the beatitude of all is enjoyed by *each* individual".[2]

"That love is single, but not private; alone yet not solitary; shared but not divided; common and singular; a single love of all and the whole love of each; growing no less by sharing, failing not through use nor growing old by time, ancient and new, desirable in affection, sweet in experience, eternal in fruit, full of mirth, refreshing and satisfying, and never cloying".[3]

Or, as St. Thomas Aquinas expresses it so clearly and beautifully in his hymn on the whole Christ, the Blessed Sacrament,

> *A sumente non concisus,*
> *non confractus, non divisus:*
> *integer accipitur.*
> *Sumit unus, sumunt mille:*
> *quantum isti, tantum ille:*
> *nec sumptus consumitur.*[4]

By reading these texts we gain some awareness of how it is possible for the Christian to see and enjoy the whole of some spiritual good at a particular moment and a particular place. For instance, at Communion I receive the *whole* Christ under the species of bread. Even if I had the power to be in two different churches at the same moment of time and to receive Communion from the hands of two different priests simultaneously, this extraordinary power would nevertheless not enable me to receive any more of Christ than at present—for I receive the *whole* Christ at a particular moment and a particular place.

Lady Julian of Norwich is expressing her awareness of this superlogical mode of spiritual happenings when she says that she "saw God in a point", and when she says of God's revelation to her, "Also in this He showed me a little thing, the quantity of an hazel-nut, in the palm of my hand; and it was as round as a ball. I looked thereupon with eye of my understanding, and thought: *What may this be?* And it was answered generally thus: *It is all that is made.* I marvelled how it might last, for methought it might suddenly have fallen to naught for littleness. And I was answered in my understanding: *It lasteth, and ever shall last for that God loveth it.* And so All-thing hath the Being by the love of God." [5]

How are these baffling features of "spiritual logic" to be explained? Surely because the *object* of this "spiritual logic", Christ, is the God-Man, "the one Man" (1 Tim. ii. 5) and the one God, the conjunction of the particular and the universal; he is universal, yet not abstract, but concrete; he is concrete, yet not limited, but infinite. He is eternal yet present at each moment of time, for he is "eternally-now" (c.f. Heb. iv. 7.). He is here-now, everywhere-eternally, the enfleshed-spirit, the Incarnate Word, who died specially for each one of us, once-for-all.

This "spiritual logic", then, derives its features from the Christ. Which does not mean, however, that the human being who operates this logic experiences a radical discontinuity between his human mode of knowing and the divine mode to which he is called by incorporation into "the one Man", Jesus Christ. For even the pagan philosopher, Aristotle, was dimly aware of the way in which the logic of material whole/part relationships is inadequate to spiritual knowledge. Obscurely, yet certainly, he accounts for human knowledge by the principle that "the soul is in a manner all things". The soul is in a manner all things, because the soul is made in the image of God, who is the whole of reality. Once the truth about the human operator of this "spiritual logic" had been revealed (that he is made in the image of God), it then became possible for Christian men to turn into poetry the sober Aristotelian statement, "The soul is in a manner all things." The Christian sings: "Mine are the heavens and mine is the earth; mine are the people, the righteous are mine and mine are the sinners; the angels are mine and the Mother of God, and all things are mine; and God himself is mine and for me, for Christ is mine and all for me. What, then, dost thou ask for and seek, my soul? Thine is all this, and it is all for thee".[6]

NOTES

[1] St. Gregory of Nyssa. Quoted by Prof. Armstrong, *Dominican Studies* I, pp. 114–5.

[2] ST. AILRED OF RIEVAULX, *On Spiritual Friendship*.

[3] HUGH OF ST. VICTOR, *The Soul's Betrothal-Gift*, trans. Sherwood Taylor, Dacre Press 1945, p. 19.

[4] "They, too, who of him partake, sever not, nor rend, nor break, but entire, their Lord receive.
Whether one, or thousands eat, all receive the self-same meat, nor the less for others leave."
(From the Sequence of the Feast of Corpus Christi). The sociological implications of the fact that the Blessed Sacrament *is* the common good are well worth considering.

[5] *Revelations of Divine Love*, ed. Warrack, Methuen, 1945.

[6] ST. JOHN OF THE CROSS, *Collected Works*, ed. E. Allison Peers, Burns Oates 1943, Vol. III, p. 244.